# Memoirs of a Red Cross Doctor

## Better to Light a Candle

Frank Ryding

PEN & SWORD
HISTORY

First published in Great Britain in 2017 by
Pen & Sword History
an imprint of
Pen & Sword Books Ltd
47 Church Street
Barnsley
South Yorkshire
S70 2AS

ISBN 9781526716880

Printed and bound in Great Britain by CPI, UK

Pen & Sword Books Ltd incorporates the Imprints of Pen & Sword Archaeology,
Atlas, Aviation, Battleground, Discovery, Family History, History, Maritime,
Military, Naval, Politics, Railways, Select, Transport, True Crime, Fiction,
Frontline Books, Leo Cooper, Praetorian Press, Seaforth Publishing, Wharncliffe
and White Owl.

For a complete list of Pen & Sword titles please contact
PEN & SWORD BOOKS LIMITED
47 Church Street, Barnsley, South Yorkshire, S70 2AS, England
E-mail: enquiries@pen-and-sword.co.uk
Website: www.pen-and-sword.co.uk

This book is a true memoir of the 35 years of work by the author as a doctor for the International Committee of the Red Cross (ICRC) and the British Red Cross

# Contents

# Introduction
## *Better To Light A Candle ...*

It was during one of the worst times, one of the seemingly hopeless times. As I was crouching for safety under an operating theatre table in a godforsaken part of Somalia, while shells exploded around us, I seriously questioned why I worked for an aid agency at all and what little use we were with violent death surrounding us. We were helping such a very small number of the victims here. My attention was illogically distracted from the gunfire outside to some graffiti written above an arched doorway in Somali script. A local nurse translated for me:

'It is better to light a single candle than to curse the darkness.'

It seemed to offer an explanation, some purpose to the years I spent before and after working with the International Red Cross in many of the most horrific wars on earth. Often it was the only motivation I had.

# PART 1

# IN THE KILLING FIELDS: CAMBODIA, 1980

SOUTH-EAST ASIA

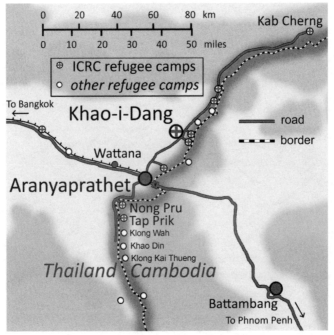

Thai/Cambodian border

*Chapter 1*

# Crossing Borders

The forest in Cambodia was noisy with exotic birdsong but the makeshift hospital in a clearing was quiet as always. Peaceful wasn't the right word: the atmosphere was subdued and wary. Already by noon I had seen more than fifty patients with malaria. Some were severely affected and I knew that two of them, despite treatment, would die before tomorrow morning. I hadn't expected that within the next hour I would see five people killed by shell and gun fire.

It could hardly be called a hospital. The wards were just four huge bamboo shelters open at the sides and covered with palm leaves for a roof. It had been built in an isolated part of western Cambodia by refugees fleeing from the chaotic and brutal fighting to the east but it was only 200 metres from the border with Thailand.

The air was hot and humid and I was so used to the incessant rasping of crickets that I hardly heard them now. The constant rhythm was suddenly broken by a deep, booming sound which I thought was thunder, but this was the wrong time of year. Everything stopped in the hospital as people listened; even the birds fell silent. The sound came again, and again. Was it getting closer? Out of the forest from the direction of a refugee village, people were running. Men with armfuls of AK-47 assault rifles were handing them out. Women were carrying babies or small children. Other older children followed them crying. The Cambodian nurse, Chantrea, who was helping me with the patients, pulled me out of the bamboo ward …

'Come with me. It's the Vietcong,' she shouted. 'They're attacking the village. They're shelling it. Get to the bridge, get into Thailand.'

'What about the patients?' I asked. Most of them were running with us but some, the very ill, were left behind.

'Go. This is not safe for you,' she said, as she pushed me towards the narrow bamboo bridge over a small ravine which marked the border with Thailand.

As I crossed the bridge with the three other members of the Red Cross team, I expected the Cambodians to follow, but a number of armed Khmer Rouge soldiers, the infamous communist fanatics who, it was said, had murdered over three million of their fellow Cambodians, stood like sentries preventing them from passing. There would be no deserters here. Everyone would have to turn and fight.

I heard shooting from the direction of the village, then distant machine-gun fire. We waited and after twenty minutes there was silence. It was an hour before the tension eased. We tentatively made our way back over the bridge and work was resumed.

Chantrea told me the attack had failed but there had been casualties. Many had been killed and they were bringing the wounded to the hospital. The first was a woman of maybe 25 who had been hit in the chest by shell fragments. It was hard to see the blood which had soaked her black shirt but a tear in the fabric showed where a large piece of metal shrapnel had entered her right lung from the front. I suspected it had hit her aorta or one of the other main blood vessels near her heart; her face was white, her voice was weak and I could hardly feel the rapid, feeble pulse in her neck. There was nothing much I could do. We could only give basic first aid here, but I doubt if even a specialized surgical unit could have saved her. As I crouched over her trying to find a vein to set up an intravenous drip, her breathing stopped, her pulse disappeared and her frightened eyes looking at me became lifeless as she died.

We dealt with ten wounded Cambodians that afternoon and five died. I asked if there had been any Vietcong casualties to deal with. Chantrea seemed surprised at the question but said that some of them had been wounded by the personnel mines that protected the forest trails leading to the village. I asked where they were.

She paused and looked straight at me. 'There will be no prisoners.'

Six weeks before, I had been working in the UK as a junior doctor in anaesthetics and intensive care in Reading. It was September 1980, I was 32 and tired. Junior doctors' hours were very long in those days – often 90 hours per week, sometimes more. The operating theatres were windowless, lit by harsh fluorescent light. In the coming winter months I would arrive in the dark and leave for home in the dark. It was all becoming stale. I felt I needed and deserved a short break.

I listlessly scanned the advertisements for appointments in the *British Medical Journal* but saw nothing at all that appealed to me until I glanced at an advertisement by the British Red Cross for general medical officers to go to Thailand for three months. I looked out of the window at the cold, rainy and gloomy dusk outside. I longed for some sun, warmth and fresh air – and a short working holiday in Thailand was very appealing.

When I casually phoned them to get more information, I admitted I probably didn't have the experience they needed but maybe they would consider accepting me – if not now then in a few years' time for a similar job. They asked how soon I could leave – they wanted people now. I had asked them at the right time. They explained the position: Cambodia was in chaos and vast numbers of Cambodians, or Khmer as they are called, were suffering. The Vietnamese army had invaded Cambodia and large numbers of refugees had fled from the warfare, mostly west to Thailand to escape. Now over 600,000 people, many ill and wounded, were crowded just inside Thailand in makeshift refugee camps.

The International Committee of the Red Cross (ICRC) in Geneva had mounted one of the biggest rescue projects in its history and was asking the national Red Cross societies, including Britain, to sponsor large numbers of medical staff to go out to their refugee camps on the Thai–Cambodian border. They reassured me that these medics were generally working in camps in the safety of Thailand.

I took just a few hours to think about it. Family and friends thought it wasn't a bad idea – have a rest and come back refreshed and eager again. One of my consultants said I was making a mistake if I stepped off the NHS career ladder – I would find it hard to get another NHS post.

Three days later I was on my way to Southeast Asia. The long-haul flight to Bangkok, with the enforced rest and nothing to do, gave me a chance to almost stop the clock for a few hours and to take stock. I'd always wanted adventure. I was born into a modest family in a small town in Lancashire where they made buses. My father was a shoe repairer who hated his job and died when I was in my teens, probably from all the leather dust he inhaled. He once told me not to do as he had done: 'If you're ever unhappy with what you're doing, then go out and do something else.' I never forgot that.

It was otherwise a contented childhood in a close family and close community revolving around the parish church, secure, unchanging and parochial, with no need to go very far from it. I had no complaints, but there was something missing, some excitement. I was born on a Thursday ... my mother used to say, 'Thursday's child has far to go' and I used to look at the horizon.

I got the A-level grades needed for medical school, and blessed with a full and free grant I was off to University College Hospital in London. It was the first adventure, but it wasn't quite enough to satisfy my curiosity about the world. It just started the craving for more.

Yet as I sat on the Thai Airlines plane, I began to have some doubts: I was still only a junior doctor with little experience and I knew almost nothing of tropical medicine. But I reminded myself that this was only a one-off experience for three months. I could regard it as a holiday. I wasn't motivated by altruism but by the need for a change of scenery and an innate curiosity. I never imagined it would be just the first of fourteen missions for the Red Cross.

Thailand was hotter than I'd expected and the ICRC headquarters in Bangkok more frenetic. I felt I was in the way. The personnel department only had time to hand me a folder of information before I was immediately sent east, still jetlagged, towards the Cambodian border. It was a five-hour journey in an ICRC minibus with half a dozen other recruits; I was the only one from the UK.

We left the world of Bangkok tourists behind and passed through flat, rich green countryside, small isolated farms and endless watery fields of rice. Two children on the veranda of a wooden house-on-stilts were happily splashing water from a huge water pot. They stopped when they saw the strange people in the bus and waved to us. We passed an ornate temple and a saffron-robed monk with his begging bowl.

It was very peaceful and pleasant and bright as I half-dozed in my seat with the sunlight and the heat and the fragrant smells coming in through the open window, a welcome change from the cold dullness of the UK and the sunless operating theatre I'd hurriedly left; but as the miles passed I thought to myself with some apprehension, 'What on earth am I doing here? I'm getting nearer and nearer to a war zone!'

ICRC was based at the Thai town of Aranyaprathet, right on the Cambodian border. Here the main highway and the railway line from Bangkok once passed through the border on to the Cambodian town of Battambang and then the capital Phnom Penh. The border area was now very tense – the nervous Thai military were very prominent. The road and railway had been closed just before the border – a blockade with signs in several languages warned people away. In those days, Cambodia was a very dangerous place to visit.

ICRC headquarters had been set up just before Aranyaprathet in the hamlet of Wattana Nakorn. ICRC had rented a former large farm here with a wide area of concreted ground and hard clay and had erected thatched huts as accommodation. A huge open-sided warehouse was used as a dining area. It was quiet and almost deserted when I arrived in the late afternoon but within an hour the medical teams started to return from the camps. Wattana became a mass of noisy, hungry, dusty, tired or elated personnel, all heading for the makeshift showers and then dinner. There were 140 multinational expatriate medical personnel based here. It was a huge and busy operation. I mingled with them trying to find a friendly English accent among all the languages – French, German, Finnish, Dutch and more. I felt lost. Then I found an Australian Water and Sanitation team. 'Sit down, mate, have a beer. We're the dunny factory.'

I slept in my own prefabricated wooden hut under a mosquito net wondering exactly how far away I was from this war zone and listening to the loud noise of crickets and rain on the thatched roof. I was woken in the middle of the night by the sound of heavy vehicles, one after another, driving along the previously quiet highway. I was convinced they were tanks – the Vietnamese must be invading Thailand. Strangely, no one in the camp seemed to be stirring and I decided against rushing out and raising the alarm. I was later told that it was just Thai black market trucks heading into Cambodia which they did every night.

My internal clock was disturbed and I couldn't go back to sleep. So I thought I'd read for a while. I found the folder of information leaflets hastily given to me in the ICRC office in Bangkok and decided I ought to find out more about the situation I was about to experience. There was no electricity in the hut so I lit a candle and read.

Cambodia or Kampuchea, the ancient empire of the Khmer nation, became independent from France in 1953 but only a few years of peace were left for this pleasant paradise with its gentle people. In the 1970s the Vietnam war spread into Cambodia and in the political chaos that followed, the communist party of Kampuchea ruthlessly took control. They were called the Khmer Rouge, led by Saloth Sar, otherwise known as the infamous Pol Pot. I never imagined at that moment that later I would actually see him in the flesh.

The Khmer Rouge immediately ordered the evacuation of all urban areas and the entire population was forced into the countryside to work on the land. Society would be brutally reshaped to conform to Pol Pot's nightmarish social vision. They lacked food, tools and basic medical care. The communes were little different from concentration camps and the name Khmer Rouge itself struck fear into the people. The result was that hundreds of thousands of Cambodians died from starvation or disease and as many were executed in the 'Killing Fields'. Most military and civilian leaders of the former regime were killed as well as anyone who opposed the Khmer Rouge or who simply did not or could not conform to their ideology. No one kept records of all those who died between 1975 and 1979 but it's estimated that the Khmer Rouge executed 1.5 million of its own countrymen and a total of perhaps 3 million died out of a population of 7.3 million.

I put the leaflet down, disturbed by what I'd read. The plight of Cambodia at the time was not well known in the West and certainly not by me; the film *The Killing Fields* describing this horror was still four years away. I also realized that tomorrow I would become personally involved in this history lesson.

I was wide awake now as I continued reading. One nightmare was replaced by another in 1979 as the Vietnamese army, victorious against the US, successfully invaded Cambodia. Pol Pot's struggling Khmer Rouge forces retreated west towards the Thai border. Along with them was a huge mass of Cambodian refugees who continued across the border for safety. The Thai authorities, eager that the conflict should not spread into their country, would let them go no further. More than half a million of them were now just a few miles from the hut where I was, at that moment, reading their tragic story. It was not the first or last time in history that frightened migrants would try to flee to safety.

The next day, the medical coordinator showed me a wall map of the Red Cross action. To the north, just off the border road, were the refugee camps with exotic names like Nong Sammet and Klong Singnang. The main ICRC hospital was situated inside Khao-i-Dang, the largest camp on the border, holding 160,000 refugees. In fact it was the largest in the world. The whole area was crowded with scores of other Voluntary Agencies, or VolAgs, of all nationalities extending right up to Laos. Some wit had termed this whole string of agencies the VolAg Archipelago.

The larger agencies like ICRC, Médecins Sans Frontières (MSF) and Save the Children were kept busy, almost overwhelmed, but some of the much smaller groups with sometimes rather vague aims struggled to find any 'customers' they could help. They would almost pounce on the poor refugees as they crossed the border. One could imagine a Cambodian trying to reach the safety of Thailand – escaping the fighting, escaping the malaria, escaping the landmines – but finally getting caught by an aid agency.

The coordinator said, 'I once came across a tiny aid organization up in the north that had cornered half a dozen miserable-looking refugees, too polite to escape, and the deal was that they would get a bowl of rice when they'd sung a few hymns. Most Cambodians are already devout Buddhists.'

He told us stories of individual medics from the West, not attached to any group, arriving at Bangkok airport with stethoscopes around their necks, taking a bus to the border and then trying vainly to find some organization that would take them on. The larger agencies wouldn't touch them: there was no way in the field to check out who these people were and whether they had any qualifications at all.

He told me I'd start work tomorrow with a small medical team that had already been here for several weeks. The team served an area, not in the north but far away in an isolated area to the south of Aranyaprathet which was visited each day. Then he casually mentioned that our team was the only one which crossed into Cambodia itself. This didn't sound good. I was expecting to work in the safety of Thailand. The team looked after two small hospitals just over the border; these were attached to two refugee camp villages, Nong Pru and Tap Prik. My team consisted of a Dutch doctor, Willy, who fortunately had some experience of tropical diseases, and three nurses, from Canada, USA and France.

*Chapter 2*

# First Day

So on my first working day the five of us gathered at the main ICRC delegation near Aranyaprathet. I'll admit the apprehension was growing – we would be crossing the border into a war zone. There was a more disturbing surprise to come. I asked Willy why these refugees were still in Cambodia, not in the safety of Thailand.

'Because the Thai government won't let them in,' said Willy.

'Why not?'

'Because they, and the whole area we work in, are under the complete control of the Khmer Rouge.' He added, 'The Khmer Rouge want to stay in Cambodia because they're still fighting the Vietnamese from there.'

This mission was already becoming something of a nightmare. Today and every morning the team would have a briefing with the Swiss security delegate for the southern area whose job it was to assimilate all the reports of military activity, assess the situation and decide whether it was safe for us to go in that day. I wasn't sure if I should be reassured by this – we had a security man to look after our interests in the field but it was worrying that we needed one in the first place. While we were waiting for Willy to collect our obligatory two-way security radios I chatted to the security delegate and asked him how long he had been here.

'Four weeks,' he said.

'Were you in security before joining the Red Cross, or in the military?' I asked.

'No, I was a ballet dancer.'

I had a dream one night where he taught us to pirouette out of the line of fire.

We loaded our two Land Cruisers – always two for security – with medical supplies from the huge ICRC warehouse at the main delegation. It was busy and noisy with perhaps twenty or thirty of the ubiquitous Land Cruisers being hurriedly loaded, filled up with fuel, and driven off at speed in a cloud of red dust. Work started very early on the border while the morning was still cool and fresh.

I wasn't sure what to do so I chatted to a New Zealander in charge of the pharmacy who was sorting out some donations of medicines from western drug companies. They were very welcome, he said, even if some of them were running close to their 'use-by' date. He did show me a surprising donation from one small company –a large shipment of slimming tablets. For refugees. It was probably sent as a tax loss, he said. He binned them.

We set off, passing through Aranyaprathet. The shops were mostly wooden shacks. The roads were compacted dirt, crowded with vehicles from other aid agencies and the Thai army. It reminded me of one of those Hollywood Wild West film sets; like the Klondike gold-rush, but it was refugees not gold that brought people here.

We bought a communal pineapple for our lunch and I bought myself a leg of chicken from a woman who ran a charcoal grill on the pavement. No wrapping, it was held in the cleft of a bamboo stick. I sat in the Land Cruiser self-consciously holding my chicken-on-a-stick, with serious misgivings.

We drove south and headed out of the town along a rust-coloured dirt road that ran alongside the border. It was wide but empty; we didn't see another vehicle for the whole journey, just the occasional black water buffalo ambling along by itself. It was open countryside, uncultivated, with no houses, just tall wild grass and reeds with the odd area of forest, copse of bamboo or isolated palm tree. Some looked dead, almost leafless, the palm fronds brown and shrivelled.

'Agent Orange,' said Willy. 'Someone's sprayed the area to defoliate it so soldiers can't hide there.'

We travelled about eight kilometres before Willy pointed out a long hill less than a kilometre away to the east. 'That hill is in Cambodia,' he said, 'and behind it are about five hundred Vietcong troops.'

'This does *not* seem at all safe,' I muttered.

After another eight kilometres, we turned off onto a much smaller track heading towards the border and a distant forest. I expected at least a high border fence but there was nothing, just what looked like a thatched bus shelter; it was a lonely Thai border post. The two border soldiers here were – appropriately – bored. They spoke no English but checked our Red Cross passes, had a cursory look in the back of the Land Cruisers and waved us on. They were used to us as this happened every morning and it was probably the only thing of interest to them all day. Not many others wanted to go into Cambodia unless it was black marketeers at night.

The narrow track was rough, winding through tall, coarse grass for about three kilometres. There had been rain recently and it was muddy and soft. In parts, logs had been placed on the ground to provide a hard surface. Willy said that the area had been mined – by whom he wasn't sure – and when I was driving I should always stick exactly to the tracks, as even just a foot or so into the grass verge could be lethal. It was also possible that the road itself had been mined, but the undisturbed tyre tracks of a recent vehicle ahead of us showed that if we followed these tracks exactly there was a greater element of safety. He mentioned that Red Cross Land Cruisers were never petrol-driven, always diesel – less of a fireball if one did happen to detonate a landmine.

Willy glanced at me. 'Are you scared?' he asked with a smile. 'You have every right to be.'

And we had to do this every day for three months? I thought about the pleasant drive every morning to the car park of the Royal Berkshire Hospital back home. We made sure there was a lot of space between the two vehicles in case one of them hit a mine. For one particular stretch of road, one of the nurses drove while Willy got out and walked thirty metres behind the vehicles: that way there was a better chance he might survive a mine explosion and get help. I noticed he walked exactly along the tyre tracks, one foot placed carefully in front of the other. Like walking a tightrope.

## Chapter 3

# Malaria, Drips and Theatre Tickets

W e soon reached the forest and Nong Pru hospital. I'd formed no firm idea of what the hospital would look like but I expected some sort of brick building at least. I was surprised to see it was hardly more than a campsite in a clearing under the trees. The wards consisted of long huts made of logs with a thatched roof as protection from the elements. The walls were simply bamboo slats, rather like Venetian blinds to let in light and air, and instead of beds there were two wooden platforms running the length of the hut about a metre off the ground, on each side of a central walkway of compacted soil. The patients lay side by side on blankets on the platforms. The four crowded huts held perhaps 300 patients in all; other huts were used as offices and storerooms. I was surprised how primitive it was, yet astonished how neat and very well organized. The dirt floors were immaculately clean with no sign of any litter or rubbish. I felt there was a military air about the place that I found unsettling, even disturbing. Most of the people wore what looked like black pyjamas. The photos of the Khmer Rouge I'd seen always showed them in these black clothes, like a uniform.

A few hundred metres from the hospital was the refugee village of Nong Pru itself, built in the forest and therefore less visible from the air. There were said to be almost 10,000 refugees here, but this wasn't a refugee camp built and run by western aid agencies like the others on the border – I later found out it was more like a guerrilla camp for the Khmer Rouge. I never actually saw the village itself as we were never invited to visit during the three months I was there. We were welcome only in the hospital because we brought supplies, food and expertise.

The team busily dispersed to start work. Our nurses organized the distribution of the supplies we'd brought and stocked up the pharmacy hut or supervised the Khmer nurses, teaching them necessary medical skills. Before Willy went off to see some new patients, he introduced me to the head man of the hospital, Mr Sam, a man in his early thirties perhaps, who would take me on my first ward round. I wondered if he was a high-ranking Khmer Rouge officer but I wasn't going to ask. The next surprise of the day was that he and many of the other Khmer spoke French but no English – but of course this used to be a

French colony, part of French Indochina. I spoke very poor French but at least they spoke it slowly, perhaps because it was not their mother tongue. I was feeling very much at a loss by now – I was expected to treat diseases I'd never seen before, using a language I wasn't used to. The thought was growing in my mind that this mission was a mistake.

Mr Sam was having difficulty making me understand him. He was very astute and no doubt realized, although I nodded, I understood very little and was just being polite. We looked at each other in frustration. He wasn't sure what to do with me. So he took me into one of the wards. It was completely full of patients lying crammed together and, as I walked in, all the Khmer faces looked up at me in almost childlike expectancy, this strange-looking foreigner with pale skin, red hair and red beard. To them I was salvation. It was a pivotal and profound moment; and it suddenly hit me. Here was a mass of humanity who had absolutely nothing – forced from their homes with no possessions, little dignity and nowhere to go, with no foreseeable chance of any hopeful future. In addition to all that, they were hungry and ill with god knows what parasites, viruses, injuries and other disabilities. It was only the first of many times that I looked into the sad faces, at the quiet distress of displaced people.

My problems by comparison were that I needed to learn a new branch of medicine and improve my French. It was very humbling. There was no question now that I would stay. But I was slow to realize the privilege I had been given – the chance to do something for these desperate people. This was no longer a holiday jaunt.

There were no experienced Khmer medical staff in the hospital, but a few had rudimentary medical knowledge and had taken on the roles of ward nurses. They showed me a man who looked very ill, sweating and shivering with fever. I looked blank and someone whispered 'malaria', as if to help me perhaps. I was floundering here.

After several more malaria cases, Mr Sam took me to see a man with a landmine injury to his arm. It was not severe; he had been thirty metres from the explosion but some metal shrapnel from the mine had hit his arm and now a week later the wound was infected, so I felt more confident when I suggested antibiotics. But this wasn't a familiar A&E department, it was a humid, tropical, cricket-chirping jungle. For the first time, the patients were not in my territory – I was in theirs. It was out of context, in the open air and it had a deeper emotional impact on me.

We all stopped for lunch and sat outside the office on bamboo benches in the shade of the huge trees. The day was becoming very hot and stifling. I asked Willy about the landmines. He told me the whole of the Thai–Cambodian border had been indiscriminately saturated with them – a ribbon almost ten kilometres wide stretching from north to south. It was the last and most deadly of obstacles to the mass of people trying to reach the safety of Thailand. It was unclear who had laid the mines, Vietnamese or Khmer Rouge or both. Many were home-made mines, explosives with splinters of bamboo embedded in them. They were often cleverly planted. They would be laid on narrow jungle trails with the direction of the explosion not aimed upward but low along the trail so that if a group of people were walking in single file, the leader would step on the mine but the blast and bamboo shrapnel would also hit all those following, causing injury to the maximum number of people. He said that we were unlikely to see the most serious mine injuries. Nong Pru and Tap Prik were surrounded by mines but the Khmer knew where they were, and anyway it was unlikely that those with serious injuries would ever manage to reach medical help.

But there was something else bothering me and making me feel uneasy. It was a moral dilemma. I had come out here with the Red Cross with the idea of simply bringing humanitarian aid to a suffering population but here we were apparently helping the Khmer Rouge who had committed the atrocities I was now aware of. I explained my concerns to Willy. He understood but said that just because these people dressed like the Khmer Rouge I shouldn't necessarily assume that they approved of them or supported them. They simply may not have had any choice: many of these people just happened to have ended up in an area controlled by them. It was advice I carried with me to other ICRC missions – that the distinction between victim and aggressor was not always clear.

I made a couple of mistakes during lunch: the Khmer staff brought a bowl of clean water for us to wash our hands. I lathered my hands with soap and splashed them in the water in the bowl.

Brenda, the American nurse, gently reprimanded me: 'You've just dirtied a whole bowl full of precious water. It may have meant a long walk for one of the refugees to bring it from the nearest clean water supply.'

The idea was to use a plastic cup to take a bit of water to rinse my hands then the rest of the water can be used for another dozen or so people. Then I made the mistake of taking my chicken leg and eating it as I strolled around the com- pound where any passing Khmer could see me and smell the chicken. These were people who had not seen meat for a long time. I even compounded it by thoughtlessly throwing the skin to a mangy dog which the Khmer kept to catch rats. I looked up to see a group of children looking soulfully at the chicken skin on the floor. I never brought chicken for lunch to the hospital again.

I was also told not to touch a Khmer's head unless unavoidable. It's where they believe the soul resides and as such it is disrespectful.

We took a few moments to relax before going back to work and Willy warned me about the dog. There had been quite a few cases of rabies in some of the refugee camps, with even one of the expatriate staff being bitten and contracting it. He added that ICRC in Geneva had sent a comprehensive teleprinter message to all delegates about the danger of rabies, risks, treatment and prevention. Unfortunately there had been a typing error in the English version and it read: 'All ICRC staff should make sure they are immunized against babies.' I was sure the social life wasn't all that exciting.

Willy told me of another misprint. One English delegate had sent an end of mission report about the abuses of human rights in Cambodia to Red Cross headquarters in Geneva and was very pleased that he'd managed to it in French. It was well received except that in a lapse of concentration he'd addressed the envelope to ICRC also in French: 'CICR (Committee Internationale de la Khmer Rouge)'. Not many principles in common actually.

The next day we travelled the same border road but this time went a few kilometres further on and turned down another track to the hospital at Tap Prik. This was also attached to a refugee village about half the size of Nong Pru. The actual border here was a small ravine, ten metres deep and twelve across, and the hospital was on the other side. The Khmer had built a bamboo footbridge across it, the only access from Thailand, so it was an important bridge for us. We would park the Land Cruisers and the Khmer would help us to carry all the supplies, medicines, dressings, food and equipment over the fragile-looking bridge and into the hospital. It swayed slightly as I tentatively walked across, keeping a strong grip on the rope handrails on each side. It looked flimsy, more like scaffolding, but this access bridge had been made at the same time as the camps and was still there so it must have been well built.

We entered the hospital. It was smaller than Nong Pru but was just as clean, just as tidy, just as regimented. The local head nurse was a soft-spoken, charming lady, about thirty years old who introduced herself as Chantrea which, she said, meant in Khmer '*clair de lune*' or 'moonlight'. She spoke French in a delightful staccato accent while she artistically gestured with hand movements like one of the traditional dancers in this part of the world. We were made very welcome but there was something odd about the atmosphere, the ambience in both the hospitals, which I couldn't quite pin down.

By the end of the week I felt much more confident. The initial fear of working in a war zone receded, there didn't seem any sign of fighting nearby and the days were peaceful. The majority of cases were malaria and minor injuries. I would spend the morning and early afternoon going round the patients in the thatched huts and the remaining time doing small operations.

The malaria was widespread and severe. The refugee population was very susceptible as they had little natural resistance to it – most had been city dwellers in Phnom Penh before the Khmer Rouge had dragged them out into the countryside to work. When they tried to escape by fleeing west after the Vietnamese invasion, they had unluckily ended up in an area endemic with malaria.

I soon learned that the type of malaria we saw wasn't constant. The mosquito-carried disease could be either the falciparum or vivax type and the preponderance of one over the other would change with the seasons. It was important to distinguish between the two as the treatment was different. Most of the day was taken up with a long 'ward round', sometimes seeing a hundred or more patients. Many of them needed intravenous treatment for their malaria especially if they were vomiting and couldn't keep tablets down or if they'd become seriously dehydrated.

The Red Cross had already successfully trained some of the Khmer staff to take a blood sample by pricking the patient's thumb then looking at it under a microscope and deciding which form of malaria it was. It often meant that the correct treatment could be started even when we weren't there. But putting up an intravenous or IV drip was another matter. If the needle cannula isn't exactly in the vein it will not work. Intravenous cannulation is a surprisingly difficult technique to master especially when a patient is dehydrated, the veins have collapsed and are invisible. It was this that took up the time when I went round the wards – I had to keep stopping to cannulate patients. I thought there must be staff with sufficient medical training – perhaps a nurse whom I could train to do it. I asked Mr Sam at Nong Pru. He thought for a while then promised that by tomorrow I'd have a cannulation nurse team for training. Next day he produced two eager girls for the IV team. I say girls rather than women because one was only thirteen years old and her sister a year younger.

This was useless, but I was becoming aware of the importance of not losing face, a very important concept in this part of the world. So I thought I'd give the girls a quick token teaching session in the ward then forget the whole idea.

I let them watch while I cannulated a patient; I put a tourniquet on the arm, felt for a suitable vein, swabbed the skin, deftly inserted a cannula, withdrew the metal stylus inside, leaving the plastic tube in the vein ready for flushing through with saline to make sure it was correctly in the vein. The bottle of saline was connected up and then, as a gesture, I let the older girl wrap a bandage around the arm to keep everything clean. The patients in the surrounding beds applauded. The girl acknowledged them with a small bow. Honour was satisfied.

I carried on with the ward round. We soon came across another patient needing an IV. I was about to put one up when the two girls stepped in. While they busily chatted to each other, conferring, they copied everything I'd done – exactly. The cannula went in and the drip worked perfectly. More applause and another bow from the girls. I was quite taken aback.

They were soon doing all the IVs. They even developed their own personal style. Instead of a tourniquet, the younger sister, the heavier of the two, would sit on the patient's arm which made the veins stand out and also stopped the patient from moving or even running away. The older sister would sometimes slap the patient's face to soften him up, shout at him, presumably to keep still, and when she'd finished, slap him again. Not exactly NHS guidelines. I would see her slap around tough-looking men whom I suspected were Khmer Rouge soldiers – ruthless sadistic killers – and I would cringe. But the men seemed to take it meekly.

The girls soon learned to cannulate the most difficult veins. They developed a point of honour of keeping up with me on ward rounds. I would order an IV and they would do it so fast I wouldn't be more than a couple of patients further along when they would catch up and stand there, arms folded with an air of nonchalance.

I also discovered that cannulation wasn't the only skill the Khmer acquired at these camps. We treated the malaria with a variety of drugs but the old method of using quinine was surprisingly effective, and cheap. Then we started hearing complaints from some of the patients – particularly ringing in the ears. This is one of the side effects of overdose of quinine. We checked that the Khmer staff were giving the correct dose but it took us a while before we worked out the cause. On one of the ward rounds I found a patient taking some strange tablets: they looked home-made with what appeared to be Chinese writing impressed onto them. Mr Sam explained that they were made by a Khmer herbalist from the village who had been handing out his own remedy, made from crushed dried bark. I was introduced to the herbalist – he had a makeshift factory behind one of the wards where he had herbs drying on large plastic sheets. He showed me how he made the tablets – as a mould to compress the powder into tablet form he used spent Chinese bullet cases which had indented Chinese characters at the end. I asked him about his malaria treatment and he showed me the crushed tree bark he was drying on one of the sheets – I eventually realized that the bark was from a cinchona tree, the source of quinine. Our patients were being given double the dose of quinine – ours and his. We came to an amicable agreement with the herbalist to stop the bell-ringing.

Malaria treatment wasn't always successful. At Tap Prik I saw a woman with severe malaria who had just given birth to a baby before she died. The baby girl was small and sickly and her first blood test was positive for the falciparum strain of malaria. She was an orphan and the camp leaders had to find a foster parent for her. One of the helpers at the hospital, was a twenty-five-year-old man with obvious learning difficulties, who himself had no family. The village committee gave him the baby to look after. He was very caring – he would sit with her all day in the children's hut at the hospital. He was taught how to feed her by taking her to one of the newly delivered mothers who had milk to spare. The baby needed an intravenous drip for her malaria treatment and he looked after the tubing and the infusion bag with great attention. He would spend the day with the baby on his lap, happily rocking her and singing to her.

The baby didn't thrive, she really had very little chance under the circumstances. A week later she died. The last time I saw them both he was still rocking the dead baby, distraught but still quietly singing to her with tears in his eyes. We were all affected by it. I noticed his T-shirt, which he'd got from some US aid agency. It read: 'Every Child is a Precious Gift'. It later occurred to me that this was the first time I'd seen a Khmer cry. We had several deaths due to malaria but I'd never seen much emotion from their relatives and friends. It struck me as rather an incongruous trait in a people who otherwise seemed to have such a pleasant disposition.

I was still unconfident about the diagnosis of tropical diseases but there was also some minor surgery to do, and here I felt much more at home – Willy was happy for me to take over all this side of the treatment. There were fractures to treat, wounds to clean which at times involved removing small pieces of shrapnel from mine injuries. We had an improvised operating theatre at Nong Pru, just blue polythene sheets hung up to make three sides of a square – the fourth side left open to let in light and air – with a polythene roof to protect us from the frequent downpours.

I was operating there one morning when I began to be aware of hushed chattering behind me. I looked up and saw twenty or more Khmer villagers standing at the entrance watching intently. I later found out that the two new young intravenous 'nurses' and their friends were selling tickets – operating theatre tickets. I casually complained to Mr Sam. He admitted he thought it was unfair – for the prices they were charging the audience should at least see an amputation, not just a wound dressing.

During these sessions, I felt it wasn't quite safe doing both the anaesthetics and the surgery at the same time. So I thought my young IV nurse might be useful. We used ketamine anaesthetic for these cases – it's fairly uncomplicated to use. I'd give the ketamine solution intravenously then get the girl to sit at the patient's head end and look after him. The important thing is to make sure the patient is breathing adequately – I tried to explain to her what I wanted but I would have loved to have one of the anaesthetic machines from home that measures the respiration. Halfway through the operation I looked up to check what she was doing – she'd taken a wisp of cotton thread from her shirt, stuck it to the patient's nose with tape and was intently watching it float up and down with every breath. Brilliant. I used it myself on later missions and called it the 'Khmer respirometer'.

It was hard work in the hospitals, seven days a week from dawn to dusk. But with increasing confidence I was now starting to enjoy it. We never stayed overnight, as it was considered too dangerous, and always drove back each evening to the delegation at Wattana. We once left it rather late and it was almost dark when we left the hospital in a rain storm. It was not safe to show headlights in the border area: artillery could mistake us for enemy combatants at that hour. I was driving fast but suddenly had to break hard and with squealing tyres, pulled up short of a huge black water buffalo, practically invisible, standing right in the middle of the road. As I sat there, shaken, I suddenly imagined how ironic and undignified it would be if I'd been killed and at my funeral they announced that it was not a mine or a shell in a war zone that had done me in – but the back end of a buffalo.

*Chapter 4*

# Time Out

Life outside working hours at Wattana was pleasant enough and Sunday could often be taken as a half day, time to catch up, do laundry, relax. Every fortnight a couple of feature films would arrive from some agency in Geneva, projected onto the wall of a whitewashed farm building. The first film night wasn't a success. Both films were war films. After a week dealing with the awful consequences of war, *Apocalypse Now* was the last thing we wanted to see, and most people ambled back to their huts leaving a few hardened film buffs. The subsequent showing of *Grease* and *Star Wars* fared better.

There was even time to relax at the hospitals if the work load occasionally decreased. Annette, the French nurse on our team, was due to leave at the end of her mission and the Khmer at Tap Prik organized a party for her in their hospital. It was very formal: we were invited to sit at the front of the gathering while they gave a concert of traditional Khmer music. They had a trio of musicians; I recognized the two-stringed violin, the *tror*. There was a *khim*, like a dulcimer, played with thin bamboo hammers, and a *takhe* the size of a small cello. All the instruments had been made in the camp, from whatever materials were to hand. The strings had come from the electric wiring of a wrecked jeep with the insulation stripped off.

The haunting music wafted up into the trees, as some dancers performed. Chantrea said they were traditional Khmer dances. The final dance was rather odd – half a dozen dancers appeared carrying what looked like backpacks but made out of our empty cardboard pharmacy boxes, brightly painted, with a piece of thin bamboo curling up and over their shoulders. The dance involved swaying from side to side and pulling the bamboo stick up and down. I asked Chantrea in a whisper what it was all about – some ancient Khmer legend? She told me reverently that it represented spraying the ponds with insecticide to kill the malaria mosquitoes.

They served us a meal of rice and vegetables and produced cans of cola for us. I had no idea where they'd got these from. But the surprise was the bowl of ice cubes – in the middle of a tropical jungle, with no electricity. They were very proud of this, and took a lot of pleasure in nonchalantly presenting it to us and watching our surprise.

I was later told that a couple of them had spent the previous night in a two-hour trek across the border to a Thai village. They had carefully broken into a petrol station, stolen ice cubes from the refrigerator and refilled the ice-trays with water. By the next morning, the water had frozen and no one knew they had been robbed. They'd trekked back to the camp before dawn with the precious ice cubes wrapped in a blanket. All for the party.

The French nurse had a shock when they gave her a leaving present – a small, brightly coloured snake in a bamboo cage. When we left after the party, she stopped the Land Cruiser down the dirt road out of sight of the hospital and rather gingerly let the snake free. A few days later, the Khmer presented us with another bamboo cage and asked us to pass it on to the French nurse – it contained what looked suspiciously like the same snake which must have found its way home. They explained that this cage was better and the snake wouldn't be able to escape again.

As the weeks passed, the weather changed and became drier. There were less malaria cases and the routine at both hospitals became easier, less hectic. They were pleasant days. We could now spare some time after the work was finished to sit with the Khmer and chat to them as the sun sank low behind the trees and the air cooled and the colours became more vibrant. The Khmer seemed more ready to talk to us now as they got to know us. Also my French was improving.

I was shown a photograph of the Angkor Wat temple which they regarded with both religious and political fervour. I'd always wanted to see it but it was ninety miles away through some of the most dangerous territory in the world. I was told that the Khmer Rouge were using the temple complex as a storage area for explosives. It would be a prime target for Vietnamese shelling. It was difficult then to imagine it as the international tourist destination it became.

Both Chantrea and Mr Sam were interested in the UK. We discussed the West, but I had the feeling that to them the conversation was surreptitious – they spoke in hushed tones. Chantrea was keen to learn English and we were often able to reserve half an hour after lunch to give unofficial English lessons. The US nurse, Brenda, would use a copy of *Huckleberry Finn*, and I had a book of short stories by Somerset Maugham sent from Bangkok. Chantrea learned quickly but ended up with a mid-Atlantic accent. I noticed that whenever anyone else came near she would hide the books and immediately switch to French.

Once after I'd finished seeing the patients in one of the wards, I chatted to the male nurse in charge. He already spoke some English which he'd learned from a book and he was keen to improve. His pronunciation wasn't very good but far better than my poor attempts at Khmer. He would only speak English to me when we were alone. He asked me if we would have some leisure time in Bangkok after the mission. He said I should make sure we met the tigers. A bizarre conversation followed:

'I'll go to the zoo and see them,' I said.

'No,' he whispered slyly, 'you can see tigers everywhere.'

'Aren't they dangerous, don't people get attacked?'

'No, they're very good, very polite. You see them on Sukhumvit Road in the city centre. Or on the beach at Pattaya, you can buy a tiger to take back to your hotel.'

'Do you mean tigers or do you mean ordinary cats?'

'No,' he said impatiently, 'not tigers – Thai girls!'

I was becoming familiar with tropical diseases by now but didn't realize I would learn even more from personal experience. In the middle of the mission I had a setback when I went down with amoebic dysentery. I'd been feeling ill all day with increasingly severe diarrhoea so I was already dehydrated when the Finnish Red Cross group invited us to a party in the evening in their home-made sauna made from tent canvas. I joined in and it was the worst thing I could have done. It was very hot in there and I lost even more fluid from sweating. The vomiting started in the night and by morning I was in a terrible state – suffering from severe water and salt loss with a vicious headache.

The rest of the team decided I should take the day off and everyone in Wattana set out for the camps, leaving the place almost deserted. As the hours went by, I realized I was in trouble: my blood pressure was dropping and every time I tried to stand up I felt faint and had to lie down again before I passed out. The hut was tropically hot inside but I seemed to have given up sweating. I crawled on all fours to the door of my hut, trying to keep my head low to prevent the dizziness, but outside there was no one to help except the Thai cook who didn't speak English. He obviously thought this foreigner crawling about the compound was strange behaviour and he avoided me.

By afternoon I was losing touch with reality and thought again how ironic it would be to die, not as I'd feared from the Khmer Rouge or Vietcong, but from some tiny amoebae.

The team arrived back from work and I vaguely heard them saying I looked deathly white. They had the sense to put up an intravenous saline drip in my arm and I was hurriedly packed off to Bangkok to recover. I don't remember the journey but I woke up in a beautifully cool room in the Bangkok Nursing Home. Still feeling disorientated, I heard the doctor telling me he would give me lots of intravenous glucose solution. I thought to myself this wasn't right but I didn't have the strength to tell him – I needed salt as well as water.

Fortunately someone from the Bangkok delegation came to visit later and I got them to bring in lots of bags of salty crisps for me. The effect was remarkable and by next morning I was feeling completely better and impatient to get back to the border. I learned a valuable lesson in tropical medicine from that – it's the dehydration that causes most of the problems. Replace what's been lost and you can save the patient.

# Chapter 5

# War Zone

I returned to work and I had forgotten the misgivings I'd had when I'd first started the mission. It was also easy to forget that I was still working in a war zone, but if the onset of the dry season discouraged the malaria mosquitoes it was bringing another threat and I realized I'd been taking the peaceful surroundings for granted. The mission was about to change radically.

We had a security alert as we arrived at the main delegation to begin the day's work, the first time since my arrival. The security delegate had heard reports of Vietnamese shelling close to the border road and for three days we were unable to go into the two hospitals. We sat around the delegation wondering what was happening to the patients. We needn't have worried – we were not as indispensable as we thought and the Khmer were more skilled and resourceful than we imagined. When we returned to Tap Prik we found the hospital office largely empty. They were all in the plastic operating theatre. It seemed that they'd diagnosed appendicitis in one of the villagers and as we hadn't been there to help, they'd decided to go ahead and operate. We were in time to watch them finishing the suturing of the abdominal layers at the end of the operation. They had an assistant shining a flashlight into the wound; he had occasionally to hit the lamp as the bulb kept going out and the battery was almost flat. They had got a book of surgery in Chinese propped up against the patient's right foot, and a Chinese/Khmer dictionary propped up against the other. Appendicectomy can be one of the most difficult of operations – but within three days the patient was walking about the hospital.

The security alert had been a preliminary warning. The peace was broken at Tap Prik one morning when I thought I heard thunder. It was the sound of shelling in the distance getting louder and it marked the beginning of a Vietnamese offensive against the Khmer Rouge. The hospital staff were keen to look after our safety and told us not to come to the hospital when there was shelling in the neighbourhood, but it couldn't be predicted and could happen suddenly. By the next day, they had built sturdy shelters for us from heavy logs – these might offer some protection from shrapnel but not from a close shell burst. For our part we draped the roof of each hut with a white sheet with a large red cross on it. The Khmer thought this might offer some protection from air raids but they

were of little use against shelling. The unease I'd felt on my first day was returning. I felt the tension everywhere – among the other team members, among the
Khmer staff and the patients themselves.

I was used to seeing minor wounds from landmines but now fresh mines
had been laid by both sides nearer to the villages. Willy's prediction had been
wrong, and we were to face much more horrific injuries.

One of the victims they brought in was a man who'd stepped on an anti-personnel mine. They laid him down on the dirt floor under the shade of a tree.
His right foot and lower leg almost up to the knee was missing. Instead there
were thin slices of skin and bleeding muscle hanging from the end almost like
the torn fabric of a trouser leg. The end of the tibia bone was sheared off, like a
bone you might buy from a butcher carelessly hacked in two, the bone marrow
exposed. Part of the other smaller bone of the leg, the fibula, was hanging loose
and was attached only by a thin shred of tendon. The stump was bleeding profusely, two arteries were pulsing blood and the man was in a bad state. In shock
from the loss of blood and the pain, his face was deathly pale, his eyes wide with
terror and he was shaking violently.

We got him into a stable condition, stopped the bleeding, reduced his pain
with morphine and brought his blood pressure up to an acceptable level. There
was nothing we could do here with our limited facilities so we decided to get
him as soon as possible to the ICRC hospital at Khao-i-Dang.

There was a delay at the small border post; the Thai soldiers had instructions not to let any Khmer past this point. We had no common language with
the Thai so we showed them the patient in the back of the Land Cruiser.
They took one look at the blood-soaked bandages and the frightened face of
the patient and hurriedly waved us through. We drove back to Aranyaprathet
then beyond, another twenty kilometres to Khao-i-Dang in the north desperately hoping the patient would survive the jolting rough road. We handed our
patient over to the ICRC surgeons. He would be operated on immediately and
eventually, when the wound had healed, he would be fitted with a prosthesis,
an artificial leg.

With the pressure off us, we had time now to wander around the camp in
the late afternoon sun. It was enormous. Although it was in Thailand, it was in
effect the second largest Cambodian 'town' after the capital Phnom Penh. It
covered almost two and a half square kilometres. It looked more like an intern-
ment camp as the Thai government had ringed it with a barbed-wire security
fence to prevent the refugees going further into Thailand. This was another
insight into the immense tragedy I had stepped into. The refugees were no longer statistics but real people.

I immediately noticed how different it was here from Nong Pru and Tap Prik: it was a huddle of thousands of untidy huts with children playing in the red dust. And it was noisy and I suddenly realized what was so odd about Nong Pru and Tap Prik – they were both unnaturally quiet. I noticed another difference – there were far more elderly people here.

I came across a children's play group organized by another aid agency. These children were up to about ten years old, and they had been through the hell of the Khmer Rouge brutality and massacres. The children were painting brightly coloured pictures. The expatriate teacher in charge showed me one of them, it was a crude picture of a large cauldron and inside were the faces of the child's parents. They had been boiled alive by the Khmer Rouge and the child had witnessed it. I looked at the child's picture, unable to comprehend this inhumanity which was outside all of my experience but now seemingly a part of life in this dreadful conflict. With the priority given to tropical diseases and surgical treatment, the aid agencies were slow to appreciate and act on the psychological problems of the Khmer victims, which could have far longer consequences than a physical war injury. It occurred to me much later that perhaps aid workers would also need counselling for the things they had seen and experienced. We heard stories of Khmer women being accepted for immigration to the US and living seemingly normal lives but then suddenly going blind. There was nothing wrong with their eyes; it was a psychological response to the horrors they had seen in the killing fields.

The conflict had now come closer to Nong Pru and Tap Prik and I was becoming more familiar with the first-aid treatment of mine, shell and bullet injuries. Sometimes as we worked we would hear shelling in the distance and I would look up. The Khmer, knowing it was too far away to mean trouble, would jokingly say, 'C'est un orage' – 'It's a thunderstorm' and I learned to laugh nervously with them.

But I felt the tension amongst the hospital staff as we worked together and on two consecutive days the Khmer hurriedly sent us back to our vehicles on the other side of the ravine for safety when the shelling came close. There were several quiet days and I thought the trouble was over. I was at Tap Prik one morning preparing to start a ward round as usual. Willy had left at the end of his mission and I was now the only doctor until a replacement arrived. There were also two new nurses, Lidia from the Netherlands and Marie from Canada. We had parked the Land Cruisers on the Thai side of the bridge as usual and were transferring supplies into the pharmacy hut.

There came the sound of shell fire – closer than I'd ever heard it before. I heard an ominous whistling and I saw the sudden plume of smoke coming from the forest before I heard the explosion. The Khmer thought it was just a few kilometres away.

Everyone stopped and looked up, then ran the other way to the opposite end of the compound and into the forest. Chantrea ran with them and we followed for more than a kilometre. There was perhaps ten minutes of silence then another explosion even louder. I thought I felt the ground shake. She urged us to leave and get back over the border but we were on the wrong side of the ravine and separated from our vehicles and our radios. I would have preferred to risk going straight back through the hospital and over the bridge but she told me the shelling was probably not over yet and it would be much easier and safer simply to go the other way and cross further upstream. There was another bridge not far away. She introduced me to one of her friends, Natha – he would show us the way. It seemed sensible to take her advice so Lidia, Marie and I followed him further into the forest. Two of Natha's friends accompanied us. He told us to keep behind him all the time and not to stray even a foot's breadth from the path. I knew why – mines. I could see he was very careful and very alert.

We walked.

After ten minutes, still under the forest canopy, I asked him how much further. It wasn't an easy conversation – he spoke only rudimentary French. Still, it was better than my few words of Khmer.

'Just a little way,' he said.

We walked some more along the tortuous narrow path. The heat was intense and there was still a lot of humidity despite the change of season. The path started to climb through the never-ending denseness of the forest. It was impossible to see too far ahead as under the palm canopy was thick bamboo and twining undergrowth. The noise of wildlife was almost deafening. We were in real jungle here.

Natha told me, 'There are still wild tigers in Cambodia.'

Just what I needed to know – real tigers, I presumed this time.

'But very few now.'

Good

'Because many are killed by landmines.'

Ahh.

But, he added encouragingly, that rare orchids on the other hand were safe and thriving.

After another twenty minutes I started to worry. I tried to talk to Natha again.

'We're not there yet,' he said. 'We're going to the next village – Klong Wah. You can cross the river there.'

I'd heard Klong Wah was very much a Khmer Rouge camp and, I suspected, not too friendly to foreigners because the Red Cross had been unable to make any contact with it. I tried to remember from a map I'd seen in the delegation, where it was. It must be close to Tap Prik. I asked Natha.

'Only seven kilometres away,' he said.

My heart sank. I was sweating profusely and in this heat that seemed an enormous distance.

'And if we can't cross there I'll take you to Khao Din village, only another seven kilometres after that.'

He could see the look of desperation in our faces. 'And if that's no good there is Klong Kai Thueng, another six kilometres further on. That is my village. You are very welcome there.'

I was becoming seriously concerned and I was also becoming disorientated as we seemed to be going too far to the east. I felt we were being led deeper and deeper into Cambodia. This was becoming a nightmare.

Natha, as if he could hear my thoughts, turned his head as he walked and said, 'My name, Natha, means great leader.'

Very reassuring, it made all the difference, I thought cynically. I gave him a wan smile.

After an hour we stopped to rest. We were making very slow progress. I sat down with Lidia and Marie and had a discussion. We had made a serious mistake making this trip. It was taking on the quality of a nightmare. We should have been patient and waited at Tap Prik for the shelling to stop but we really had no option now but to carry on. We certainly couldn't find our way back along the path alone. I began to wonder what would happen at the delegation when they realized we had disappeared. It was another hour before we stopped again, we must have walked far more than seven kilometres.

We were becoming exhausted and dehydrated and bitten by insects. Natha spoke softly to us, he seemed rather embarrassed. He's got us completely lost, I thought in despair. But I was wrong. He explained that we'd almost reached Klong Wah and traditional Khmer hospitality meant that we would normally have been welcomed into the village. But the Khmer Rouge here could be 'difficult' (rather an understatement). He suggested, if it wouldn't offend us, that we skirt round the village instead and go straight to the river. I couldn't agree more. We suddenly emerged into grassland. There was a welcome breeze but if anything it was hotter here as there was no shade. I thought to myself, 'This seems an extreme way to get away from a dull UK operating theatre just for some sunshine and fresh air.'

The path was difficult to follow. Natha suddenly stopped, looked at the ground and held us back. He wasn't happy and he wasn't prepared to go on – he suspected landmines. I could see absolutely nothing unusual about the path at all. It made me realize how little I knew of this alien environment and how vulnerable we were. I had a new respect for Natha. He led us back the way we came for perhaps half a kilometre until he found another, safer, route.

We walked on through undisturbed tall grass. Another half hour and I had had enough. I told Natha we had to stop, that we could go no further. He pointed to a line of trees only about a hundred metres ahead.

He spoke some French words which I'll never forget: '*Là-bas c'est la sécurité.*' 'Over there is safety,' he said, then paused. '*Il y a la Thaïlande.*' 'There is Thailand.'

Within minutes we reached the trees and the river and crossed it using a bridge even more rickety than the one we knew at Tap Prik. With a startling clarity, I could immediately imagine how it must be for the hundreds of thousands of refugees who had made the arduous and dangerous journey right across Cambodia. I could feel the same relief when they realized that they were now standing on Thai soil and were safe. A short distance and we had joined a red dirt road.

Natha pointed up the road and said, 'Aranyaprathet.'

I almost fell on my knees and kissed the dirt. I thanked him and he hurried back. He still had a journey of perhaps 15 kilometres or more and he seemed as fresh as when he'd started.

We began walking along the dusty road expecting a long and tiring journey ahead. But at least here we felt safe. It wasn't long before a pick-up truck came up behind us. A Thai farmer who spoke only incomprehensible Thai gave us a lift all the way back to Aranyaprathet. He kept an expressionless face but occasionally glanced at us. He must have been wondering what on earth these odd-looking, exhausted foreigners were doing miles from anywhere. We thanked him profusely as he dropped us off in town. Lidia started to take money out of her pocket as payment, but I knew enough about the Thai by now to stop her. The lift he'd given us was a gift. Paying him would devalue the gift and would offend him.

We returned to Tap Prik the next morning by the more usual route. Our Land Cruisers were still there undamaged but we were stunned to find that the bridge had disappeared. It had been hit by a shell the previous day, leaving charred and shattered timbers down below in the river. The bridge was essential – without it, we would have to manhandle all the heavy boxes down the ravine, across the stream at the bottom and laboriously up the other steep side. It took more than two hours to unload the trucks. This wouldn't do. The lack of confidence I'd experienced at the start of the mission had now disappeared and with the enthusiasm and perhaps overconfidence that followed, I took it upon myself to organize the building of a new bridge – in the best traditions of colonialism.

A team of Khmer workmen appeared from the village, led by their foreman, an elderly 'greybeard' with a stooping back and vacant expression. I drew a plan of a new bamboo bridge and I was rather proud of it. It's all a matter of triangles. I showed it to the foreman and set them to work while I went into the hospital to start the day's ward round. Around mid-morning I returned to the bridge. The work had begun, but someone had altered the plan and the framework didn't look right. I took the old foreman aside and pointed out that I wanted a large piece of timber, a tree trunk, right in the middle of the stream to take the weight. He said something in French about floods. I replied firmly it would be better to stick exactly to the plan.

It was a difficult morning in the wards. It was hot and humid again. I returned at lunchtime and the bridge was finished but nothing like I'd planned it. In Southeast Asian society, it's not done to lose one's temper – it means a loss of face. I lost my temper. I was hot, sweating and irritable. I have no other excuse. The villagers gathered round as I argued with the foreman. There were some giggles – watching this red-faced Westerner embarrassing himself was great fun. When the Khmer get angry, they paradoxically lower their voice. I raised my voice and the foreman's voice was down to a whisper. I should have known. But this was after all my first mission.

'I want this bridge built properly. I don't want it to fall down!' I shouted.

'I think it will be satisfactory,' he said almost inaudibly.

'I doubt it! Have you ever built a bridge before?'

'Yes'

'Where?'

He whispered, 'I will take you to see it one day. It is a steel and concrete suspension bridge for four lanes of railway traffic. I built it when I was a professor of civil engineering.'

More giggles from the audience. I tore up my drawing and apologized.

They never let me forget it. For the rest of my time at Tap Prik we would arrive each morning, park the vehicles and approach the bridge. The Khmer would stop us, jump up and down on the bridge to make sure it was safe, giggle, then wave us on. As far as I know the bridge is still standing.

*Chapter 6*

# Khmer Rouge

We were always warmly welcomed and treated very politely at both Nong Pru and Tap Prik so it was easy to forget that we were there under sufferance to a large extent because we were useful. The Khmer Rouge presence had always been there, in the background, almost invisible – but with the sudden onset of fighting they became more prominent and their influence at the hospital increased. It was now not unusual to see men carrying Kalashnikov rifles in the hospital.

One day the staff at Nong Pru disappeared. In the afternoon they suddenly upped and headed for the village, leaving us staring after them. I could see them in the distance through the trees gathered round a figure, listening to him speak. Half an hour later they returned without an explanation. When I asked Mr Sam who the figure was, he said confidingly that it was an important visitor whom they'd all been obliged to greet.

'Who?' I asked.

'Pol Pot.'

That was the only information I could get out of him. It was as though I had unknowingly seen Hitler in Nazi Germany.

The Khmer hospital staff we worked with almost never mentioned the Khmer Rouge, but there was a dark side to this mission which was becoming apparent as the conflict came nearer. The Khmer at both hospitals would talk happily about everything except the Khmer Rouge. I was advised quietly and politely not to mention the name.

I was alone in the dimly lit pharmacy hut, checking lists of medicine with Mr Sam who seemed to have great difficulty reading them. I knew he wasn't illiterate – he had been very well educated in Phnom Penn. In a rare moment Mr Sam reluctantly admitted, when he was alone with me, that he had worn glasses when he was an accountant in Phnom Penn, but this was before the Khmer Rouge had started victimizing wearers of spectacles, regarding these people as suspected undesirable 'intellectuals'. He didn't want to take the risk now.

We had become good friends in the past months and it was becoming easier for him to confide in me.

He checked to make sure no one could overhear him: 'During the worst times of the Khmer Rouge, people could be rounded up and killed not only for wearing glasses, but for speaking a foreign language. We are allowed to speak French to you but we would be suspect if we were found learning English.'

He told me it had been an ideological crime to scavenge for food. One of his friends had been shot for growing his own vegetables. It was a crime to be old and sick. It was even a crime to shed tears for loved ones who die, especially those whom the Khmer Rouge had killed. Ironically, even some Khmer Rouge loyalists were killed for failing to find enough 'counter-revolutionaries' to execute.

There were a number of orphans in the hospital. One was being treated for malaria – a small boy of about eight years old who never spoke. I asked if anyone knew what had happened to his parents. One of the female nurses said she'd known him from when they both lived in the town of Battambang. I thought at the time it was unusual for anyone to talk about the past. But she continued. His parents had both been shot and killed by the Khmer Rouge. She said they'd also killed her own parents and all her brothers and sisters. The ward went silent. She hid her head completely in her headscarf and I could hear quiet sobbing. I now knew enough about this society to know she was being very indiscreet. The next day the nurse wasn't there and we never saw her again. She had simply disappeared. When I asked Mr Sam about her, he subtly changed the subject.

Then we had a young woman patient at Tap Prik who had been having low abdominal pain. She was a diagnostic puzzle; she had a urine infection but it hadn't cleared up with the routine antibiotics and I had, unusually, sent a urine specimen to Bangkok for testing. On the morning ward round, we came to the young woman and I showed the lab report to Chantrea. It was gonorrhoea infection.

She took me to one side and whispered, 'Change the diagnosis.'

I asked her what she meant.

She looked around to make sure we were alone. 'Gonorrhoea is an anti-social disease to the Khmer Rouge. They treat it with an injection of lead.'

I was puzzled but she put two fingers up to her temple in imitation of a gun, then she took the lab report I was holding, discreetly tore it into small pieces and hid it in her pocket.

Another incident was more serious. In any medical set-up there is always a lot of rubbish – empty boxes, old bandages and dressings which have to be cleared away – but used and broken glass ampoules and needles would be a particular problem here. People, especially children, walked about freely in bare feet and it was easy for them to step on something sharp. So I advised the workers that we should be sure to collect all the sharps in a plastic box. From then on I never saw any sharp rubbish.

Then at Nong Pru, an eight year-old child was brought in, injured. They told me she'd wandered off away from the village and stepped on a small mine. She had a wound to her leg and it was probable that she had some shrapnel in there. It was getting late in the day but we were happy to stay to operate on the little girl; it wouldn't take long. But the behaviour of the local nurses was strange. They said they could deal with it themselves – there was a lot of quiet talking between them. They didn't seem to want me to be involved but I went ahead. I put the girl to sleep and examined the wound; it wasn't severe – a cut to the thigh but anything in there has to be removed before infection sets in. I had a metal probe which I put into the hole in the muscle and I felt something grating against the probe deep inside. I managed to grasp it with a pair of forceps and drew it out. At first I couldn't make it out. I rinsed it with water and then I froze. I saw it was a shard of glass from an ampoule with the Red Cross penicillin label still attached. Exactly the type we were using. It took me a few moments to realize the significance – the Khmer were using the sharps from the hospital mixed with explosive to make home-made mines.

It had gone quiet.

When I turned round, all the staff had silently left. They all knew. All of us expatriates felt a betrayal of trust. It affected us deeply. At the Red Cross head-quarters they weren't as surprised as we were. They'd had reports from another camp that the six-inch nails supplied for building and the metal tips of ballpoint pens given to the children had instead been used as shrapnel in mines. They were very effective at penetrating human tissue. We followed advice and stayed away from both Nong Pru and Tap Prik for three days, as a subtle message.

We returned and carried on as usual but the mood was never quite the same again for the remaining few days of my mission. Marie, the Canadian nurse, ended her mission early.

On my last day, Mr Sam said an awkward goodbye. He'd said nothing up to that point about the ampoule incident, obviously embarrassed. As I walked with him for the last time from the hospital to the Land Cruisers, he broke the silence, apologized, and said quietly, 'Don't judge us too harshly. Sometimes we have little choice if we want to survive. For it is our misfortune that we ordinary people are at the mercy of both the Vietnamese and the Khmer Rouge and we have nowhere else to go.'

Sometimes the culture shock is greater when you come home. I came back to a cold, foggy UK and soon took a position as anaesthetist at a hospital in

Hereford. At the interview I was asked about my time in Cambodia but strangely I found I couldn't begin to explain. I didn't know where to start. I later went for a walk and found myself on a woodland path. No thick, green undergrowth here, no sweltering heat, no birdsong, no crickets. But I realized that I was subconsciously looking carefully at the ground in front of my feet. Life had changed.

# PART 2

# KHAO-I-DANG REFUGEE CAMP: THAI–CAMBODIAN BORDER, 1987

*Chapter 7*

# The Dog's Back

It was six years until I worked for the Red Cross again. In the meantime I'd specialized in anaesthetics and I was what is termed 'clinically independent'– I could do it without any help or supervision. I was well on the way to taking a permanent consultant anaesthetist post in a hospital in the UK. I was working in the tranquillity of Herefordshire and I'd even bought a house there. Before me there were another twenty-five to thirty years working in an operating theatre. It wasn't long before I was feeling restless again. I needed some fresh air.

Then I was unexpectedly phoned by the Red Cross; this time they were looking for a qualified anaesthetist, for the Thai–Cambodian border again, as part of a UK surgical team for three months in the ICRC hospital at Khao-i-Dang.

I didn't hesitate. I said yes.

The hospital was the same one I'd visited back in 1980 on the Thai side of the border twenty kilometres north along the busy road north of Aranyaprathet. It was part of the huge refugee camp established by the United Nations High Commissioner for Refugees (UNHCR) in 1979. Khao-i-Dang means 'dog's back' in Thai because of the shape of the hill behind the camp. It was featured in the 1984 film *The Killing Fields* which has become iconic of the Cambodian tragedy. At the end the main character, Dith Pran, flees across Cambodia, sees the red cross on the hospital at Khao-i-Dang and realizes he is safely in Thailand. It was strange watching the film and seeing the same veranda where we would drink tea in the evenings. The actor and doctor Haing S. Ngor, who played the part of Dith Pran, was himself a refugee and his story is very much the same. He worked in Khao-i-Dang hospital in 1979 and visited in 1983.

I was surprised that the border area was still full of refugees. But it was much quieter than when I'd first visited. It was no longer news and many of the smaller organizations had left. The main refugee camp at Khao-i-Dang was still full with over 10,000 displaced Cambodians. It was a good example of the problem of going into a war area and setting up a hospital. In fact, it is very easy to set up a refugee hospital but very difficult to take it out.

The landmine injuries continued to come in, long after the fighting had stopped. And it's not easy to shut the hospital doors one day and say, 'That's it, you'll have to find somewhere else to go.' There was nowhere else.

We had also created a problem ourselves. Thousands of people had settled in the border area. Some of the children had grown up in the camp. The refugees were fed and they had excellent medical facilities. There was no incentive to go back home. We had no 'exit strategy' as the phrase has it. We had unavoidably become the national health service of the border region. It was many years more until it could eventually be closed but the Red Cross learned a lesson at Khao-i-Dang and were careful not to repeat the mistake in subsequent conflicts.

There were three surgical teams, British, Canadian and Finnish, each with a surgeon, anaesthetist and theatre nurse. There were also three expatriate ward nurses and a physiotherapist. The theatre nurse was Anne Kerr who had done many missions as a Red Cross worker, the surgeon was Robin Coupland – on one of his first missions, but who, because of his eventual wide experience of war injuries with the Red Cross, became the expert in this field and organized training of Red Cross surgeons. He jokingly told me he loved surgery, fishing and women, but not necessarily in that order.

The huge accommodation area at Wattana had long since closed as the number of medical delegates had been greatly reduced over the years, and we now lived at the delegation just outside Aranyaprathet in comfortable prefabricated huts with straw roofs and we commuted each day by Red Cross minibus the twenty kilometres to the hospital.

There was a rota system where one team would be on call to accept, treat and operate on any admissions and stay at the hospital overnight for any more casualties. The second team did a huge ward round of post-operative cases and perform any repeat operations needed. The third team which had been on-call the night before would do the same but go home after lunch for some sleep if it had been a busy night. It also gave us enough leeway for one team to go away for a few days in the middle of the mission.

On our first day at the delegation we had another briefing so we could meet everyone, and arrangements were made for us all to go to Khao-i-Dang for an introductory visit and a hand-over of all the patients. We were due to travel from the delegation courtyard to the hospital with the outgoing French team but there were several ICRC minibuses waiting – there was still a lot of activity at that time, field delegates were going off to meet Khmer contacts over the border and detention delegates were trying to trace prisoners of war. Which was our bus? We were confused but tried the most likely one. There were three silent, scowling people sitting in there whom we took to be the French team. I asked with a smile if this was the bus going to Khao-i-Dang.

There was a pause, a withering, bored look and a sarcastic reply: 'Well, it is certainly not going off to Bangkok for a holiday!'

Oh dear, attitude. They'd not had a good mission and after three months they all hated each other.

At the hospital we had another briefing. This would be the fifth – we had been briefed at the British Red Cross headquarters in London, then at ICRC in Geneva, then at the delegation in Bangkok, then at the Aranyaprathet delegation and now at the hospital. All very commendable of course but the joke was made that we would continue to have introductory briefings right up until the midpoint of the mission when they would subtly change to debriefing meetings that would continue until we returned home.

We settled in and had no problems throughout the three months. We would sometimes even swap members within the teams for variety and learn from each other.

It was busy. The vast majority of cases were landmine injuries. They were often horrific. I was used to seeing extensive wounds in the UK but they were fresh – after a car accident, for example, the ambulance would bring them to A&E in a very short time, measured in minutes. These landmine wounds were days old. They were infected and many had the awful smell of gangrene. The patient might have been carried or even walked themselves for days on end, in pain with no painkillers. They would arrive at Khao-i-Dang, sometimes in a very bad state with blood loss, dehydration and infection. A typical case would be resuscitated, and go to the theatre for debridement of the wound or even amputation of part or whole of a limb. It was absolutely essential to take away all the dead tissue – to debride the wound. The surgeon had to be ruthless otherwise infection would set in. The skin was never stitched closed at this stage. The wound would be bandaged with sterile dressings and then left for four days. Then, under anaesthetic, the dressings were removed in the operating theatre and if all was well the wound would look clean and healthy and we would close the skin in a procedure called delayed primary suture or DPC. There was a saying in Red Cross circles that if the wound became infected the surgeon would blame the ward nurse for not keeping the dressings clean and the nurse would blame the surgeon for not doing a radical enough debridement.

ICRC surgery was still in its infancy at the time and we were still learning. Surgeons coined the term 'salami surgery'; inexperienced surgeons trying to save as much tissue as possible, might, for example, do a below-knee amputation instead of above-knee. In a few days the wound would start smelling with infection. The patient would go back to theatre for another slice of tissue to be debrided to remove the infection. This might happen several times, the patient deteriorating each time, and there is only so far up the leg or arm one can go.

Surgeons soon learned the lesson. In Geneva, before they set out on a mission they would undergo an intense training, thanks to people like Robin Coupland.

The Thai nurses spoke excellent English, but one of them, eager to learn 'ICRC English', couldn't understand the word 'debridement' because with a dictionary she had concluded it must mean to take away the woman from her husband on the wedding day. Presumably she thought debriefing was losing your pants.

Of course many wounded people never survived to get help. Innumerable Khmer stepped on mines and if not killed instantly died soon after. The bodies were never found. I heard of a Buddhist monk wounded by a mine who, carried by his friends, had almost made it to the hospital. They had stopped in the first village across the border and asked for medical help in the village shop. The shop had somehow got hold of a bottle of an intravenous plasma expander – a blood substitute – and sold it to them. These solutions have a short lifespan and must be absolutely sterile. This bottle was months old and instead of being almost colourless had become green with bacteria. It must have been similar to the green scum on ditchwater. The friends injected this into the monk who was dead within four hours.

Sometimes there was a happier outcome. One evening an ambulance rushed in with a seven-year-old girl. She came from a village in the north, right on the border and had been playing in front of her house when there had suddenly been some cross-border shooting. The little girl had been shot in the head and was deeply unconscious. There is realistically almost no hope at all here for someone with a bullet in the brain and we assumed she would die very soon. But we put her on a table in the emergency room and took an X-ray of her head. The bullet was not where we thought it was. It hadn't even penetrated the skull but had gone through the scalp at a sharp angle, ricocheted along the bone and was lying just under the skin further back. As we looked in amazement at the picture, the girl suddenly woke up, saw some strange-looking Europeans staring at her, jumped off the table and ran off into the courtyard screaming. We eventually persuaded her to come back and have the bullet removed. She kept it as a souvenir. A very lucky girl.

The anaesthetic side was in many ways simpler than in a hospital in the UK. We used the injectable anaesthetic ketamine, this in the days before it was subject to substance abuse. It has intense painkilling properties – someone once described the feeling as totally losing all bodily sensation, feeling like nothing but two eyeballs on stalks. It is perfect for limb injuries, not so good for abdominal operations. The blood pressure stays up, the patient continues to breathe and the swallowing reflex is still there, so there is less chance of inhaling saliva or vomit. The only drawback is that it can afterwards make patients disorientated and cause nightmares, often terrifying, which is why it isn't used as much in the UK. It never seemed to cause a problem in Khao-i-Dang. I wondered if the experiences they had suffered in real life were such a nightmare in themselves that ketamine didn't even come close.

Life was actually pleasant in Khao-i-Dang. The operating theatre had been built with air-conditioning, as the outside temperatures could soar. Such was the delegation's concern for the wellbeing of its medical staff that it had employed a chef, who at one time had worked at one of Bangkok's best restaurants, to cook for us. We would order our Thai food in the morning before leaving the delegation and it would be delivered hot for the evening meal. I ate far better there than back in the UK. On Wednesdays, for a change, he would make superb pizzas. After the mission, being debriefed in Geneva, we were asked if we had any complaints about the food. Someone as a joke said we could only get pizzas on Wednesday. The Swiss debriefer nodded and solemnly wrote it down.

When we were very busy, we might operate on a dozen patients during the day, then have another half dozen repeat operations, maybe DPCs, well into the evening. When on call the team slept in a communal room next to the theatre, still in our theatre clothes. Maybe in the middle of the night we would be half-woken by the noise of an ambulance entering the hospital. Desperate for sleep we would hear it approach. If it stopped short we knew it was a medical rather than surgical case as it parked outside the MSF hospital next door and we could lapse back into grateful sleep. If the ambulance carried on, it was for us and we would be up for at least a couple of hours.

The surgical teams were not exclusively western, one of our team members was a Japanese nurse. She had been sent on her own to Khao-i-Dang by the Japanese Red Cross who had a rather different policy – they allowed less choice of mission than the rest of the Red Cross national societies. She was alone and spoke no English at all, the idea being that she should learn English on the job as soon as possible. It didn't work. We managed to communicate a little by sign language but it was very difficult to integrate her into the team and when things got hectic with a large influx of badly injured patients there just wasn't time. She was naturally shy and introverted and came across as very formal and distant. She spent a lot of the time alone. She got the occasional phone call from her parents or the Japanese Red Cross and one evening when I went to her hut to call her to the phone, I found her sitting in the half-dark looking at a certificate she had been given before she'd set out. We found out later it was a commendation for taking on the mission and expecting her to distinguish herself and be a credit to her family. She was quietly crying.

Two things changed the situation. I was in the hospital admissions room when a severely injured patient was hurriedly brought in. The Japanese nurse was wandering about aimlessly outside. She ran in and came to the same conclusion I had – haemothorax – the lung was punctured and both air and blood were leaking into the pleural space just inside the rib-cage squashing the lung. This is a real emergency. We didn't need any language. She brought me exactly what I needed – chest drain, drip set, intubation equipment. When we'd finished, and the patient started to improve, we looked at each other in relief – no words necessary. I later told the medical coordinator and he let out a satisfied sigh. He said he was having great difficulty writing an assessment report about her which had to be sent both to Geneva and to the Japanese Red Cross. He'd heard no comments either positive or negative from most of the teams, but at least here was something to go on. I said I understood that and he asked me if I'd consider a medical coordinator's job in a future mission. I said I might have a go.

The other occasion was when we were having a party in the delegation. Some of the field delegates were leaving at the end of their mission. Work hard, play hard. It got very noisy. At some point, one of our Dutch nurses found a can of shaving foam and started squirting it on people's heads. The Japanese nurse was standing forlornly in the corner, with a drink in her hand, miserable. As the Dutch nurse passed her she casually squirted her with foam. There was a second's pause and then the Japanese nurse took a handful of foam and plastered it on someone else. It was the first time I'd ever seen her smile. I suppose it was a baptism – she felt she had been accepted. Things suddenly got much easier from that day on.

We had very few cases of post-operative wound infection. I expected there to be more, after all this was a makeshift hospital, in the middle of a dusty area only just out of the jungle. But there wasn't time for the bacteria to get established. The most susceptible clinical area – calling it an intensive care or high dependency unit would perhaps be stretching terminology a bit far – was simply a concrete floor, the walls were bamboo poles strung together and the roof was corrugated iron. So germs had a hard time of it – the corrugated roof was blazing hot under the scorching sun, therefore self-sterilizing; the bamboo was taken away, burned and replaced every two months or when it started to fall apart. As for the concrete floor, the Khmer had a unique way of washing it. Every Sunday morning, they would divert a local stream which would flood the whole hospital floor. Patients soon learned not to put their rice bowl or other belongings on the floor next to their bed on Sunday otherwise they would lose it all as it floated outside and downstream.

When a patient had a limb amputated, a prosthetic limb was fitted at the reha-bilitation workshop next to the hospital. We had a couple of expatriate experts from Geneva but most of the technicians were Khmer recruited from the camp and trained to make the prostheses – they were all amputees with prostheses of their own. The idea was that there's nothing like having to wear a prosthesis yourself to appreciate the finer points of getting one to fit comfortably. The ones we made were very basic. An above-knee model would be a simple leather cup-shape where the amputated leg stump would fit into, a simple metal hinge to represent the knee joint, a piece of thick bamboo for the lower leg and a life-like rubber foot. They all wore long trousers so when fitted it was quite difficult to see that it was a false leg. Because they were so simple they were much easier to repair especially if the wearer had gone back into Cambodia and had no access to a hospital. Some of the limbs made by some of the other aid agencies were more complicated – no use to a poor Khmer farmer if it had to be sent back to Germany for repair! A piece of bamboo could be found anywhere.

Ours were surprisingly robust considering the constant hard use. It was the knee joint that usually went first. There was a persistent rumour, probably apoc-ryphal, that if you were an amputee who needed to replace your 'knee' hinge and you could get hold of an old Toyota Land Cruiser – of which there were many in the region – there was a bracket that supported the exhaust pipe which could be adapted to fit the prosthesis. We had visions of marauding bands of amputees hijacking Toyotas. Conversely of course there could have been bands of Toyota parts dealers mugging amputees for their knee joints.

Child amputees presented a special problem. As they grew up, they would need larger prostheses and as their bones grew they would often need repeated operations to adjust the stump and this would continue until they were past puberty. In fact we found that children did quite well; they adapted much more quickly than adults to the fact that they'd lost a limb, took the prostheses in their stride – as it were – and, being children, couldn't sit still so they did their own physiotherapy by running around and playing. Prosthetic arms and hands were a different and difficult matter; they were not as simple to make and maintain. But they improved over the years.

*Chapter 8*

# Kru Khmer

There was a third unofficial hospital at Khao-i-Dang run by the 'Kru Khmer' who practised traditional medicine, Cambodian style. It is very old and uses a form of naturopathy that combines different roots, barks, leaves of various trees, herbs and other natural ingredients. They had a bamboo hut at the other end of the compound where the chief doctor would sit Buddha-style with his plastic pots full of home-made medicines by his side and dispense wisdom and cures.

We had a very good relationship. He recognized his limits – someone came to him with abdominal pains and he immediately brought them over to us: it turned out to be appendicitis. At the same time he was very useful to us when we were faced with a problem that couldn't be solved by surgery. Psychological trauma or severe depression was common and was something we had neither the time nor expertise to deal with. The Kru Khmer would take them and of course understood their culture far better than we did. The Kru Khmer doctor was very interested in our methods – he came to visit several times. He particularly liked the idea of a set of patient's notes. He produced his own version with boxes to tick; he had one for the patient's astrological star-sign.

He was very good at dealing with long-term pain. In fact, on my first visit to his clinic, he found out I suffered from regular migraines so he insisted on preparing a treatment for me. I was to come back in a week. He would prepare some ingredients for a 'magic shower'. When I returned, he took me to a back room where several cauldrons were boiling filled with twigs and leaves. The smell was pungent and the wood smoke choking. He told me what was in my treatment – wood bark and herbs which were okay – but then more exotic things like powdered snake skin and bits of dead mouse. The whole mixture was a thick, black liquid. I was totally skeptical, my main concern being how to get out of the place without offending him. He handed me the bottle so I could smell it. It was rancid and foul. I said I was sorry but couldn't possibly drink it.

He was surprised. 'No, no, you don't drink it – I do!' He took a mouthful and sprayed it directly into my face – the magic shower.

I walked back to our hospital for a real shower. The strange thing was I didn't have a migraine for the rest of the three months I was there. I didn't realize it until I went home and then desperately wished I could remember exactly what he'd put in the magic shower.

Not even the Kru Khmer could help us with one patient, a man in his thirties who'd come to us after a mine injury. Some shrapnel had severed his spinal cord at the neck and he was permanently paralyzed from the neck down. His other wounds healed but there was little else we could do. If he went back to his family he would need constant skilled care; there was talk of transferring him to a spinal unit in Europe but the Kru Khmer doctor shook his head. One morning we arrived at the hospital to find he wasn't there. The family had taken him away and the rumour was that the solution they'd decided on was euthanasia. Another case was a young woman who had lost both hands from a landmine. Her father told us that no amount of rehabilitation would help her – she would never be married because no potential husband would accept that she could look after children with no hands.

However, we had a young boy of about fifteen who'd lost his right leg above the knee from a landmine. He was acutely depressed and wouldn't take any interest in rehabilitation exercises, he refused a prosthesis and lay on his bed all day, face to the wall. The Kru Khmer doctor sat and talked to him and persuaded him to go outside where a football match was taking place. At first the boy was very upset, crying that he'd never play football again, until the Kru Khmer called one of the players off the field, rolled up his trouser leg and showed the young boy the prosthetic leg. Every person playing on that team had lost a leg. And they were winning 2-0. The boy got his prosthesis and did very well.

The border area seemed much quieter than on my first mission and the town of Aranyaprathet was less busy and not constantly grid-locked with vehicles. After work, when not on-call, we would often drive into town. The expatriate women would often frequent the 'beauty parlours' to be pampered by a hairdresser or manicurist. We would all meet up at the ice-cream parlour where the brave would even try the durian-fruit-flavoured variety. This curious fruit smells dreadful, like rotting flesh – it is banned from some hotels in Thailand – but it actually doesn't taste too bad. During festival days there were stalls in the street selling fried locusts – to be tried at least once – and there was a regularly visiting Chinese opera company performing in a makeshift street theatre with colourful costumes but with music which very few of us found anything but unbearably shrill and irritating.

But the border was still next to a war zone and we were occasionally reminded of this.

We were coming back from Khao-i-Dang one day and giving a lift to a couple of newly arrived Belgian doctors from another aid agency back to Aranyaprathet.

Along this road there was always an air of tension as it was only a kilometre from the border. We had to pull over to the side of the road as a long convoy of Thai tanks passed us from the other direction. This was not unusual; they were nervously guarding the border against both Vietnamese and Khmer Rouge military incursions. One of the Belgians got out of the car to stretch his legs. He was behaving like a tourist, took out his Pentax camera and started taking photos of the tanks. Even as a beginner I knew you should never take photos of anything even slightly military-looking, especially anywhere near a war zone. Before I could get out to stop him, one of the tanks came to a halt opposite us. I had visions of us all being arrested, but out of the tank climbed an obviously high-ranking Thai commander. With a calm but serious expression he came over to us. Without saying a word, he took the camera from the Belgian, placed it on the ground in the middle of the road and waved his tank forward which drove right over it. By the time it passed there was absolutely nothing worth salvaging of the camera. Lesson learned.

One of the Khmer hospital staff, unusually, had a camera but thankfully he was far more discrete with it. In the days before digital cameras he had managed to get hold of a roll of 35mm Kodak film and had taken photos around the hospital. He had no way of getting the film developed himself, so we offered to have it sent to Bangkok via the ICRC bus. The film came back after a week, but it was blank – a complete white-out. Not too surprising as it was rather old film and the conditions were hot and humid. We bought him another roll. He took his photos, the film went to Bangkok, and came back blank again. When a third film came back blank we thought we ought to check his technique. The camera seemed perfectly 'light-tight' and he loaded the film correctly. He always took the lens cap off and took his pictures at a reasonable 125th sec at f8. Everything seemed fine until we saw that after each photo he would open the back of the camera to see if an image had appeared on the film.

Once a week, one of us would travel further north up the border road with other ICRC field delegates to our first-aid camp at Kab Cherng a hundred kilometres away. We would hold a clinic there and decide if any of the wounded needed to be sent to Khao-i-Dang for surgery.

In the centre of Site B, one of the nearby refugee camps, among the trees was a large elaborate wooden stage, decorated with flowers with a wooden throne in the centre. It had only one purpose – it had been built to receive Prince Sihanouk, the former ruler of Cambodia, on the off-chance that he ever visited the camp. It had been there for several years, unused. I don't think it ever was.

These free camps were so different from the Khmer Rouge camps of Nong Pru and Tap Prik where I'd been six years before. There was a much more relaxed and brighter atmosphere. There was even a small zoo. The head of the ICRC Kab Cherng sub-delegation had made a collection of orphaned monkeys. When I arrived, he jokingly lent me a tiny six-week-old monkey to carry around while I was working. He placed it on my shoulder and with its natural instinct to grasp onto anything, it stayed there happily all day. If I had to do some minor operating, I could simply stick it to a tree, rather like a rubbed balloon sticking to a wall; it would cling to anything – just find a branch and plonk it on. The thing he forgot to tell me was not to go to the toilet with a baby monkey on your shoulder – it thinks you're its mother and imitates everything you do.

Even though the work we were doing at Khao-i-Dang was not new, I learned that eventually on a Red Cross mission we would encounter some media interest, for better or worse. In Geneva we'd even had briefings about how to deal with it. The obvious thing to remember was not to jeopardize ICRC's neutrality by making political statements. Even describing how one side of a conflict was shelling another could be misinterpreted as partisanship and lead to ICRC being denied access to the wounded or prisoners of war. But it was often difficult to follow the safe rule, 'Describe what you do, not what you see.'

I had my first interview while I was at Khao-i-Dang. Not too difficult – it was one of my local UK radio stations who wanted to do a live interview by phone about the work we were doing. The PR delegate gave me some advice: don't take this lightly. It could possibly be some very keen junior journalist on his meteoric way up the career ladder to become political editor of one of the major newspapers or a broadcaster. Research all the history of the Cambodian conflict thoroughly, because it doesn't look good if he's done his homework and you haven't. Get all the facts and figures down on paper in front of you, numbers of refugees coming in, numbers of wounded, types of wound, mortality rate etc. so that he can't catch you out with questions.

This made me nervous but I got everything ready, copious notes in front of me. I sat in the office, the call came through. We were live on air throughout the West Midlands.

The interviewer started:

'I have Doctor Frank Ryding on the line – welcome to the programme – and he's talking to us all the way from Cambodia. So tell me, Frank, Cambodia is in which part of Africa exactly?'

'It's in Southeast Asia.'

'Is it? Short break now and over to the weather and traffic news …'

We lost the phone connection and that was the whole interview.

During a day off I made a nostalgic trip accompanying a field delegate to the south of Aranyaprathet but the villages and hospitals of Nong Pru and Tap Prik were no longer there. They had been closed in 1985, five years after I left, and the refugees had been relocated across the border in Thailand to a new camp, Site 8. I made enquiries about Mr Sam and Chantrea but no one could remember them. I could find no one I knew but I very much hoped they had escaped the Khmer Rouge.

After I left Khao-i-Dang, the camp, together with the hospital, continued but with decreasing numbers of refugees. The camp finally closed six years later in March 1993 when all the refugees were transferred to another camp pending repatriation to Cambodia. A child born in the camp when it opened would be 15 years old when it closed. At the closing ceremony, the UNHCR Special Envoy called Khao-i-Dang a 'powerful and tragic symbol of the "Cambodian Exodus" and the international humanitarian response'.

# PART 3

# THE AFGHAN CONFLICT: QUETTA, 1989

AFGHANISTAN - PAKISTAN

# Chapter 9

# A Peshawar Head

In Thailand I'd got on well with the medical coordinator and he'd recommended me to ICRC for a similar coordinator post. It was a big step. I felt I could fit into a surgical team as anaesthetist well enough. But managing a team and deciding how the surgery fitted in with the overall response to a conflict was another matter. I still couldn't settle into the NHS and in 1989 I was offered and accepted my first post as medical coordinator. I was to be based in Quetta in Pakistan where ICRC had set up a surgical hospital to receive war-wounded from Afghanistan.

Afghanistan has had a troubled history. Being at the crossroads of Asia, it has always been surrounded by far larger and more powerful neighbours 'like a poor pawn in a great game'. In 1978, after years of instability and repeated coups, the communist People's Democratic Party of Afghanistan (PDPA) took control and invited the Soviet Union to assist in modernizing the country. Violent opposition to the regime increased from early 1979 by loosely allied groups of staunchly Muslim rebels who called themselves the mujahideen, 'fighters for Islam'. In December of that year, the Soviet Union, at the request of the PDPA, entered its southern neighbour with 100,000 troops. The ten-year occupation that followed was a war of attrition resulting in an estimated 600,000 to two million Afghan deaths. Faced with mounting international pressure and the casualties on both sides, the Soviet Union withdrew in 1989 but continued to support the communist president Mohammad Najibullah. The conflict and the number of wounded escalated as the mujahideen took on the government forces.

I was not new to the region or to the conflict. A year before I'd done a short one-month mission as anaesthetist in the ICRC hospital in Peshawar further north. Here I was part of a UK surgical team sent to relieve the teams already there who were exhausted due to the enormous number of wounded coming through the Khyber Pass to Peshawar. So I was fortunate to know already the background of the war – and also how busy it was going to be in Quetta. Both the problems of anaesthesia and the way the ICRC operating theatres worked in a war zone were both now very familiar to me. The role of medical coordinator was unknown territory. I understood that it was my responsibility to make sure it all ran smoothly.

So I spent the first week simply learning how the place worked and getting to know the teams. Quetta is in the southern Pakistan province of Baluchistan and a few miles from the Afghan border. There were two main exits from Afghanistan into Pakistan – the Khyber Pass to Peshawar and the Kojak Pass to Quetta. The wounded came to Quetta from the south of Afghanistan especially the Kandahar and Helmand provinces. We had several outlying first-aid posts, the main one being at the village of Chaman just on the border. There, the wounded would receive emergency treatment to stabilize their condition if necessary, before being brought by ICRC ambulance sixty miles to us in Quetta. Usually there were so many wounded that it became a shuttle service.

It was remarkable how some of these patients survived the struggle to get to us. They would trek or be carried for days across the dusty, inhospitable terrain of Afghanistan. It was impossible to calculate how many severely wounded had simply not made it and died on the way – from infection, starvation or exhaustion.

One elderly injured man had been brought in a wheelbarrow pushed by his teenage grandson down mountains and across plains. It had taken two weeks to get to Pakistan. When I was in Peshawar, an Afghan girl was brought into the admissions room – she had been shot in the back. But I could see no ambulance outside; she had walked to the Khyber Pass then caught a bus to Peshawar and got off at the stop opposite the hospital. We took a bullet out from under her shoulder blade and she recovered.

With some patients we had to be careful for political reasons. Once or twice in Quetta we received wounded soldiers via Chaman who were obviously not mujahideen but their enemy serving in the government army from Kabul – they had either been separated from their units or had deserted. It was easy for them to discard their uniforms but they were still easily identified by their short haircuts and absence of beards. We suspected they would not have been treated gently if recognized, so we never put them in the hospital wards; they convalesced in a safe house in another part of Quetta.

We had a major problem with some unknown first-aider in Afghanistan. I noticed it first in Peshawar, then in Quetta. He was putting tourniquets on the thighs of patients whose feet and lower legs had been blown away by mines. The correct first-aid treatment in the field was to put pressure directly on the bleeding stump, or sometimes it was acceptable to apply a tourniquet just above the stump for a very short time, certainly less than two hours, to stop the bleeding until they could reach help. But someone was placing high tourniquets on limbs and leaving them on for days on end while the patient was slowly transported to us. With no blood going to what was potentially a recoverable and viable leg below the tourniquet, the leg would soon die and become gangrenous. So the loss of a foot or lower leg, which should have ended up being a below-knee amputation and a simple prosthetic leg, would turn into a full leg amputation and a more complex above-knee prosthesis as a result of the tourniquet being placed high up the thigh. The problem was made worse because this first-aider was going about teaching others to do the same. Two ICRC field delegates were sent from Peshawar into Afghanistan via the Khyber Pass with the enormously difficult task of trying to find the man and tell him to stop it. At the same time they mounted a counter-campaign to teach people the correct first aid. Such cases became less common, gradually decreasing, and the rogue first-aider disappeared, perhaps himself a victim of the war.

As we had so many patients with amputations, I thought I would make an early visit to our ICRC orthopaedic workshop next to the hospital and it was impressive. The quality of the leg prostheses made by ICRC throughout the world was improving all the time. The simpler prostheses were made with just the foot looking like a foot, made out of rubber. The rest was made out of wood or bamboo and leather, depending on the materials locally available, and would be hidden by the trouser leg. Then they had changed the colour of the rubber solution to match the country where it was being used. A foot used in Africa would be darker than in Southeast Asia. As I was watching them in our workshop in Quetta, I noticed there was a subtle difference from the Cambodian models – it was in the knee joint. Instead of bending to 90 degrees, these bent double to almost 180 degrees. I asked the technician the reason. He said that ICRC had adapted them for a Muslim country. It meant that when the wearer went to mosque he could kneel down to pray like all the others. I was impressed by that.

There are occasions when you think that it is someone's exceptionally lucky day. We were advised that a patient was coming in who'd lost a leg in a mine explosion. He did come in – hopping and carrying his leg under his arm. He also had numerous cuts and bruises, but he seemed more irritated than distressed. This was the second time he'd stepped on a mine, a small anti-personnel mine, with the same left leg but now with a prosthetic above-knee leg that he'd had fitted a year previously. The explosion had snapped the wooden shaft of the leg in two and twisted the metal knee joint. After we'd treated his minor injuries he went along to the orthopaedic workshop and they swapped his leg for a new one.

I made a point of going on the daily ward rounds and they could be a source of wonder. I had gone to Peshawar again to meet my equivalent medical coordinator there and I joined him on one of the post-operative rounds. The hospital was in an old disused post office building and sorting hall that ICRC had taken over. It still had a photograph of Queen Elizabeth in a frame high up on the wall of the ward, still there from former days. The patient lying in the bed opposite pointed to it and said, 'We like English people, and that lovely lady there – yes, we love Margaret Thatcher.'

In another bed sat an Afghan with a smart peaked military cap with red band around it and cap badge. I looked carefully at it – it was that of a colonel but of the army of the communist government in Kabul. Normally these soldiers, enemies of the mujahideen, would be kept in a separate hospital for safety. The man had a beard, and the patients around him were obviously his friends – he was a mujahideen. I asked him where he'd got the cap from.

'I took it from a government soldier,' he said.

'How did you persuade him to give it to you?'

'I took his head as well … would you like to see it? I have it in a bag in my house.'

'Not just for the moment, thank you.'

One of the first problems I had to deal with was orthopaedic equipment. Elementary orthopaedics: one of the ways to treat fractured bones is by 'external fixators'. They are particularly effective when it comes to war injuries, especially when there's an open wound as well, a common occurrence where they are caused by landmines.

Closed fractures of, say, a lower leg that perhaps can't be treated in a plaster of Paris cast, can be operated on and a titanium metal plate screwed to the bone across the fracture – an internal fixation – it works very well and the recovery time is much shorter. The metal plate can be left in there after the bone has healed. But it all needs to be infection free – infected bone with screws and a plate on it doesn't do well at all and is very difficult to treat. When the skin over the fracture is broken, especially after a landmine injury where there may be quite extensive damage to the muscles as well, infection is bound to have been introduced into the wound so internal fixation is not an option. Instead metal titanium pins like large six-inch nails are screwed through the bone well above and below the fracture out of the possibly infected area. These protrude through the skin and are joined together rigidly on the outside by a long piece of titanium metalwork like a bridge. This is an external fixator and it keeps the fracture stable and immobile while it's healing and avoids plaster of Paris getting in the way of wound cleaning. Then after several weeks the bridge can be dismantled and the pins through the bone can easily be removed without the need for an anaesthetic; the metalwork bridge is then re-sterilized and used again. It works very well. The patient can even hobble about on crutches with the external fixator in place.

But we began to discover that certain patients, due for the removal of their external fixators, were disappearing from the hospital and couldn't be found. And it seemed to happen when these patients heard they would be going to theatre next day for their fixation removal.

The reason was eventually discovered when one of the expatriates was wandering through the bazaar. A chemist's shop was selling medical instruments and there in the window was an external fixator, suspiciously like the ones we used in the hospital. Word had got around that these external fixators were very expensive, the scrap metal value alone of titanium is high. So some patients were absconding from the hospital, getting a friend to remove the pins from their leg or arm with a pair of pliers, then selling the fixator on the black market. We couldn't stop patients leaving the hospital but they couldn't take the fixator with them. As the traditional baggy trousers could easily hide the fixator we had to have a guard on the main gate with a metal detector. It was not fool proof. One patient had removed his fixator under his bedclothes and one of the guards caught him throwing it over the hospital wall to an accomplice in the middle of the night.

Because of the nature of the wounds we saw, cleanliness was our paramount concern; the wards were scrupulously swept and cleaned each day, sheets and blankets regularly washed. The local ward nurses were taught how to change wound dressings with an absolutely sterile technique, fresh sterile bandages were handled only with sterile forceps and the wounds carefully washed clean with antiseptic. I was following the dressing ward round early one morning to see if the nurses were following the rules; it was coming winter and the weather was getting much colder, especially at night. There were huge heaters at either end of the ward blowing warm air. One of the nurses was cleaning a wound; behind her was a tripod with a stainless steel dressing bowl on it. She had filled it with sterile dressings hot from the autoclave. Everything seemed to be satisfactory as I watched her renewing the dressing, all done with a very clean and sterile technique ... until I passed the dressing bowl. Nestling among the warm sterile gauze dressings was a cat asleep with five kittens.

We occasionally had patients being brought in paraplegic – usually from spinal injuries due to shrapnel wounds. The treatment is very specialized and long term, so ICRC was sponsoring a paraplegic centre in Peshawar to the north. It is over 700 kilometres from Quetta and a twelve-hour journey on a stretcher in an ambulance. It was an ordeal for patients so I asked for funds to try taking them by air, using scheduled flights. The first patient we took was a ten-year-old boy who'd been injured in the spine by a mine in Helmand Province. When his wounds had healed well enough we booked him on a flight and I accompanied him, with an interpreter to make sure it all ran smoothly. Two things we hadn't bargained for: the first was that when some of the other passengers heard who he was, there was a surprising amount of resentment – in Pakistan you had to be very rich to afford admission to a paraplegic centre, let alone flying there in a passenger aircraft. The second surprise was the reaction to the flight of the boy himself. He was from a poor family and had never flown before. At Quetta airport we had a lot of taxiing to do to get to the end of the runway and the boy thought it would take a long time at this speed to get to Peshawar … air travel was apparently slower than a car. But when we eventually took off he was amazed and thrilled as he felt this heavy machine suddenly lift off and up into the sky. It was very satisfying to watch his excitement as he eagerly looked out of the window.

Then as we flew round and over Quetta far below, he pretended to shoot with a machine gun out of the window – *rattatatt … rattattat* – and exclaimed it would be very easy to shoot everybody from up here. This loss of innocence depressed me for the rest of the flight and beyond.

# Chapter 10

# Criteria

CRC had a specific policy for whom it would treat when it set up a hospital for any conflict area – the 'criteria for admission' which, as medical coordinator I had to uphold. Patients had to be a resident of the country or countries at war, they had to have a wound specifically caused by war, and it had to have happened less than thirty days ago. There was a logical reason for this, and it developed after mistakes made in the early days of ICRC activity. For instance, in Quetta when the hospital was first set up, one of the surgeons – with previous experience of plastic surgery – was getting a little bored during one of the rare quiet periods. He would wander around the town and if he saw, for instance, a person with a cleft palate, he would bring them to the hospital and operate on them.

The problem with this was that when the Pakistan health officials heard of it they weren't happy at all. We were taking potential patients away from their hospitals, and when our surgeon left at the end of his mission, these same hospitals would have to undertake all the follow-up treatment. Then when word got round, the ICRC hospital was getting besieged by patients wanting free treatment. And car accident victims were being brought straight to our hospital instead of the city's A&E. It would have been very noble of us to take in all these patients but from a purely practical view we simply didn't have the finance or the beds or the surgical staff to deal with anything other than what we had been sent out to do – treat war victims. We had to make it clear what the admission policy was.

Even some of the injured coming from Afghanistan would push their luck. One Afghan insisted his injuries were a direct result of the war. He had been sitting on a wall with his newspaper; when he read that the town of Jalalabad had been attacked by the mujahideen, he was so shocked he fell off the wall. He insisted he satisfied the criteria. We disagreed. Another man thought ICRC might repair his motorcycle which he had driven into a shell crater in the middle of the road. It was made in 'Afghanistan, damaged by the war, less than thirty days ago' so surely it satisfied the criteria? No it didn't. It was sometimes not easy to say no. I had a request from the wife of one of the officials of a US aid group in Quetta. She was in late pregnancy and had asked if she could have a Caesarean section, if it proved necessary, at our hospital rather than the City hospital in Quetta. I had to refuse. Our surgeons were not primarily obstetricians and there was the problem of legal action if anything didn't go exactly to plan. She was an American citizen and compensation claims brought in a US court against the medical staff concerned and against ICRC, even for damages occurring outside the USA could be phenomenally high. I advised her to have the baby in the US.

I didn't always get it right. I'd heard that one of the surgeons was busy in theatre taking out a kidney stone from a patient. This was definitely not a war wound and I went in and confronted the surgeon.

'No, you're wrong,' he explained, 'this wasn't a kidney stone, it was a stone in the kidney – it was a piece of rock from the road. A landmine exploded, the rock penetrated his back and landed in his kidney. Now will you kindly let me carry on!'

I stood corrected.

One evening a group of us went to the Afghan Restaurant in Quetta. The owner was the one who'd fallen off the wall reading the paper. We had mutton kebab but it tasted really bad. We complained that we shouldn't have to pay for it. The owner said that the mutton was from an Afghan sheep, it had been killed with a bullet, within the last thirty days, so according to his criteria we would have to pay up.

The Afghan Restaurant was quite popular with expatriates, and there was in fact far less chance of getting food poisoning there than in some of the expensive Quetta hotels – the meat was usually freshly cooked, very well done, and heavily laced with salt. It was a poorly lit, dingy place, down a dirty, dark alley. It was very bare with only long wooden tables and benches. No decoration at all. And it was full of huge, bearded, solemn Afghans who seemed to spend the time putting even more salt on their meat. I used to take newly arrived expatriates there just for fun, to see their expression … and watch their surprise as the waiter would serve nan and paratha bread straight from the kitchen door by throwing them across the room at the customers like a frisbee.

The policy of only treating war victims was now being extended to most of ICRC missions in conflict areas, not just Afghanistan. I heard that a teleprinter message stating this policy had gone out to all ICRC hospitals. Unfortunately there'd been a mix-up in Geneva with the various messages and the medical coordinator in Khao-i-Dang in Thailand had received a message informing him he should only accept wounded Afghans in the hospital. His response was that if a wounded Afghan had struggled all the way to Thailand, he could hardly be refused.

I had expected primitive accommodation but, like Cambodia, our living conditions were very good. ICRC had rented several private houses in town about a mile or so from the hospital itself. Security was an issue, not from any political aspect so much as from ordinary bandits. So each house had a guard or *chokidar* sitting outside in the garden all night in a makeshift sentry box, with a powerful heater and blankets. I doubted if they could keep awake all night anyway, but it actually served another purpose: they were almost exclusively Afghan refugees with extended families so this was a way of supporting them financially without it appearing to be a handout which might have seemed undignified and embarrassing to them.

Soon, the delegate in charge of our accommodation called and asked if we would mind having a cook – an Afghan widow they wanted to help. No problem. Then another woman who would clean the house and make the beds. Then a laundry woman. Then a gardener. Family and friends in the UK would write asking if it wasn't too uncomfortable in Quetta. I was somewhat embarrassed at the time to tell them. The real hardship occurred at the end of mission when we all went home and realized that back in the UK we'd have to start doing our own cooking and cleaning and laundry again.

Quetta was a pleasant town, especially in spring when the cold of the winter was giving way to milder temperatures before the summer heat. And it was relatively safe, certainly compared to Peshawar. It was easy for the female expatriates to wander around the shops in the town centre. There was only one exception to this – the infamous Tailor of Quetta. The ICRC women found that he would make them superb clothes very cheaply either by copying those worn by their friends or simply from pictures in fashion magazines. They would buy the material from the fabric shops in the bazaar and he would produce the clothes in a matter of days. The problem was that he had wandering hands, especially when the women went for measuring and fittings. So it became *de rigeur* for one of the male expatriates to accompany them whenever they set foot in his shop. I seemed to spend hours there in the evenings acting as chaperone to many of the women. His face would light up as the women entered only to fall when he saw me following. The only time he ever spoke to me was to ask testily, 'How many wives do you have?!'

It wasn't long before the first major alert came in from the field delegates. There was about to be a major mujahideen offensive in Kandahar province. So we prepared for a large increase in casualties. I stopped all holiday leave for the surgical teams – one tired team was about to take a well-earned break in the north of Pakistan. The days went by and nothing happened, then a week, then two. The teams wanted to know what was happening. The head of the delegation suggested I have a meeting with one of the mujahideen commanders who he'd heard was still in Quetta. I was apprehensive. It was the first time I'd actually met a warlord. This was politics not medicine and I felt underqualified. My Afghan interpreter, Gulam Mohammed, drove me into the suburbs and I was welcomed into a dingy and untidy office. It was very civilized. We were given tea and sweets, we had the obligatory small talk then I got down to business.

'The Red Cross has heard rumours about possible fighting in Kandahar. We've heard nothing since and we are getting rather concerned.'

The commander poured more tea for us and nodded with a serious look on his face, 'I understand,' he said, 'but there have been problems. My wife has been ill and my daughter is getting married, so I've been rather busy. But I can reassure the Red Cross that I will start fighting as soon as I possibly can.'

I felt as if I was in Alice in Wonderland.

'Could you then tell me where the fighting will be so that we can put a first-aid post in the area?'

He thought for a while, 'Tell me where you want to put the first-aid post and we can fight around there.'

I asked him not to go to any effort on our account. Fortunately, that particular attack never materialized. We finished the meeting and as I was about to leave I asked, 'Now that the Russian army has left do you think there will be an end to the fighting?'

'No, I don't think there's any need to worry, we'll always be able to find someone else to fight.'

I later found there was another unusual reason for us to go on standby – when there was an Afghan wedding in the area. They could get quite noisy and dangerous. There was frequently celebratory shooting up in the air, but the bullets could actually go anywhere and there was a high risk that someone could accidentally get shot. There was one tragic case where a stray bullet had hit a box of bullets and grenades. The explosion had killed several guests including the bride's father. I was invited with other expatriate staff to one of the weddings – of one of our male Afghan nurses. I was surprised that I never actually saw the bride. The expatriate females joined the bridal party, and we men were put in a separate room with the groom. It seemed they had been roasting a sheep for a day or two in a pit in the ground with hot stones around it. We were first given a bowl of dull, grey-coloured liquid with globules of fat floating in it. I seriously thought it was dirty washing-up water. It was the soup. Of course, to be courteous it had to be drunk. But as we were honoured guests we were also given the delicacy – a sheep's eyeball. I wondered if the best way to deal with this was to perhaps secretly bring a small jar of pickled onions:

with a bit of legerdemain it should be possible to substitute a pickled onion for the eyeball which also gives an authentic crunch as you bite into it. I hadn't had that foresight so I had to eat the eye. To take my mind off it as I swallowed it, I had a vision of an Afghan as a wedding guest in the UK, with a secret bottle of sheeps' eyeballs in his pocket.

Most of my work in Quetta involved the main hospital but a large proportion of the rest was with other hospitals and organizations. We didn't have an eye surgeon and often landmine and shelling injuries resulted in eye damage. I had several meetings at the main Quetta City hospital trying to persuade the ophthalmic department there to take our eye patients. There was no free NHS service here and it seemed impossible to get them to take penniless Afghans. The Pakistan army medical service couldn't help either. Eventually I persuaded a doctor at the Christian Hospital to take an interest and in fact he would come to the ICRC hospital in his own time to operate gratis.

There was always good cooperation between the aid agencies. There was a Saudi Arabian organization who had a mobile field hospital outside Quetta. It was impressive, larger than a container truck, from which it was adapted. It was state of the art with an operating theatre and intensive care unit. The surprising aspect was that the walls were lead lined as it also served as a mobile nuclear bunker. They had intended to take it into Afghanistan but it was so cumbersome that it couldn't get through the Kojak Pass, so Quetta was as far as it got.

We seemed to be continually short of beds, especially when the fighting escalated. Over and above the buildings, every spare inch of space was taken up with large marquee tents. We couldn't expand further because the hospital grounds were surrounded by a four-metre-high security wall. While I was trying to sort out the problem of beds I had a visit from a UK author who was researching material for a commissioned feature film set in a hospital serving Afghan war victims. He got a lot of material but just as he was leaving I asked where it was being filmed. Apparently this was the ideal location. But there was no way filming could be done in the hospital; we had precious little space as it was. The proposal, he said, was to build an identical film-set hospital next to the ICRC one. My first reaction was that there was something quite bizarre about the whole idea. But on reflection, I suppose we could have taken it over when they had finished filming and doubled our bed space. As it was, the project never got off the ground.

The bed shortage became critical; the buildings we had acquired for the hospital could only take a limited number of beds even when squashed together. The two marquees in the grounds could take thirty patients each, but when they were recovering and didn't need our expertise any longer, there was nowhere else for them to go to convalesce. I had what I thought was a brilliant idea. We could transfer them to the mujahideen hospitals. I knew of several of these hospitals in Quetta. There were at least nine different political factions of mujahideen, most of which were at odds with each other, some outright hostile, and there seemed very little in the way of co-operation. Each had its own hospital for its own injured members. But I found they were very small, ill-equipped miserable places and could deal with only very minor injuries.

I went with Gulam Mohammed to a typical hospital. It was simply a rented house in the suburbs, empty except for nine rickety beds with not very clean mattresses. The beds were crowded together in three rooms with hardly any floor space between them. The floors were dusty, the walls were bare, and the patients sat there sadly in their uncared-for bandages.

I talked to the doctor at each hospital but didn't get far. They couldn't take any more patients because they had very little funds, not even enough to buy food let alone medicine and dressings.

At each place I was afforded the usual hospitality – several cups of tea which looked like weak milky water and had about six sugars in it. It was a case of 'if you don't take sugar, don't stir it'. I was feeling queasy by the end of the day. Gulam pointed out after the first visit that I had probably offended them by refusing a biscuit and I had offended him by not writing his name in the visitors' book along with mine. It was a rather depressing day with endless talking and endless biscuits and cups of hot white water. Eventually I agreed to provide some food from our own hospital and a limited supply of medical essentials in return for them taking some of the convalescing patients. The plan didn't turn out well. Within a few weeks I was back after they had refused any more patients but were still taking the supplies, and it became an endless negotiation about how much food we would give them.

My first real test came a few weeks into the mission. It was about midnight and I'd gone to bed when there was a knock on the door. A messenger had come from the hospital – there were armed mujahideen at the hospital gate demanding to be let in. Gulam Mohammed was there with the car. We headed for the hospital. Half-asleep I wondered what on earth I should do. I told Gulam to turn the car round; perhaps we should get the Quetta police, or even the military. At least I should make sure the head of the delegation knew about this.

Gulam was calm; he suggested we just drive to the hospital. But how were we to handle this, I asked.

'First we make them tea,' he said.

We were still arguing about it as we arrived at the hospital.

'If we offer them tea and hospitality,' explained Gulam, 'they become our guests, and it would be very difficult for them to shoot us.'

We approached the main gate. The guards were still arguing with the gunmen. We intervened. Gulam brought tea and biscuits from the hospital and we all sat down in the sand.

The gunmen had travelled all day from Afghanistan to see one of their wounded colleagues whom we'd recently operated on. It appeared that there were two problems: it was long past visiting hours ... and they were carrying guns. Red Cross rules were very specific – no guns in the hospital, the guards were adamant. It was sorted out very quickly. They left their Kalashnikovs at the gate and we gave them a guided tour of the hospital. We found the wounded man, who had had a debridement of a gunshot wound to his leg. He was in one of the tents, sitting up in bed quite happy and doing well. The gunmen were more or less satisfied, except that they asked why he was in the tent and not in the more comfortable main building. He was after all a special case ... considering all the service he'd rendered to the Red Cross since the fighting began. It suddenly occurred to me that he might be an official of the Afghan Red Crescent. He wasn't. But they told me that it was this wounded man who had laid half the landmines in Helmand province and if it wasn't for him, the Red Cross would probably be out of a job and not be here at all. So could he have a private room?

No, he couldn't.

Gulam Mohammad, my interpreter, was priceless. If you wanted to make a film about the mujahideen you couldn't get a better extra from central casting than Gulam – a huge man with a bushy Hagrid beard, dyed red as he'd been to Mecca, traditional pancake-type hat, and a black scarf to keep out the dust when wind whipped it up. He was a devout Muslim and on long trips he would stop the Land Cruiser in the middle of nowhere, take out his mat and pray at the side of the road. During the miles of travelling we used to have discussions about religion. He was impressed that I could quote the Quran 2:62 about tolerating Christians – the 'children of the book'. But then he would discuss different world religions, like Christianity, and would ask questions like 'Who exactly is Santa Claus and why does he come down the chimney?' He was puzzled that the Red Cross was not a religious order and had no connection to the crusades, and why did the expatriate sisters in the theatre and ward, whom he presumed were nuns, not behave with more decorum.

He talked about the CIA presence in Afghanistan and their support of the mujahideen. The CIA vehicles were occasionally spotted, supposedly anonymous but, as Gulam pointed out, they were easily recognizable: they were white, impeccably clean and all had darkened windows. He said if the Americans wanted to stop the Afghan production of heroin, which found its way to the US, there should be a compromise – the Afghans would cease making heroin in his country if the US would stop all production and sales of alcohol in theirs.

As an interpreter he was excellent. Once during a discussion with some muja-hideen, I made a point about the various groups fighting each other, but Gulam quietly said to me, 'I will not translate that as these people would misinterpret it as an insult.' On the other hand, some conversations would be puzzling. I once asked a simple question at one of the hospitals: how many patients did they admit each week. Gulam spoke in Pharsee to them. There was a response, Gulam replied. The exchange went on and on for several minutes – in fact it seemed to get very heated at one point, hand gestures were getting quite ani-mated, then it calmed down. Gulam turned to me and said, 'Eight.' I thought it best not to ask what the conversation was all about.

*Chapter 11*

# Into Afghanistan

We had several trips together to the Afghan border and beyond. A few times I went to the border village of Chaman, to sort out some problems at our first-aid post there. Some of the local drivers were using the ambulances as a bus service to ferry friends and relatives to Quetta. The journey took a few hours from Quetta; the road snaked along, following a railway track for part of the way before descending steeply through the Kojak Pass, the equivalent of the Khyber Pass from Peshawar, down onto the flat, red, arid plain and into the province of Kandahar in Afghanistan. Another problem at the first-aid post was with returning patients. After they had recovered at our ICRC hospital in Quetta, they would be taken in our ambulances back to the Chaman first-aid post where they had first come under our care. They were then left to return to wherever they had come from in Afghanistan. It was too dangerous at that time for the ambulances to drive them all the way to Kandahar. But they must at least be given tea and a supply of nan bread for the journey.

I decided to cross the border into Afghanistan to the nearest, or rather the only, town on the map in that area – Spin Boldak, a further seven miles away. I wanted to see if there was any sort of bus service. There wasn't. In fact there wasn't anything of any use or interest whatever in Spin Boldak. We saw a few mud houses, a donkey, some scraggy chickens and very little else. We met a couple of ICRC field delegates coming the other way, coming back from Kandahar where they had had discussions with the local chief. It had been a rough time for them. It was very unsafe and there was heavy fighting between rival mujahideen around Kandahar. They'd been warned that one of the groups was intent on kidnapping any westerners they could find, and the field delegates had been ambushed and shot at. Only some very good, fast driving down a dried-up riverbed had got them out of trouble. They said that the best thing they and we could do for the moment was get back to the safety of Pakistan as soon as possible. We were standing in what could only optimistically be called the high street of Spin Boldak. The field delegate looked around at the dusty, dirty, desolate village and with a heartfelt sigh said, 'If ever Afghanistan needed an enema, they would shove the nozzle in at Spin Boldak.'

We were wise to leave as a few months later some ICRC delegates were kidnapped and it took some very intense negotiations to get them released.

We spent the night in the relative safety of the Chaman first-aid post. We were just about to leave around lunchtime next day when a truck drove up to the gate from the direction of the border. Instead of wounded Afghans emerging, I was amazed to see a dozen UK teenagers. They were tourists on their gap year. They had been on what was advertised in a dubious travel brochure as the 'journey of a lifetime' – an overland trip from Turkey, through Iran and astonishingly through Afghanistan, in the back of a truck. They were weary, dirty, and rather disappointed. They couldn't see much from the truck – it had no windows – and they hadn't seen any fighting as promised in the brochure. How they could have survived touring through a war zone where even ICRC feared to tread I can't imagine. Rather like going on a tourist trip through the trenches during the First World War. They'd come to the first-aid post because they'd had a disaster: the truck had gone over a large pot-hole in the road (probably from recent shelling) and one of the girls had hit her head on the roof of the truck. They should be so lucky. Not exactly a war wound, but we put two stitches into the cut on her head and they were on their way. They were supposed to be driving up to Peshawar, and from there into Afghanistan again and on to Kabul. We tried our best to persuade them to head for Karachi and call it a day. I hope they did, but I never found out what happened to them.

I had three surgical teams to coordinate. Two of the teams were mixed nationality, German, Dutch, Swedish and Finnish. The other team was all Italian. They would all usually be on a three-month contract sponsored by their own national Red Cross society. I was often under pressure from headquarters to reduce the teams to two, especially when there was a lull in the fighting. But it would always pick up again and they would be busy. The team on call might have to operate well into the night when ambulances would come in with wounded from Chaman just before nightfall. My main aim was to keep the hospital working efficiently and harmoniously. I didn't realize when I took the job on just how much time I would spend sorting out personal problems, squabbles and crises within the surgical teams themselves.

I had problems with two expatriates, a Swedish anaesthetist and a German theatre nurse. They simply didn't get on. In the theatre and on the ward it was a constant war of criticism, argument and sarcasm. I sent them on holiday together up north to the beautiful mountain town of Gilgit – in the same hotel. By the time they got back they were practically engaged. But I didn't get an invitation to the wedding ... if there ever was one.

There were close attachments, perhaps affairs, among the expatriate medical staff which were not a problem if they were reasonably discreet, but occasionally things were more serious. One of the male medical expatriates had become friendly with one of the female Afghan nurses and had taken her out to dinner in one of the Quetta hotels, unchaperoned. It was quite unpardonable behaviour on his part – he should have known that in Afghan society this sort of liaison is only tolerated if it ends in marriage. The girl's family could easily take offence, come after him, guns loaded, and threaten the whole ICRC action in Quetta. It had happened to one of the other NGOs in the past. I gave him two choices – either stop the affair or be sent home. He was furious. He cut his mission short a few weeks later.

We had an Afghan nurse in charge of the post-operative ward. She was very quiet, very shy but dedicated, intelligent and very competent. She was ethnically a Hazaran. They are a distinct people from the Bamian region in the centre of Afghanistan. Often treated as inferiors, they look different with narrow eyes, flat noses, broad cheeks – more Asiatic, and legend has it they are descended from the Mongolians of Ghengis Khan. There had been one or two minor problems on the morning ward round – a patient's dressing hadn't been changed, another patient hadn't been kept 'nil by mouth' before an operation. One of the expatriates lost his temper and angrily asked the Hazaran nurse in charge if she thought this was the way to run a surgical ward – this was in front of all the other nurses and patients.

The Hazarans also have the Far Eastern tradition about not losing face. She was visibly shaken and embarrassed. I took the expatriate aside after the ward round and explained that a more effective way – in fact a more considerate and dignified way – would have been to talk to me first and I would have sorted the matter out more privately. The damage was done. More than I realized – when I went to talk to the Hazaran nurse, she said that after her humiliation she couldn't possibly work in the ward and would have to leave the hospital. We lost one of the best nurses we had.

One of the surgical teams in Quetta was always Italian. This was traditional as there had been an Italian Red Cross surgical unit here for a year or so before ICRC moved in and the team had been absorbed into the mission. I'd never worked with Italians before. They were fun, animated, and hospitable. I might be having a discussion with them at the hospital over some minor problem and suddenly it would become a blazing row, voices raised, hands gesticulating. Then, just as suddenly, the row would be over and I'd be invited to dinner with them that evening. And they knew how to entertain. I would be served a beautiful veal and pasta dish, feel very full and then realize it was only an appetizer for the enormous steak carbonara to follow.

They liked to sing in the operating theatre which puzzled the Afghans. But there was a cardiac arrest one day, and things were quite different. It is almost a matter of course in UK hospitals for cardiac arrest calls to be treated very calmly, with quiet efficiency, follow the protocols logically – panic doesn't help at all. The Italian team were the opposite – there was shouting, gesticulating, almost wailing, '*Mamma mia*! Where is the adrenaline?' The Italian surgeon, Gino, looked at me and shrugged as if to say this was usual.

'Rossini could set this to music,' he whispered. 'It would make a grand opera – or commedia dell'arte.'

Gino was a live wire, passionate about surgery, with a creative soul. He announced to us that he was organizing a cultural concert in Quetta. He had come across two Afghans who were musicians and who sang traditional Afghan folk songs. It was an unmissable opportunity. This sort of native music was in danger of disappearing forever, he said, as he sold tickets to everyone, not just to ICRC people but to all the other aid agencies in Quetta, the Italian consulate, and through the army's medical unit he even sold tickets to the Pakistan military. He had rented a hall in the Serena Hotel, the largest and grandest hotel in Quetta. We were all there. Up onto the dais strode the two rough-looking musicians, dressed in their traditional, rather dirty clothes, colourful scarves around their necks, huge black beards almost covering their dark, sunburned, wrinkled faces, pancake hats on their heads. One carried a stringed instrument like a small guitar which I recognized as an Afghan *sarinda* – I'd seen one for sale in the bazaar. The other carried a traditional flute, a *tula*.

One of the Afghan theatre nurses welcomed us and introduced the musicians who would sing a traditional Afghan lament about a poor man who was pining for the love of a high-born lady. They started playing, accompanied by chanting. It was very emotional. I'll admit it was a long way from western harmony theory and I couldn't detect any sort of melody, but people listened intently. Someone whispered that it was so wonderfully ethnic, someone even recorded the songs on a tape recorder. We applauded enthusiastically when it was finished. The nurse introduced another lament about another man pining for another woman. We had more of the same for about a couple of hours, maybe people were getting a bit restless but there was absolute quiet in the audience. The recital came to an end. There was a hearty applause. Before the musicians left the dais, one of them thanked us in perfect English with an Italian accent. The beard had slipped slightly askew during the performance. Gino and his anaesthetist had gone to a lot of trouble with their make-up and dress. They were totally unrecognizable. The music was rubbish. The storm afterwards had to be calmed by the head of delegation, who had to go and apologize, particularly to the Pakistan military who didn't see the joke at all. None of us got our ticket money back but it was worth it. Gino sent the money to a favourite charity and was unrepentant.

I came across him again two years later when I was medical coordinator in Kabul. He had stopped working for ICRC, not as far as I can gather because of his pseudo-ethnic concert, but he had founded his own medical charity and was back helping the Afghans. At a party one evening, after he'd had a little wine, he confided that he'd had a wonderful idea of disguising himself as the former King of Afghanistan, Zahir Shah, now living in exile in Italy – there *was* a certain likeness there. He was going to request a formal reception for himself at the ICRC headquarters in Kabul. Shades of the famous *Dreadnought* hoax perhaps. This was a lot more serious than his previous escapade however, and he was firmly advised to abandon this dangerous idea; he would more than likely end up shot or arrested by the Afghans. I heard that someone blew the whistle on him well in time.

There had been some dissension in the delegation. All caused by carpets. Delegates had found that a lot of high-quality Persian carpets had been coming in via southern Afghanistan and were being sold at bargain prices in Quetta. Most expatriates had bought one, some had bought several, one had bought twenty. It was relaxing after work to go to the bazaar and spend an hour looking at carpets, bargaining with the carpet seller and drinking his tea. The problem was in getting all the customs paperwork done before they could be exported to Europe. This had fallen to the already over-worked delegation secretary. She was spending hours shuttling to and from the relevant customs offices and was not too happy about it. The head of delegation stepped in. In future she would only do this for one carpet per delegate. It caused a lot of complaints and arguments. The entire conversation at lunch was carpets.

You could be forgiven for thinking this was contrary to the Geneva Convention – depriving people of the right to buy carpets. Eventually the carpet question became like the Dreyfus Affair. It was not to be mentioned.

Into the middle of this minor fracas came a visit from a Japanese TV film crew. They were making a feature on the sole Japanese Red Cross nurse in the hospital. Incidentally, this nurse, called Mariko, spoke very good English and was enjoying the whole experience but she was very nervous about the TV crew. She took it very seriously, and told me she had to make a good impression for the sake of her family back home; it was a matter of honour. She was prepared for any questions they might ask. She had worked hard studying and had all the statistics at her fingertips. The three-man crew were treated as VIPs by the head of delegation. I was there to help, together with Mariko, when he received them in his office. To Mariko's relief, he gave them a very thorough briefing about the work of the Red Cross in Quetta. After I'd given a comprehensive summary of the work we were doing in the medical field, he lectured them on the work of the field delegates, then the detention delegates doing prison visits in Kandahar, then the dissemination team promoting Red Cross principles. After a couple of hours he paused to draw breath and asked the TV crew if they had any questions. They thought for a while, then one of them leaned forwards eagerly and said, 'Can you tell us where in Quetta we can buy carpets?'

Mariko was always a very careful worker, very formal and very keen to get everything right. She asked me to improve her English, she taught me some rudimentary Japanese and even had sent over her equipment for the intricate tea ceremony from Japan. Four of us sat cross-legged in our residence while she directed proceedings and enjoyed showing us the correct conversation. I once asked her, in fun, for some slang Japanese words. She said she didn't know any swear words, the strongest she knew was *shimata* – 'I have made a mistake'. It became a catchphrase in the hospital when things went wrong. But before the Japanese camera crew arrived, she begged me not to say *shimata* – the camera crew would immediately know who'd taught me the word.

She came to the hospital one day very agitated – she'd been driving the team's Land Cruiser and while going round a roundabout, a truck had pulled out in front of her and hit the side of the car. Both the car and the truck were extensively damaged. The truck driver wanted compensation. It seemed obvious to us that Mariko wasn't at fault, as she had right of way on the roundabout. So I went with the head of delegation to the Quetta police station to find out who legally had right of way – who gives way to whom on a roundabout? The police official was surprised at the question.

'You say the other vehicle was a large truck?'

'Yes,' we said.

'Then the answer is simple. If the other fellow is in a bigger vehicle, you give way to him.' Silly question.

A memo was urgently sent to all delegates.

One day the head of delegation called me urgently, a group of mujahideen were taking some of our patients away. It appeared that they had come to the hospital during visiting hours, taken photographs of patients and were talking to them trying to persuade them to leave – they were being offered transport and entry visas to enter Egypt where they would get better treatment and a better life. Fifteen of them had accepted and were leaving the hospital. The head of delegation was very agitated – those patients were under ICRC care and protection, it's a fundamental mandate of the Red Cross, and it was his ultimate responsibility. But of course they always have the perfect right to leave that protection if they want. We could in no way insist that they stay. The problem was that the surgical care wasn't complete, some of them were between operations, being made ready for skin grafts, for example. One of the patients was paraplegic. He had been promised that in Egypt they had 'electrical treatment' that would enable him to walk immediately. We had to let them go.

We heard weeks later that the patients had got as far as Karachi, where, being Afghan and not Pakistan citizens, they were stranded with no chance of being granted exit visas. They never made it to Egypt and despite enquiries, they were never heard from again.

A significant proportion of the patients at Quetta were mujahideen soldiers and it was inevitable that the question would be asked at the dinner table one evening why we were treating soldiers, maybe saving their lives, getting them fit enough to go back into Afghanistan where they would continue fighting, wounding and killing others. It was a question I would hear asked and discussed on other missions in other conflicts. It was a question I asked myself. But we always accepted every patient from a conflict area. The only criterion was that they were wounded – not who they were. And I think that's because the question is not black and white. To begin with, it's not always easy to determine who is a soldier, as they seldom wear uniforms. In many parts of the world the fact that a man has a gun is not proof he's a fighter. And even if he is part of a military group, he may have been conscripted against his will, either legally or by threats and intimidation. Or it may be that he became a soldier to ensure the safety of himself or his family. I wonder how far people in the UK would go to protect their wives and children. If one discriminated against someone because he is a soldier, it's not a big step to extend it to his religion or his politics or his race. One is at risk of playing God, and that's not what we were there for.

# PART 4

# LAND OF SAND AND SLAUGHTER: SOMALIA, 1991

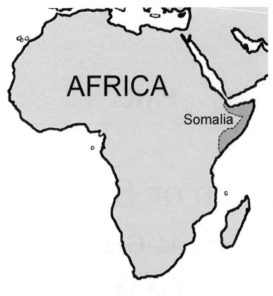

# SOMALIA

*Chapter 12*

# The White Pearl

I'd had a run of good missions. It had occurred to me that I ought to call it a day and belatedly concentrate on an NHS career. But I enjoyed the excitement of being sent to exotic places, even though they were in no sense holidays away from the operating theatre. They were places tourists would fear to tread. Not long back from Quetta, hardly settling into life in Herefordshire, in December 1990 I was offered another six-month post as medical coordinator in Somalia, in the Horn of Africa. I needed little persuading. I had a briefing at the British Red Cross Headquarters in Grosvenor Crescent, just off London's Hyde Park Corner. It was a relaxed meeting where I learned that I would be working in an ICRC surgical hospital in Berbera in the north of Somalia. There had been some sporadic rebel activity and there were some casualties there. But it was a relatively safe mission, not too busy: all that was required was to keep the place ticking over nicely.

Modern history begins when the ancient empire of Somalia was colonized towards the end of the nineteenth century. The north became British Somaliland and the south Italian Somalia. In 1960 the two protectorates united into the independent Somali Republic under a civilian government. Mogadishu became the capital. In a *coup d'état* in 1969, the president was assassinated and the army seized power, led by Major General Siad Barré who established the Somali Democratic Republic. Disillusionment with his regime grew as corruption and mismanagement increased. Armed opposition started in 1986 after Siad Barré began ruthlessly attacking clan-based dissident groups opposed to his rule. By the end of 1990, only Mogadishu, the surrounding region and some of the larger towns like Berbera were still safely in government hands.

I was to fly to Mogadishu on 28 December 1990 via Frankfurt. The first leg of the flight on British Airways was uneventful, but there was a problem with Somali Airlines with regard to the onward flight from Frankfurt. I learned that the problem was not technical – Somali Airlines did not have enough credit with Frankfurt airport to be refuelled. A good start. The next day, ready cash was forthcoming and the flight left for Mogadishu.

I arrived in Somalia at 9 a.m. on 30 December 1990. The attack on Mogadishu and outright civil war started at 2 p.m. that day.

I was welcomed at Mogadishu International Airport by a member of the ICRC delegation. Like most African airports it was crowded, noisy, rather chaotic but friendly. There seemed to be no attempt to form queues, just a general pushing. But all my luggage was there. I was eager not to lose any; I'd brought quite a lot, probably too much but enough to keep me occupied for six months because it was likely to get rather tedious with so little going on – lots of my favourite books, music, camera equipment, paints and canvas, magic tricks to amuse the local children, even my best suit for the important meetings with Somali authorities – it always went down well.

I was driven to my hotel through the city of Mogadishu. It's been called the 'White Pearl of the Indian Ocean' and it lived up to its name – brilliant white stucco buildings with an Arabic flavour to its architecture, reflecting its past when Arab dhows would sail down this east African coast and maybe trade for incense then journey on to Zanzibar, the Spice Islands. The sky was a brilliant indigo blue and the sea a subtle turquoise. I had the window down and I caught the strong scent of a brilliant red-flowered bush climbing up the wall of a smart white residence. We passed a bustling, thriving market with traders in long white smocks drinking coffee, perhaps completing business before the day became too hot. I thought to myself, 'I'm going to enjoy this pleasant country. The 'welcome' delegate suggested I take a tour round the city, it was beautiful and quite safe.

But I was tired from the overnight flight and the delay in Frankfurt, so I had breakfast and went to my room to sleep for a few hours. I would have a look round in the late afternoon when it was cooler.

I was woken at two o'clock in the afternoon. I thought someone in the room above had dropped one of their shoes onto the floor. A few seconds later I heard the other shoe drop. Then a third. This was curious. I was still only half awake but the noises didn't sound right, like there was an echo. It sounded like shelling. Surely not … but I was right.

I got dressed and was about to go down to reception when there was a knock at the door. It was one of the expatriate delegation officers. There was no time for pleasantries or even introductions. He told me the city was being attacked and he'd come to take me to the delegation. I bundled all my excess luggage into the back of his ICRC pickup truck and he drove very fast for the mile or so to the Wardhigley district. There was confusion. The few people on the streets looked agitated and confused, running to find shelter. A woman was crying loudly and shaking her arms in front of her face. We heard more shelling then repeated gunfire as we arrived at the delegation. As I stepped out of the pickup I smelled the strong odour of cordite; there was a grey haze around us.

The delegation was a large white rented house with separate annexes in ample grounds and I was pleased to see that it was surrounded by a solid three-metre-high steel wall. The white gate, also solid steel, had on it the large reassuring logo of ICRC. I was hurried in. No time for the usual exhaustive ICRC arrival briefing. There were very few people inside and I realized it was Sunday.

The shelling increased. It seemed much nearer and we all took shelter. I was advised to sit underneath one of the sturdy metal tables in an office in case the ceiling came down. I was under no illusion that if the delegation received a direct hit the table would be of no use. The shelling was intermittent. Then there would be gunfire, sometimes distant, sometimes closer. During a lull I looked around. There was a kettle and I made a cup of coffee. I was in the Dissemination and Tracing Office. There were filing cabinets against the walls, I supposed filled with the thousands of cards of lost relatives that every delegation seems to contain. On the table were leaflets and booklets. I picked one up. Just then the shelling started again. I ducked underneath the table again with my coffee and the book. I looked at the title, *A Memory of Solferino* by Henri Dunant, an account of the 1859 battle of Solferino that was published in 1862 as *Un Souvenir de Solferino* and which was the inspiration for him to found the Red Cross movement. So I read the description of that battle, the noise of the cannons and the smell of the gunpowder while I could actually feel the thud of artillery vibrating under my feet and smell the cordite outside. It was a surreal sensation. It would have been the ultimate in virtual entertainment had it not been so bloody scary.

Thankfully things quietened down that night but I was unable to sleep on the hard floor. The next morning I talked to Peter, the Swiss head of delegation. He said he didn't know what the situation was but it would be best for me if I were taken directly to the airport while it was quiet and the ICRC plane would take me to the safety of Berbera.

I was driven in the pickup but this time I was advised to lie down on the floor in the back surrounded by my luggage to act as sandbags and keep my head down. The truck raced away. The only bit of Mogadishu I saw was the blue sky above. The airport outside the city had been attacked. The small ICRC Beechcraft plane was at the far end of the airfield waiting. I could see the terminal building where I'd gone through customs twenty-four hours before. It seemed deserted and there was shell damage to the walls. Then I saw the Somali Airlines passenger jet, I presume the one that had brought me in. The tailfin had been completely blown away and the large hole revealed the seats at the rear of the cabin. I think I'd had the honour of flying on the very last flight of Somali Airlines. We took off and headed north. I have to say I was relieved. The thought of six months of relaxed, uneventful work in Berbera seemed even more enticing now.

*Chapter 13*

# Berbera

Berbera is a town of less than 70,000 on the southern coast of the Gulf of Aden and the only sea port and deep harbour on this coast. It was for a time the capital of British Somaliland. It's not a particularly attractive place, surrounded by desert and sparse shrubs. As we came in to land I was surprised at the airstrip: it is truly enormous – no, gigantic – very, very long and so wide that the small plane could probably have landed sideways across it. It was made of paved asphalt and was in first-class condition. The pilot told me it was over four kilometres long, some two and a half miles, built originally by the Soviet Union but since 1970 enlarged and used by the US as an emergency landing strip for the space shuttle.

The hospital was small with two surgeons and one anaesthetic nurse, a jolly Icelandic woman. It looked as though I'd also be helping out with the anaesthetics to give her some time off. The delegation was a kilometre down a dusty street and there I finally got my introductory briefing. I went to bed early; it seemed as if I'd hardly slept since leaving London three days before. I was woken at midnight by loud noises – for one awful moment I thought … but no, it was a very noisy party with lots of cheering. I wondered if this went on every night. I looked at my watch and saw it was midnight. I suddenly realized it was New Year's Eve and we'd just passed into 1991.

The hospital had about thirty beds, and patients would either be brought in by truck from the outlying areas or flown in by ICRC plane from other towns like Hargeisa, Burco and Las Anod. They had mostly gunshot wounds or shell injuries from skirmishes. Quite a few of the wounds couldn't really be classified as war wounds as they weren't political, rather fights between rival tribes. But we were hardly overworked so we took patients until we had filled up the beds. But already there were the first signs of malnutrition; the infrastructure of the country was gradually falling apart and as usual it showed first in the women, children and elderly. One little Somali girl was brought in. She was eight years old but looked like five. She was skeletally thin; as I took hold of her upper arm, my finger and thumb met. She had a combination of tuberculosis and starvation. In theory she didn't come under our criteria for admission. She had no surgical condition so we invented a fictitious one, admitted her to the ward and gave her a high calorie/protein diet. It was satisfying breaking the rules.

It was almost a leisurely time. The work stopped at lunchtime for a two-hour siesta during the worst of the heat. There was time in the evenings before dinner when the sun was going down when we could sit on the flat roof of one of the residences in the coolness and watch the sun set on the desert. We could even take a half day off on Sundays. Not much to do in Berbera but the docks were picturesque and there was a market where one could wander and wonder what on earth one could possibly want to buy.

I made some trips with the ICRC planes. We had two six-seater Cessnas which were kept at the enormous airstrip some eight kilometres out of town. We seemed to have the whole airfield to ourselves. There were three of us besides the pilot –the expatriate 'flying' nurse who went out with the planes almost every day, myself, and a local Somali who sat at the rear with a blank expression and said not a word the whole trip. We flew out to Las Anod, 330 kilometres to the south-east. After landing we went to one of the hospitals we were supporting, a small place with nothing but the basics of surgical care. The doctor was waiting to show us four patients whom he hoped we would take. There was a patient with a badly shattered upper arm, the result of a machine-gun bullet. The arm and hand were dusky blue, the bullet had gone through the arteries and I knew that she would lose the arm. We would take her back to Berbera and the arm would be amputated before the onset of gangrene killed her. There was a small child with a simple greenstick fracture of the forearm; easy to treat but the child would need an anaesthetic, so he would come too. The other two cases were not surgical problems. One man had a kidney infection and another recurrent diarrhoea. I could only give advice and a box of medical supplies.

We flew back to Berbera. From the air there was a certain wild, barren beauty about the endless red desert with the occasional patch of green around the odd village. I was busy taking out my camera to get some aerial photos but the nurse quickly threw her jacket over it to hide it. With her eyes she motioned to the silent man behind her and shook her head ever so slightly. She later told me that the man was sent by the Berbera military to monitor us on every trip to make sure we were not photographing military installations or anything that might be useful to the rebels. Not that I'd recognize anything anyway. We approached the runway. The pilot said it was the perfect place for a flying school and for a beginner to practise landing: the runway was so large it would actually be difficult to miss it.

A few days later I flew to Hargeisa, the former capital before Berbera. There had been rebel activity and fighting here in the late 1980s. In 1988, the Somali National Air Force had extensively bombed the city and large parts of it were in ruins. Nearly 10,000 civilians had been killed. As we flew over the suburbs, looking down onto a housing area, I saw that the roofs were missing, destroyed by the bombing. We could see inside the houses, the interior walls painted in bright colours – reds, blues and greens. It somehow seemed intrusive looking inside.

The days passed slowly. There was another small hospital near ours, and we had an arrangement that in return for food they would take some of our convalescent patients to relieve our crowded bed state. Almost every day, like a ritual, I would be told they had refused to accept any patients, I would go over there and talk to the director and remind him of the agreement. He would say they hadn't received any food, I would check that in fact they had and he would reluctantly admit he had made a mistake.

I visited the mayor a couple of times. He liked to meet new ICRC delegates, give them tea and practise his English.

I inspected a large inflatable dinghy that belonged to ICRC and was stored in a shed at the port – it was intended as a means of escape by sea if trouble broke out and we had to leave quickly. Up to that moment the possibility hadn't entered my head.

*Chapter 14*

# Front Line

On 23 January, just over three weeks after I had arrived, things changed and the mission started to turn into a nightmare. We heard for the first time distant rumbling early one morning. Thunderstorms are not uncommon here but this was the middle of the dry season. During the day it became louder and we knew it was artillery fire.

At dusk the head of delegation called a meeting. He said he was receiving reports of rebel forces advancing in this direction. This didn't mean they were necessarily heading for Berbera but as a precaution we should all spend the night in the hospital which was half a mile from the residences. It was safer because it was surrounded by a high wall and better to have everyone in the same place rather than scattered in different houses. We would only bring essentials; all luggage was to be left in the residences which were guarded by local employees – and we didn't want to give anyone the idea we were leaving town which might worry the local population. We travelled in a high-profile convoy of ICRC trucks, lights blazing, spotlights on the ICRC flags to make sure no one mistook us for an invading army. There was almost a party atmosphere among us in the hospital. The cook brought an evening meal for everyone from the main residence; we sat and ate in the court-yard with candles and we set up camp beds in some of the hospital offices.

Then at about 5 a.m. we were woken by odd whooshing sounds. Someone pointed up and we saw what looked like red flares passing high overhead. In my half-asleep state I thought it was a fireworks display. Then I heard a distant thud. Shells were passing over us. The explosions became louder as the morning progressed and we realized we were in trouble. It's so difficult being in the middle of a battle yet not knowing what is going on. We couldn't see over the walls but we later learned that the rebel forces were attacking Berbera from the west and that the government had advanced with artillery to protect it. They had placed one of their large artillery pieces on the other side of the hospital wall for cover and were firing directly over our heads. This also meant we were in the direct line of fire of the rebel artillery trying to take out the gun. We were well and truly in the front line. We were a target.

I had by this time experienced from a relatively safe distance the aftermath and injuries resulting from shelling in Cambodia and Afghanistan; this was the first time I had been in the middle of it, a potential victim. It's impossible to describe the intense noise that comes from a shell firing or exploding very close. It's not so much hearing it as feeling it deep inside your head. It is sudden and gives no warning. I can understand why stun grenades leave one helpless for a few seconds. Every time there was a detonation, I experienced a sudden strange feeling of anger and I felt like shouting, 'Will you bloody well stop that!' and banging on the ceiling as though it was a noisy neighbour in an upstairs flat. With each shell, windows would shake – one window simply shattered – and paint and plaster fell from the ceiling

Of course it didn't take long to realize that if we received a direct hit we would suddenly cease to exist – the cliché is we wouldn't hear the noise of the one that hit us. I remember each second passing and almost calmly thinking that it might happen in the next second or the next or the next. It's so unreal that it's like being in a war film but not knowing the ending; or thinking about being able to tell grandchildren in fifty years' time the boring story yet again of the time I was in Somalia … or maybe not, depending on the randomness of where the next shell might land. We saw afterwards that a shell had exploded ten metres from the hospital making a crater right across the road. They say people react differently to stress. I felt tired, almost sleepy and very hungry, both of which surprised me.

As the morning progressed, the shelling seemed to decrease but in many ways that was more disturbing. If there are no explosions for half an hour and you relax, the sudden bang takes you more by surprise than constant bombardment and the sudden prickling of the skin and rush of adrenaline is more noticeable. A new danger took over. There were now gun battles in the streets outside. One of the female expatriates was in a room at the outer part of the hospital. She suddenly heard a bullet enter through the thin walls; it was close enough for her to hear the whistling as it passed inches above her head. It wasn't long before the hospital gates were breached. I saw an armed Somali climb over the wall and shoot off the lock. All the ICRC Land Cruisers were stolen. We had purposely left the keys in the cars but one of the gunmen couldn't understand this. He came up to one of the expatriates shouting and demanding the keys. Where is an interpreter when you need one? He only turned away when he saw some of the cars being driven out of the compound and ran after them.

Another gunman arrived, threatened the head of delegation and demanded his two-way radio. There was nothing to be done but give it up. A gunfight started in the main courtyard between rivals trying to take the remaining cars.

It was then we realized that this was a more complex and more dangerous situation than two armies trying to take the town. These gunmen were civilians or renegade soldiers in the process of looting everything they could find. It was degenerating from civil war into tribal warfare. We all gathered in a smaller courtyard in the centre of the hospital away from the outside walls and the front gate.

We were standing behind the operating theatre and I was next to the theatre window but could see nothing as all the windows had frosted glass. I remembered something from some Red Cross security course I'd been on sometime in the distant past – 'during shooting or shelling, never stand next to a window'. I idly moved to the side. Less than a minute later, I heard a very quiet crack and saw a small hole in the window. One of the French surgeons, Louis, was next to me. He calmly announced that he thought he'd been shot. We thought he was simply relieving the tension with a joke. But his face was turning ashen white. He was wearing green operating theatre clothes, and from under his left armpit a dull red spot was expanding wider and wider, spreading onto his chest and arm. He said he felt faint and we got him down on the floor. A bullet had passed through the side of his chest wall but ricocheted off a rib and passed through the biceps muscle of his upper arm. He was standing exactly where I had been a moment before. Louis' wound was bleeding profusely so we got him into the theatre – difficult as we were all on our knees crouching to keep below the level of the windows. We didn't want to use general anaesthetic – if we had to evacuate the hospital quickly and run for safety, we needed everyone on their feet and fully conscious. So I injected as much local anaesthetic as I dared into the wounds so that the bleeding vessels could be clamped and any stray pieces of metal removed. It wasn't enough anaesthetic and Louis was gritting his teeth through the pain.

We operated on him on the floor, actually under the operating table rather than on it as there was a bout of more shelling. He was most concerned about his arm: he couldn't feel any sensation in his forearm and hand; he thought the bullet had severed the nerves. As a surgeon, he could see the possible end of his professional career. He impressed us all with his sense of humour: he told me that as the bullet was coming through the window he was reaching to the right to take an offered cigarette. If he hadn't, the path of the bullet would probably have gone right through his heart instead.

'Never again tell me that cigarettes are dangerous for my health,' he said.

He told me his main fear now was that he was experiencing the worse nightmare for a surgeon – being operated on by a bloody anaesthetist. I said it could be far worse – he could be being anaesthetized by a surgeon. In-house joke. (Eventually Louis was to make a full recovery.)

We had both seen and treated many gunshot wounds while working for ICRC. Now we were experiencing gunshots close up. Louis said that at first he didn't feel any pain from the bullet as he might have expected – it felt like a small, almost soft explosion under his arm. For my part I was surprised I had hardly heard any noise. But of course the detonation of the bullet occurs where the gun is, not where it hits, and that was quite a way away. It was also lucky that as the bullet was fired from the other courtyard, it had passed through two windows thus losing enough momentum to avoid the destructive cavitation effect as it hit Louis' body.

More gunmen entered the compound. They were shouting and obviously drunk or had been chewing *khat* – leaves from a local flowering shrub containing an amphetamine-type stimulant – and were very excitable. One of the locals told us the men had come to kill those hospital patients who were members of a rival clan. I had a horrific vision of a bloody massacre, of a travesty of a ward round where the diagnosis of 'wrong tribe' meant death. However, at that moment a car drove erratically in through the gates, there was more shooting, the car reversed out pursued by the gunmen. We didn't see them again. I was sheltering in a doorway as this was happening but I could see the adjacent concrete wall of the courtyard. A bullet hit the wall as I was watching. It made a centimetre-wide hole in the concrete about three centimetres deep. I felt curiously detached from reality as I speculated on how long it would have taken with a masonry drill to make such a hole, then imagined doing the same thing, using the same force, to a human head.

The shooting subsided after a few hours. The shelling seemed further away. We took stock. The medical warehouse had been completely looted; what hadn't been stolen was destroyed. The garage and construction warehouse were now completely empty. We also heard that some of the looters were our local hospital staff. The water tower that supplied the hospital had been shelled: this was very serious – a hospital without water can hardly function.

One of the locals had arrived from our residences. He said everything had been looted including all our personal belongings. Gunmen had found the bar and alcohol store and had been drinking heavily there and then fighting among themselves. Later some of us went to the residences to see what could be recovered. The rooms were completely empty; even the furniture had been taken; there was nothing except a few personal letters and papers strewn on the floor. So much for all my precious belongings and excess baggage. We were overjoyed to see two feared-missing delegates and a local member of the Somali Red Crescent walking through the gates from the ICRC delegation offices up the road. They had been sheltering in the office when gunmen broke in and took everything. One of the delegates had had the foresight to save our passports and the long-range radio – our only link with the outside world – by sitting on them while the looting was going on around them.

Very soon people started bringing the wounded into the hospital – and they kept coming. Within two hours we had sixty wounded patients, seven of them life-threatening. Three of them died as we examined them. The courtyards and corridors were covered with stretchers. It was almost a relief to be able to work again after the inactivity during the shelling and shooting. We could go into medical mode. We were now in familiar territory, but in the post-stress phase of extreme tiredness it wasn't easy. There was an overwhelming and continuous influx of patients and they had to be dealt with as quickly as possible.

There is a well-recognized system for dealing with this situation so that medical staff can be as effective as possible. It's called triage. In its simplest form, the patients are separated into three categories: 1) those patients with minor injuries that will not do any significant harm to them and can often be treated by the patient themselves, 2) those patients whose condition is critical but whose lives or limbs can probably be saved by surgery, and 3) those patients who are so seriously injured, for example, with severe head or chest injuries, that surgery would be very prolonged and the patient would likely die in any case. Only those in category 2 went to the theatre; category 1 were sent away, category 3 were made comfortable, given pain killers and TLC. We invented a category 4: those patients whose relatives have a gun and put it up against your head. It happened to us, and these patients went to theatre first. Of course this is dangerous, because if word gets around that your relative won't get treatment unless you threaten the medics with a gun ...

All the medics were doing the triage, doctors and nurses. This was as far removed as you can probably get from UK NHS practice. There were no patients' records here, no consent forms, no X-ray request forms. Just get on with it. We all had coloured felt-tipped pens. If there was an obvious fracture or wound needing surgery, it was marked in red. If an X-ray was needed, the part of the anatomy was marked in green. If antibiotics had been given a large 'A' was written on the patient's forehead. If morphine had been given a large 'M'. For an intravenous drip needed, 'IV'. This caused a slight problem. It was brought to our attention by the X-ray delegate who complained that patients were coming to him with green and red marks on every limb, he couldn't keep up. It seems the patients' relatives had seen the coloured marks and thought they were some kind of treatment. So they'd found some pens, handed them round and were busy scribbling all over the patients' skin. Actually this wasn't entirely without its merits – one patient had a scribble under his left ribs where he had pain and we found a small shrapnel wound round the back which we could well have missed. Otherwise, all the marks had to be washed off, pens confiscated, and we started again.

We worked all day. It was slow going with one of the two surgeons now out of action. The other surgeon operated on the difficult cases, the theatre nurses operated on the rest – mostly wound debridements and cleaning. One of them said to me, 'You know, I'd never be allowed to do this back in Switzerland. No matter how many courses I'd been on, or certificates I'd got.' She was competent, she'd seen enough debridements on previous missions, and the results were excellent. 'Go for it!' I told her. One of the expatriate pilots told me he felt useless while all this frenetic medical activity was going on. I said I'd teach him to put up intravenous drips – that would be very useful to us. He said he didn't think he could do something as specialised as that.

'If a thirteen year old Cambodian girl can do it, so can you – and I'll explain that some other time.' I showed him on one of the patients how to do it; he got the idea and he was away.

'This is amazing!' he said. 'If we ever get out of here I'll show you how to fly a plane.'

There were a few irritations. Some of the local hospital staff refused to come in to work – they were busy looting in the town. Others were working hard for us even though they could have been at home trying to protect their property. I came across a patient on a stretcher in the courtyard who needed an X-ray. There were three men next to him, friends or relatives who had brought him in. They were lying down dozing. I asked them to carry their friend to the X-ray department.

They declined: 'We've been out all night fighting; you ICRC have been sleeping, so you carry him there.'

'Then no X-ray and no operation.' I wasn't even going to argue with them.

One of the expatriate nurses was actually mugged in the hospital. A man had threatened her with a knife – she had no money to steal but he'd demanded her passport. As she passed it to him she ripped out the front page and tore it up. 'If I can't use the passport then neither will you.' She was a very feisty lady.

A little later, an open truck reversed into the compound. There were wounded men lying in the back. The men who'd brought them in were armed. As the patients were offloaded we could see what they had been lying on – our looted suitcases with the ICRC stickers on them. For a moment we thought they were being returned. There was a moment of eye contact with the gunmen before they quickly offloaded the last patient and drove away, giving us no chance to even reason with them to get our cases back. I have never felt so angry on any mission. Maybe never so angry in my life. A local nurse told us later the next day that he'd seen all our looted belongings for sale in the market.

We had a visit from the commander of the government forces. The rebels had overrun the town but his forces had taken it back again. He had brought back three of our Land Cruisers and guaranteed there'd be no more fighting. Okay, if you say so. He said he felt ashamed at the looting, especially of our residences.

We worked on into the evening and into the night but the shelling started again in the distance. The rumour going around was that the rebels had regrouped and were going to mount another attack on the town. The next day was still busy but we seemed to be making headway and the influx of patients had all but stopped. It was time to think, make decisions about our position and make arrangements for possible escape.

Our two ICRC planes had been in the path of the two armies and were unlikely to be still usable. The inflatable boat by the quayside had disappeared. There was a possibility of a French naval boat rescuing us from Djibouti, the French protectorate along the coast west from Somalia, but it was the time of the First Gulf War and most of the French fleet was on its way there. Then we heard from the government commander again – he told us our two Cessna planes were still at the airfield and appeared undamaged. Our hospital was now running out of supplies and with the reserves of water depleted, it was doubtful if it could carry on for long. There was a possibility of transferring to Hargeisa where there were more wounded and there was a functioning hospital we could work in. One plane would go to Djibouti with Louis who needed more extensive surgery to his arm.

That afternoon, we decided that twelve of us would try to get to the airfield, while five very brave medical expatriates would stay at the hospital in Berbera to look after the patients still there. There was a prolonged lull in the shelling late in the afternoon and there was no shooting to be heard so we decided to make a run for the airfield. No packing to do; we had nothing to pack. We were advised to sit very low in our seats – less of a target.

Berbera had changed, we emerged into an apocalypse. Several houses nearby had been completely destroyed by shelling. From the centre of the town, smoke curled upwards. We had to drive round rubble and craters in the road. It seemed miraculous that the hospital had not been hit. Then we saw the dead bodies in the street and at the side of the road. There had been no attempt to bury them or even to cover them. We were driving purposely slowly but as we rounded a corner we narrowly missed a body in the middle of the road – glazed eyes stared at us, blood from the head had formed a congealed pool in the dirt. We must have seen thirty or forty bodies before we emerged onto the desert road. There seemed to be a checkpoint ahead, a group of three armed men blocking the road. The delegate who was driving turned to us: did anyone remember to bring cigarettes? Fortunately yes, Louis' lucky cigarettes. The driver slowed right down to approach, put his head out of the window pointed to the Red Cross on the car door, said 'hospital' and offered them cigarettes. There was a moment's pause as we held our breath and time seemed to stop. Then they let us through.

The two Cessna aircraft were standing on the runway. The pilots did a check on them and there were some problems. One plane's radio was missing. On the other someone had been inside, had turned the lights on and left them on – the battery was completely flat.

It was then we heard shelling again and saw clouds of dust in the distance to the west. It looked like tanks and they were approaching. It was another attack on Berbera. Time was now running short. With twelve of us plus the pilots we needed both planes and even then they would be overloaded and overweight. The pilots were determined to get them both in the air. The plan was to start one plane and keep the engine running while we swapped the batteries and started the other. I knew it was like a car: once started the engine would generate its own electricity from its alternator. Some of the tools had gone from the planes. Despair; then they found a wrench left behind. While the rest of us sat anxiously on the ground watching the dust cloud get bigger, the pilots got the first plane started then the battery was unbolted and taken to the other plane. It was just bolted in place when the first plane's engine stalled. One of the pilots cursed with frustration. Okay, unbolt the battery and take it back to the first plane – no, start the second engine then transfer the battery. The bolts took an infuriatingly long time to turn. Someone commented that it felt like we were in some bizarre but deadly TV show with contestants struggling with some complex task. As the pilots were working, one of them said, 'There are three main NGOs: ICRC, Médecins Sans Frontières, and Jeux Sans Frontières' (this, the latter, was the European version of the UK game show *It's a Knockout*, popular at the time).

The battery was in place; both engines were running. The shelling was louder. There was very little time now. We had to get airborne before we found ourselves in the middle of another battle. We all squeezed into the two Cessnas; there would have been no room for luggage even if we had any. It was then that our pilot noticed clear liquid dripping from the right wing. There were two bullet holes under the wing and fuel was leaking from the wing tank. There was no choice now. We took off. As the pilot banked away from the advancing army, he told me he would try to fly with the plane leaning to the left and the damaged wing elevated to shift the fuel and reduce the loss. As we gained height, he relieved the tension by announcing, 'Welcome to ICRC flight 999. We will shortly be serving dinner and showing a war film.' I was in the plane with the flat battery – please don't stall!

It was decided that the two planes would escort each other to Djibouti. With one of the radios missing, communication between the two planes was through the window – a surreal conversation conducted like a game of charades. The question was whether we had enough fuel to get to Djibouti, 275 miles away. Everyone had the sense not to ask the pilot. Below us was featureless desert with very little in the way of civilization if we had to make an emergency landing.

We made it, with the fuel gauge on empty. I believe we glided rather than flew down onto the Djibouti airfield and the pilot freewheeled exactly to his parking place.

From Djibouti, I was called back to Geneva for a week to discuss the future of the medical action in Somalia. When the medical staff and I arrived in Geneva, it was a snowy January day. We had only the clothes we stood up in. We were shivering in our shirt sleeves. The cabin crew of the Swissair flight to Geneva gave us the in-flight blankets against the cold and at customs I remarked to the official that we must look like refugees.

'No,' he said, 'usually refugees have at least got some luggage.'

I heard that the hospital and staff had survived the capture of Berbera by the rebel group, the Somali National Movement (SNM). There had been little in the way of fighting: the government troops had simply retreated, and the town became relatively peaceful, but the whole Somalia mission needed rethinking. Wisely, a new surgical team was later sent in to augment and replace the team left behind. ICRC action in Berbera continued for another eight weeks until 21 March when the security situation deteriorated; two ICRC vehicles were attacked. The SNM said they could no longer guarantee ICRC safety and all personnel were withdrawn. For myself, meanwhile, I had a couple of days in the UK to replace all my clothes and lost luggage. From that day on I always travelled light on ICRC missions with nothing of any monetary or sentimental value.

I had always made a point in the UK of not mentioning much about the awful conditions I came across in war zones; it somehow felt like preaching. However, I was in a supermarket at home and found myself in a small queue at a checkout. The woman in front of me was complaining that they should open another checkout if there were more than two customers waiting.

She turned to me and said, 'Don't you think it's absolutely disgusting!'

I thought of the malnourished girl with TB in Berbera. I was very tired and still stressed from our escape and for once I completely and regrettably lost my cool: 'Oh, shut up, you silly woman. Go off to Somalia – they don't even have supermarkets there!'

I received a call while in the UK, from BBC Radio 4 and it was the start of a long and enjoyable association with Simon Elmes, the Creative Director. He was interested in the work I was doing in Somalia and gave me a BBC Marantz tape recorder and a hurried five-minute tutorial on how to use it and how to make documentaries before I rushed off to Heathrow to return, with apprehension, to Somalia.

# Chapter 15

# Mogadishu

First, I flew into Nairobi, Kenya. The ICRC mission for Somalia was now split into two parts – the north was administered from Djibouti, but the main delegation responsible for the south, including Mogadishu, had been evacuated to Nairobi and was sharing the offices of the main ICRC Kenya delegation. I was pleased to see Peter, the head of the Somalia desk, again. I always got on well with him which was important in the weeks ahead. He had also had a bad time. His house in Mogadishu had been destroyed together with most of his belongings and he was lucky to have got out with the rest of the delegation.

I took the opportunity while in Nairobi, on Simon Elmes's advice, to make contact with Peter Byles, the BBC's East African correspondent. He had been covering the Somali civil war and his advice was invaluable. He also realized I was a complete novice so he showed me which was the record button on the tape recorder, gave me more blank cassette tapes and suggested I just keep the recorder running.

It was no longer safe to have our base in Mogadishu; the president had fled Somalia on 26 January and the country was in chaos. We could fly into Somalia on an ICRC Beechcraft from either Nairobi or Mombasa on the coast but we rarely stayed overnight. The main objectives were to get food aid into Somalia and to get the hospitals running again with medical supplies. There were initially just four of us delegates working out of Kenya, besides Peter, the head of delegation. Work was divided into medical, food and fuel, and construction.

That first day I flew into Mogadishu with the rest of the team was a shock. There was no longer a functioning airport terminal, all the windows were broken and a whole corner was missing from the main block where a shell had hit. The still-active Somali Red Crescent provided a car for us. It was an ancient model with the letters USC – United Somali Congress – painted on the side. It was considered to be the safest political faction to be seen to be supporting at the time.

We drove into the centre. From being the picturesque city I'd glimpsed on my first day it had become a ruin. Much of the city had been destroyed by shell fire, the rest was in a bad state; there was hardly a wall which didn't have bullet holes across it. The 'White Pearl of the Indian Ocean' was no more. There wasn't the usual bustle of a normal African capital; there were few cars and few people on the streets. Almost blocking a main road was a military tank. It was burned out and it was already brown with rust. There was sand blowing into the streets as though the desert was beginning to take over again. In an almost surreal image, a tree was festooned with long thin black streamers being blown by the desert wind, fluttering across the road. This was thousands of feet of cine film from a nearby cinema, shelled and looted.

During the attack on Mogadishu, it is estimated that 2,000 people had been killed, 1,500 wounded and the population of two and a half million reduced by half as people fled into the countryside. The economy of Somalia had collapsed.

There was now only one hotel for us to stay at and most of the staff had left. It seemed like the only place where there was any activity. There was a large crowd of people outside who seemed to be waiting for something – anything – to happen. We entered the foyer through glass doors, one of which was shattered with a wooden board blocking it up, the other with a crack along its length. Inside it was gloomy, there was no electricity and the only light was that which came through the small windows. In the old cracked leather-upholstered chairs and sofas there seemed to be a formal discussion going on. It was a meeting of the provisional government of the USC, the United Somali Congress, one of the rebel groups that had attacked the city. The crowd outside were waiting for them to make decisions, to restore order among the chaos, to bring life back to some normality. Our driver told us they were appointing the various ministers and arguing about who was going to be Minister of Sport and Leisure. A pickup drove past the hotel, very fast. There were gunmen in the back shooting into the air as the crowd quickly ran for cover. The civil war had become a mix of inter-tribal fighting and banditry. After dark there were no lights in the hotel. In the huge dining room there was a line of tables pushed together in the centre lit by a couple of candles where everyone in the hotel ate at the same time, ourselves and the would-be government of Somalia. It was goat stew served by a sad, solitary, slow waiter – at least we inside the hotel had something to eat.

The night was noisy with gunfire and the sound of vehicles driving very fast in the surrounding streets. We were reassured this was normal and happened every night. At breakfast we were about to take our chunks of bread and sour milk into the inner courtyard but we were told this was dangerous. Bullets fired up in the air had to come down somewhere and someone had been hit by a bullet falling directly onto the top of his head a few days before.

It became apparent over the next few days that the USC had very little power in the city. There were other rival factions, often clan-based or even rival sub-clans, with a confusion of initials: SNM – Somali National Movement, SPM – Somali Patriotic Movement and SSDF – Somali Salvation Democratic Front.

At one time there were over twelve rival groups vying for control of their own part of Mogadishu. This was the first time I'd seen pure anarchy – and I use the word deliberately. In civilization there are normally constraints that prevent one person killing another even if it is only the fear of consequences from the police, from the military, or from an embassy if the person killed is a foreigner. In Somalia and especially Mogadishu there were now no such constraints. No police, no effective army and the foreign embassies had all left. Every day was a risk and our ICRC identity gave us no protection. Imagine a kindergarten full of hyperactive children all carrying loaded guns and the teacher has left. That was the impression I had of Somalia.

During the attack on the city, our ICRC Land Cruisers had been stolen. We soon learned that one of the factions had adapted one of them. They had removed the rear part of the roof and seats and bolted a heavy machine gun to the floor. They were in the habit of driving round the streets of Mogadishu shooting at enemies or just to incite fear. As the Land Cruiser still had its ICRC emblem on the sides, front and top, this didn't do our image much good. Contact was made with these rebels and they were asked nicely to return the Land Cruiser. When this was refused they were asked at least to paint over the ICRC logos. Their cynical response was that they would let us paint over the logos if we gave them 200 US dollars. The money was paid.

During the following weeks, I joined the team as we made more visits to Mogadishu. My task was to find the hospitals that were still working or which could be helped to start work. But the instability was increasing and we soon avoided staying in Somalia after dark – instead flying back to the safety of Kenya each day.

In Mogadishu, I always had the same local Somali driver, Ali, who in more peaceful times had been a member of the Somali Red Crescent. In his decrepit black car, with its obligatory USC initials crudely whitewashed onto the side, he would take me around Mogadishu. He was a good interpreter. We also had his brother riding shotgun – literally. It was a point of contention: it has always been a rule in ICRC as in all Red Cross divisions that we are not associated with any armaments and we don't allow guns to be carried in our vehicles. Ali made it quite clear – if people knew we weren't armed we would be attacked and the car would be taken. It was his car not an ICRC car and if I didn't like it …

So Ali's brother would sit in the front with his Kalashnikov rifle very visible. Sometimes the brother would go looting at night and put the proceeds in the boot of the car. He once showed us what he'd got.

'Look, a television.'

'No, that's a computer monitor,' said Ali.

'Look, a telephone'

'No, that's a shower head.' Ali was by far the smarter of the two brothers.

'Look, American passports.' They really were – twenty or thirty blank American passports which he'd found in the ruins of the American embassy. He was going to sell them for a dollar each.

As we drove through Mogadishu, Ali would sometimes stop, get out of the car and produce a can of whitewash from the boot. I would watch as he wiped off the USC initials from the door panels and paint SNM – he knew we were entering SNM territory. During a hurried return across the city one day he was interrupted in his repainting and we unwittingly drove into the city centre with USC on the right door panel and SNM on the left. One day Ali said his brother was staying at home as he was too tired from a night of looting. He said I would have to carry the gun. I refused. He insisted. Either that or we go straight back to the plane. Against all my instincts I took the Kalashnikov from the back seat.

Ali said, 'Stick the gun out of the window so everyone can see it ... no, the other end, stupid!' He said I was useless, I just didn't look as though I knew how to shoot someone with it. 'Not even a little girl would be scared of you!' he said, rolling his eyes upwards. He didn't have a very high regard for me at all.

During our trips around Mogadishu, I was looking first of all for a hospital to use as a base for operations. I found it in a part of the city less damaged than the rest. It was called the Martini hospital, an old colonial building built in 1936, now very faded with a long neglected air about it, but at least it was still standing and still functioning up to a point. It ticked all the boxes: it stood in its own grounds with a high wall around it, it had a large warehouse to store the medical aid and even food aid we would bring in, it was close to both the airport and the docks and it backed onto the sea so in terms of security there was one less side to think about. Most importantly it was a former Somali Red Crescent hospital and was even flying the Red Crescent flag. This meant it had an impeccable neutrality – it had never been connected to the former regime's Ministry of Health or any of the new warring political parties. I was lucky to find it and they welcomed me with open arms. There were ten doctors and surgeons and ten qualified nurses still there looking after about a hundred patients. These patients almost exclusively had gunshot wounds and the hospital was admitting at least six more each day. There were also thirty paraplegic patients still there from pre-war days.

The chief surgeon showed me round: there had been some damage which wasn't immediately apparent from outside – the roof of one of the wards had been hit by a shell, the floor was covered with debris, someone had made a half-hearted attempt to sweep it up. Several iron beds stood useless with twisted, blackened frames, the rest had been rescued and taken elsewhere. I didn't like to ask if anyone had been in the beds when it happened, but an area of the floor had been partly washed and I suspect it had been to remove the blood. In the operating theatre they showed me a metre-wide gaping hole high up in one corner where a bazooka shell had come through. The operating table was damaged together with the only anaesthetic machine and a sterilizer for the instruments. So they were now using a smaller operating theatre next door. They were still able to do debridements and amputations but under local anaesthetic only – abdominal injuries were beyond them. In their admissions room, they showed me an elderly man unconscious with a head injury. He'd been hit by a bullet as he'd tried to run across the street to get home during a gun battle. The bullet had entered his skull. Removing the bullet was out of the question – they had neither the equipment nor expertise and it would inevitably cause more damage if they tried it. The hospital staff were struggling because they'd been partly looted during the initial fighting. They'd managed to keep some of their stock because they'd never deserted the hospital, but dressings were few, medicines almost non-existent now and they were having to turn many patients away simply because they didn't have enough food for them. But much of this could be put right without much difficulty.

It's one of the joys of an ICRC mission, when dealing with a hospital which is eager to get working again, to arrive from the airport with a crate of supplies, basic surgical instruments, a replacement sterilizer and a new generator so they wouldn't have to work by candlelight. It wasn't all easy going. I had a problem with the hospital administrator. He held the only keys to the pharmacy storeroom and kept all the storekeeping books to himself. It was impossible to tell if some of the supplies we brought in were going astray. I solved the problem by delivering the supplies straight to the wards. Eventually we had to have words – he'd locked all the donated surgical instruments in his office.

'They are being held in reserve for later.'

Sorry, chum, either they are put in the operating theatre now or the donations all stop. He backed down. He also had a peculiar idea about what ICRC was there for. There was a shell hole at one point in the wall surrounding the compound. It was a security risk so I said our construction delegate would supply the building materials for the hospital staff to rebuild the wall. The administrator didn't like that at all and wanted ICRC to do all the repair work. I'd done too many ICRC missions by now to accept that. I saw little of him after that. I think he left, but the hospital managed just the same without him, in fact the hospital worked quite well. In the days that followed, the chief surgeon invited me to watch them operate – the surgery they were doing was good and closely followed ICRC standards. Except I noticed that although they did good debridements of gunshot wounds I saw a couple of cases where they didn't wait the four to five days before finally closing the wounds but did so after only twenty-four hours. The surgeon explained that they would like to wait longer but the patients' not-so-patient relatives threatened to come back with a gun if he didn't get a move on.

It was at this stage that the idea was considered in Geneva that we put expatriate surgical teams into Mogadishu as the Martini Hospital was an ideal location. I advised against it and I think it was the right decision. I had enough ICRC experience now to see the disadvantages, particularly in the case of Khao-i-Dang hospital in Thailand which could not be closed even after many years. I could see that Mogadishu would present an even more difficult problem especially if security deteriorated, as indeed it did. We might become the Health Service of Somalia without a very good exit strategy. With Berbera in mind, we might not even have any physical exit possible either. I don't think it needed expatriate surgeons in any case. The local Somali medical and surgical staff were competent and eager to work; they just didn't have the equipment and supplies. We could provide that, and as the Martini Hospital was part of the Red Cross/Red Crescent movement anyway, we could be confident that it wouldn't go astray.

One day I was outside the front of the hospital with the chief surgeon looking up at some structural damage to the roof. I'd got into the habit of carrying round the BBC tape recorder on a shoulder strap. It had the recognizable BBC Radio logo on the side. I felt quite proud of it – I could almost imagine myself as a John Simpson or a Kate Adie. There was a small crowd of curious people watching us.

One of the men came forward. He pointed to the tape recorder: 'BBC?'

'It certainly is,' I said, in my new role as documentary programme-maker.

The man continued and the chief surgeon translated for me: 'He wants to know if you are Peter Byles.'

Still in my imaginary role, I thought it might be a pity to disappoint him and rather fun to say, 'Yes that's me.' At the same time we were rather busy and didn't have much time to chat like this so I said, 'I'm sorry, but I'm not Peter Byles. Have you met him before?'

The surgeon replied, 'He says, no, but when they find him they're going to shoot him.'

So close. Apparently Peter Byles had recently broadcast a programme on the BBC World Service about the political situation in Somali which they didn't like. The surgeon suggested we go back inside. I made a mental note to mention it to Peter Byles when I got back to Nairobi.

*Chapter 16*

# Sloop *Steve B*

The first of the large ICRC relief deliveries came in soon afterwards. A small ship, the SS *Steve B* was chartered out of Mombasa and steamed up the coast to Mogadishu with five tons of medical supplies and 300 tons of fuel and food – beans, maize, oil and rice. Mogadishu harbour was derelict; it was full of shipping containers left over from the peaceful days, but every one had been broken into and looted. I stood at the end of the dock for hours, expecting the ship to appear; there was even a US media camera crew waiting for a news story. When the ship appeared in the distance and was recognized, the staff of the Martini Hospital, who were with me to help, whooped with excitement – I don't think they had actually believed it existed. Most importantly, they had arranged for some friendly armed guards to protect the harbour gates in case word of the arrival had got around. The ship docked and we spent all day unloading it. As the cases and sacks were unloaded by crane from the hold, I noticed some sacks of rice had small holes in the corners. As they were swung over the dock, a tiny stream of rice trickled onto the concrete each time. There were some children there who'd come to see what was happening and had got past the guards. As I turned I saw a boy of about six clothed in torn dirty rags picking single grains of uncooked rice off the dirty, sand-covered ground. He would eat a few then give some to his younger sister sitting next to him. They were eating more dirt than rice. Someone said they were orphans. They came back with us to the Martini Hospital. I still see ghosts – nothing supernatural, just the memories of people I've come across during the various Red Cross missions – and as I write this, I wonder what happened to those two children, twenty-five years on.

The journey to the Martini was only a kilometre or less but it was a dangerous trip; the trucks all had armed guards on them. We used the Martini's huge warehouse for all the aid we had brought in and from there we could distribute it to the rest of Mogadishu. The camera crew were still with us. They asked us if we could distribute some of the food, as it would make a good story. I think the BBC tape recorder idea had gone to my head so I staged a scene for them. It was a mistake. There was a rather thin Somali woman sitting outside the gates of the hospital with a baby in her arms. So I opened the first sack – it was rice – and someone cooked a bowl-full in the kitchen. With the cameras rolling I proudly gave it to the woman. She looked at it, then looked at me a bit disappointed and said something in Somali which was translated for the camera: 'Have you got any pasta?'

I'd forgotten this was an ex-Italian colony and rice was largely unknown here. Stick to medical matters, Dr Ryding.

I made visits to the other hospitals. The main university hospital had been thoroughly looted. A corridor was blocked by a bulky X-ray machine which someone had tried to steal but they had given up and left it. I couldn't imagine why they wanted it. A small hospital at the other end of the city had been shelled. They had three patients whom they'd operated on before running out of materials. The ward had been destroyed and the post-operative patients were in a corridor open on one side to a courtyard. They were sitting on the concrete floor leaning against the wall. The nurse explained as she changed their dressings that this was their Intensive Care Unit. A cow ambled over from the courtyard and along the corridor past the patients and made a mess.

As we feared, malnutrition was increasing in the vulnerable groups, the women, children and elderly, despite the tons of food aid the NGOs were bringing in. This in turn meant that resistance to disease was low and cholera, typhoid, malaria and tuberculosis were becoming common. By April there were frequent epidemics of sickness and diarrhoea in children.

There were a couple of hospitals run by other NGOs: SOS Village was run single-handedly by a German expatriate with Somali surgeons and was taking most of the wounded in the city. MSF France were using the Medina Hospital. They were resident there and stayed overnight. I didn't envy them. They invited me for tea. One of the expatriate nurses was sitting in the tearoom, hunched up, looking pale and anxious, shaking slightly. It had been a bad night with shooting close to their sleeping quarters. She looked very young and I wondered if this was her first mission. She was scared and showing signs of stress. These two hospitals were very busy, admitting thirty to fifty patients a day, with 95 per cent of all admissions being gunshot wounds. They said their main problem was not having enough beds for the new patients because they had difficulty discharging the old ones. None of the patients wanted to leave after their surgery because they feared for their safety and they would no longer be fed. The other hospitals were struggling to cope with the extensive destruction and looting – it made me realize that the Martini Hospital had got off lightly.

When I went back to the Martini I was surprised and worried to see three vicious-looking gunmen outside the front gate. Two had Kalashnikovs, the third had a machine gun, loaded and ready, with two belts of bullets draped over his shoulders. It looked like trouble – except that the machine gun was standing on a rickety table along with more guns and boxes of more bullets, for all the world like a terrorist car boot sale. The chief surgeon met me at the gate and reassured me that they were on our side, guarding the hospital. In fact the one with the machine gun was his teenage son – the others were his friends. They spoke a little English and I chatted to them for a while. I was standing in front of the machine gun until someone gently moved me to one side. Never stand in front of a loaded weapon – I should have known by now.

We did our first run distributing the medicines to the other hospitals and I had to argue with the ICRC food delegate to get a fair share of the food for them as well. It almost turned into a fun run. I'd told the chief surgeon that I wanted to distribute it as quickly as possible to avoid being hijacked along the way. So he had recruited a group of a dozen able-bodied teenagers, relatives and friends of the hospital staff, to help. We had a large truck loaded high with boxes all colour-coded and labelled with the names of the hospitals we would deliver to. Before we started, they all had a good meal from the supplies we'd brought in, the 'food-for-work' idea favoured by ICRC. We had two gunmen on the truck. It was against all ICRC policy but I didn't feel I could argue with anyone.

Off we went resembling another *Jeux Sans Frontières*. At each hospital the team would jump off the truck with a whoop and form a chain, throwing boxes down and along the line and into the hospital building. It looked like a rugby team or a circus act – tossing the boxes a long distance and catching them with a flourish and a shout. I should have had a cine camera rather than a tape recorder. I checked the numbers of the boxes as they came off the truck, reading the contents from a list. The boys liked the strange English words and would repeat them with each throw. The word got more corrupted as the box was thrown down the line: antibiotics … andibiotics … andibotics … anjiblotics. And on to the next hospital. Laughing and shouting through the city, but not looting and shooting like the bandits, instead throwing boxes of aid. I couldn't understand it. Was it something in the food we'd given them? Here were these kids in a war-destroyed city with little prospect of peace or hope for the future – simply having fun. I couldn't help joining in the euphoria. We probably didn't need the gun-toting guards: the distribution was done so quickly and with such panache that any would-be hijackers would have had no time to attack us or they would have been too bemused to know what we were doing.

However, it wasn't easy to travel through the city. Some days the situation was very tense, security quickly deteriorated and fighting enveloped whole districts. I always feared being trapped and unable to get back to the plane at the end of the day. It was also difficult identifying the remaining clinics and smaller hospitals. It was all done on hearsay – there was no longer a Ministry of Health with a register of them all.

I unexpectedly came across a damaged building with the sign for 'Clinic' outside. I went inside to look but it was deserted, the doors had been torn down and there was rubbish on the floor. I entered a room and I felt my heart pounding as I saw blood – lots of it. The floor was inches deep in blood. But no bodies, just broken glass and the remains of some laboratory equipment. The blood hadn't clotted and I realized with some relief that this was the Mogadishu Blood Transfusion Service and Blood Bank. Looters thought there was little of value here so they had smashed bottle after bottle of precious stored blood. The next unexpected find was a building with legs and arms scattered about the floor – artificial limbs. It was the Norwegian orthopaedic workshop; the machines and tools had been stolen but the artificial limbs were of no value to the looters. We found the central pharmacy but it had been broken into. As I walked through the smashed door and into the storeroom my feet crunched on broken glass. On the floor were hundreds of broken ampoules – they were intravenous antibiotics, penicillin, streptomycin, cephalosporin. The looters had no idea what valuable medicines they were destroying underfoot.

One day I passed through the Wardhigley district and recognised the ICRC delegation where I'd sheltered during my first day in Somalia. The ICRC emblem was still on the gate, but the gate was wide open. I went inside. The house was derelict. The whole building had been gutted by fire. Nothing undamaged remained. I found the room where I'd hidden under the table – it was black with ash; the tracing department's filing cabinets had all been opened and emptied. The filing cards and papers had been scattered about the floor and burnt.

I made some heart-warming visits. I was once directed to the grand imposing house of a rich Somali businessman. Inside the large walled compound he was sheltering over 800 women and 200 children in tents. They were from the low-caste Hawiyen clan; the husbands had been killed, mostly because they had fought for the former regime of Siad Barré. The businessman had been protecting and feeding them with dwindling supplies as they were too afraid to leave the compound even to get medical help; there were some cases of tuberculosis and many of the children had diarrhoea.

Then we found by chance a small deserted psychiatric hospital in an obscure part of the outer suburbs. At least we thought it was deserted, until a man saw us and hurried over. He took us round to the back of the building. There we saw five severely disturbed patients in a terrible, dirty state, hardly clothed, emaciated and agitated. They were chained to iron rings set into the wall. The man had been visiting them occasionally with water and what little food he had. It took a long time to find a hacksaw to cut the chains and release them so they could be taken to the Martini Hospital.

I had some narrow escapes. My driver Ali had borrowed a covered pickup truck. We had been delivering boxes of medicines to a small clinic in what I thought was a safe area. I was sitting in the back of the empty pickup on one of the benches along the side while Ali went off to deliver the last box. The tree-lined street seemed peaceful. I closed my eyes for a moment but then heard a gunshot close by. I saw three men armed with Kalashnikovs approaching the front of the truck. They stopped to look, peered inside at the driver's seat, then came round the back. I just had time to put the tape recorder and my camera out of sight under the seat. The three men looked into the back of the truck. I barely had time to think through the psychology involved here. The crucial point was not to show fear because if I expected them to be violent then that would put the idea into their heads. I went for extreme nonchalance, put my arm casually along the back of the seat, yawned, said 'hi', reached into my pocket to find I'd remembered the mandatory blessed packet of cigarettes and offered them each one. I even had a souvenir Red Cross lighter for them. I still don't know how I managed to keep calm; as a non-smoker, I would even have smoked a cigarette with them if I thought I could do it without choking. I should have got an Oscar. They could see there was nothing in the truck and they were proba-bly nonplussed to unexpectedly come across a strange-looking foreigner. They accepted the cigarettes with a nod and a gesture of thanks and just moved on. They looked back once to see me apparently peacefully dozing ... with a pulse rate of 120.

It was tiring work, not so much physical but tiredness from tension. The plane journeys from Kenya each day made the time we had in Mogadishu much shorter and intense and as the weeks passed the increase in violence made it dif-ficult to move around the city. At the end of the day we would fly south to Kenya following the desert coast but over the ocean for security reasons. Occasionally I would see giant manta rays swimming idly and feeding in the green-blue water. Then across to Nairobi and into Wilson airport which is also used to fly tourists out to the game parks like the Masai Mara. We always had lots of empty medical crates to bring back and the airport staff would try to clear a path through the waiting tourists in the small airport building. We usually looked tired, dusty and dishevelled, wheeling the crates with the Red Cross logos on the side. It usually took the crowd by surprise wondering what disaster we'd come from. I heard a tourist say almost in awe to a companion, 'They've just come out of Somalia!' as though we'd come out of hell. I suppose we had. But I'll admit it caused a trickle of pride to soak through the exhaustion.

It was good to spend the occasional day in Nairobi at the main ICRC dele-gation, doing paperwork and writing reports for Geneva. All main delegations seem to be pleasant places. The grounds here were completely shaded by banana trees with trellises and pergolas for the sweet-scented climbing plants. There were flowers planted everywhere which were kept constantly watered giving off the wonderful scent of wet earth. I would sit there working outside the 'Somalia Office' and smell the flowers and the deep red bougainvilleas. We had meetings in Nairobi with the other NGOs to coordinate all the activities. This made it easier to try to cover the different areas both geographically and in the type of aid each was giving. Even some of the smaller agencies who might have very specific or limited agendas – treatment of tuberculosis, for example – could relieve the larger NGOs of having to cover this.

One small NGO had a surprising plan. They announced at a meeting that they were about to go into Mogadishu with food aid and were going to swap food for guns and hopefully end the violence. Someone pointed out that there was a serious flaw in this idea: the gunman is going to take your food and you might get a bullet in return but certainly not the gun.

There were other towns in southern Somalia affected by the civil war. Most had no suitable airstrip and access by road was difficult and extremely danger-ous. At Belet Huen there were many landmine injuries, a new and disturbing development. Baidoa was struggling to cope with burns injuries from shell-ing. Garowe had so many starving and wounded people that an airdrop was attempted with the risk that the supplies might not go to the right people. I felt sorry for a refugee camp of Ethiopians who had fled from famine in previous years and who now were caught up in a war.

We couldn't visit Mogadishu at all for several days because of rumours of an imminent large-scale attack on the city. The Somali National Front based in Kismayo had advanced to the town of Afgoi within twenty-five kilometres of Mogadishu. There was unease in the city and many of the fighters were prepar-ing to move out. As we were getting ready to leave Mogadishu we came across a demonstration in front of the main hotel. I always assumed that Somali women were desperate for peace but a group of maybe fifty was now marching through the city centre, angrily mobbing cars and shouting, or more accurately, ululat-ing – that strange, high-pitched, trilling howl produced by the tongue. There was the even stranger sight of them waving their petticoats above their heads. They were calling the men cowards for not fighting and offering to swap their petticoats for the men's guns so they could do the fighting themselves.

# Chapter 17

# Rotting Fish

Kismayo, Somalia's second largest town, is more than 500 kilometres south-west of Mogadishu on the coast and exactly on the equator. It is about the size of Bournemouth but there the similarity ends. Three of us in the team – medical, food and fuel delegates – flew into the town where we spent a few days. It was a dry, dusty, crowded and very hot place, but it had mostly escaped the intense damage of Mogadishu. There had been some damage from shelling including a nearby fish-processing factory by the shore where tons of fish now lay rotting. There seemed to be just two factions in control here, the Somali National Front (SNF) which had evolved from Barré's ex-government, in an uneasy peace with the Somali Patriotic Movement (SPM). In the unfathomable plethora of Somali political parties, it occurred to me that if you started with the letter S for Somalia and followed it with two more completely random letters, the chances are you would come up with one of the political groups.

However, there was still sporadic shooting to be heard and we were advised not to travel the streets alone. There was no clear distinction between military activity and simple banditry. I'd heard there had been a sudden influx of 200 wounded so I went to the largest hospital. Ninety-four per cent of adult patients were war wounded, mostly gunshot wounds with a few shell and mine injuries; but there were also a large number of children with dysentery, pneumonia and malaria. They had a lot of Somali medical and surgical staff but a high turnover of nurses who were not being paid. They told me that initially they had enough medical supplies as a lot of it had been looted from Mogadishu and brought to Kismayo – nice to know it had gone to a good home – but it had almost all been used up by the recent influx of patients. A lot of their stores had been re-looted by a group of bandits from outside the town. I was concerned about this – if we brought in more medical supplies they might be looted again.

'No,' said the hospital director, 'it would not happen again.'

I asked how he could be so sure.

'Because we told the police chief who went after them with a posse and shot the lot.'

They were short of food – it was available but at highly inflated prices: flour was £80 a sack and sugar was £50 per kilo. They had no operating table and very few surgical instruments. They could do amputations even though they had no bone saw – they had bought a carpentry saw from a hardware store. That went on the top of my list. They were sterilizing their instruments in a saucepan in the kitchen. It was actually a depressing day. The thought of the rumoured attack on Mogadishu with more looting and destruction made the work we'd done so far seem rather futile. I was getting compassion fatigue.

It's not possible to keep enthusiasm at a high level for long periods. It didn't help though that there were issues with the ICRC team I was in. It makes all the difference on any mission if you can work with a close, friendly team with good morale. Often if certain team members leave at the end of a mission things can improve. But the opposite occurred here: within a few weeks of starting the Mogadishu action, the other medical delegate, a friendly Swiss woman with a sense of humour and easy manner, cut short her mission because of team problems. I missed her: communication within the team was now becoming almost non-existent. I felt isolated, even excluded. It was hard to know, in such a stressful environment, whether I was being paranoid but it was depressing sitting down at mealtimes with the other two team members who would speak only rapid French. I was convinced it was done to exclude me. Fortunately I got on well with the local medical staff and Peter, the head of delegation, was always ready to listen and advise.

At the end of the day in Kismayo, I returned to the hotel very late. It was a primitive hotel, half a star, if that. There was no food and I had to make do with a dry sandwich left over from lunch. The team had to share rooms. The others retired early. I went quietly to the shared bedroom but the others were already asleep. The air was thick, to the extent of being a fog, with the cigarette smoke of their Gauloises. I just couldn't face it; in fact I was suddenly quite angry at the thoughtlessness of it. I returned to the bare foyer and found a wicker chair which would have to serve as a bed. It was stiflingly hot, even with the windows open, but the pervasive smell of rotting fish blowing in from the ruined factory was marginally better than the cigarette smoke. I had a bad headache. I talked for a while to Brian, a British aid worker who had lived in Somalia for over thirty years. He was visiting Kismayo and like me had had a busy day. We talked about the deteriorating security situation. He said it was safer here than in Mogadishu where he lived. A few weeks later I heard that he'd been shot and killed by robbers at his home.

I found it difficult to sleep in the uncomfortable chair. There was an interview going on between a journalist and a Somali politician who was leaning back comfortably in an armchair and talking lazily in what seemed to be only clichés. As I dozed, I heard words like 'committee' and 'renewing the infrastructure' and 'dialogue to unite all parties'.

'Rubbish!' I thought.

I considered the situation we were in. At first, foreign aid workers were regarded as curiosities but now we were becoming targets. It was once said that the Red Cross emblem on a shirt was better than a bulletproof vest. No longer. Rumours were beginning to emerge of kidnappings and killings of foreigners.

If ever there was a low point in my whole career with the Red Cross – in this spiky wicker chair and this bad fish smell and this heat, with this headache – then this was the moment. I hated the other two members of the team with a vengeance, I cursed them, I vowed I would never ever again be on the same mission with them. I didn't care if they studiously ignored me at the meal table, I didn't care if they could hardly find the good manners to speak to me at all. Then in that brief moment of clarity that sometimes comes just before sleep, I reluctantly had to concede that they were supremely good at their jobs. They had got enormous amounts of food, fuel and materials into Somalia against all the odds and had pushed it in when other NGOs were pulling out. That was what mattered in the end. But I'd still never again work with them . . .

I slept.

We left Kismayo the next day. It was becoming unsafe, even here. There was more gunfire in town and the pilots were eager to leave as soon as possible. Just as the plane started to move forward to take off, I saw a thin, destitute man nearby on the tarmac opposite my window. I thought at first he was begging, but he was holding a dirty, blood-stained pad of dressings against his neck. Our eyes met and he took the pad of dressings off to reveal beneath a raw, fulminating area larger than a saucer. The skin was gone from over the suppurating muscles underneath and the edges were bleeding. Even at that distance I could see it was probably a virulent cancer, maybe of the thyroid. Beyond all hope of cure. He raised his hands, palms together as a plea for help. I couldn't stop the plane and we left for Kenya. On the next visit to Kismayo he wasn't there. His face has haunted me ever since.

For the first time ever in ICRC I counted down the days before the end of the mission. I had done three and a half months, I was tired and rather discouraged and I had another two and a half months to go. It seemed a very long time. Then, *deus ex machina*, a few days later I received a priority message from Geneva. They urgently needed me as medical coordinator for Afghanistan, based in Kabul, starting as soon as possible. I was warned it was not a safe mission. Was that compared to Mogadishu? I doubted it could be worse. I accepted. I thought the reversed 'fire into the frying pan' aptly summed up my position.

I had a few days to make arrangements. I would need a replacement. Most of the work here had been done; the delivery of medical supplies to Mogadishu was almost running on automatic. Peter, the head of delegation, suggested the medical work could be done if the medical coordinator for southern Sudan – she was based in the town of Lokichokio on the northern border of Kenya – could take on the additional work in Somalia.

I took a few days off to go up to see her in Lokichokio. I flew direct from Nairobi in a small ICRC plane. It was good not to be flying into Somalia for once. We flew low up the Rift Valley with its fantastic mountainous scenery, so low that as we flew over Lake Nakuru I could see the mass of pink flamingos. We landed at a small airstrip at the small desert town of Lokichokio. This had previously been merely a village on the road into Sudan a few miles north and inhabited by Turkhana tribespeople who were traditional cattle herders. The place had been chosen as a convenient base for ICRC and other NGOs. There were a few huts and shacks, nothing else, but it attracted the Turkhana as ICRC had dug a deep well from where they could take their water. The ICRC delegation was small with a relaxed atmosphere, secure and not too busy at that time. It was a welcome change from Somalia. It seemed very quiet and I realized why: there was no sound of gunfire. I was given an appointment to meet the medical coordinator at precisely three o'clock in the afternoon in the delegation. I had two hours to wait and one of the field officers asked if I'd like to see the hospital. Good idea, so I got into the Land Cruiser but didn't realize that the hospital was over two kilometres from the town. It consisted of tents with a small building for the operating theatre. I was surprised to find the jolly Icelandic anaesthetic nurse – I hadn't seen her since the escape from Berbera. She was glad to see me especially since they had a patient for operation which she felt was too difficult for her and she asked me to help. She was right not to tackle this anaesthetic alone: he was a man who had been shot through the jaw three days before. These cases can be notoriously dangerous to anaesthetize. Everything might be fine when the patient is conscious but as soon as the anaesthetic is given, the fractured jaw bone and the surrounding massively swollen tissue can cause obstruction to the airway and the patient will suffocate. The inflamed muscles of the jaw are tight and they don't relax with the anaesthetic so it's often impossible to get the mouth open to relieve the obstruction. To an anaesthetist it's what nightmares are made of. It felt good to be doing some practical anaesthetics and good to be in a safe environment again as I helped her with the case: with care we got the patient asleep, still alive for surgery. By the time we'd finished and I'd arranged a lift back to the delegation I was very late for the appointment and it didn't go down well at all. However, I persuaded the medical coordinator to visit Somalia and to hopefully continue where I'd left off.

I arranged one more trip to Kismayo to finish the work there, then to Mogadishu where I could say goodbye to the Martini Hospital staff.

*Chapter 18*

# Last Day in Mogadishu

So I had one last day in Somalia. The security situation was deteriorating rapidly because of the violent inter-party warfare and just plain banditry and it would be extremely dangerous to stay overnight. The small twin-engined Red Cross plane took me from Nairobi into Mogadishu as usual but it was a very tense day there. There'd been heavy fighting all morning and there were rumours of tanks being seen south of the city. In Mogadishu, I asked Ali to be my driver as usual. We loaded the truck with as many crates and boxes of medical supplies as we could to deliver to the hospitals and we set off cautiously into the ruins of the city.

I gave a last load of medicines and dressings to the Martini Hospital, still run by the Somali Red Crescent. When we arrived I was glad to see that they were busy operating and functioning well and all the beds were full. It took time because I had to say emotional goodbyes to all the Somali medical staff I'd got to know in the last few months. I said I was sorry I couldn't have helped them more. It seemed that we'd achieved so little compared to the infinite amount of suffering in that godforsaken country.

It was now late afternoon and I had just one last task. I had a huge wooden crate of medicines left which I'd promised to deliver to a clinic that I'd heard had started up again in the Huriwa district. This was right at the far northern end of the city and I was torn between completing everything I had to do before leaving and being sensible about the security situation. It meant a long and unsafe drive and I was determined not to be shot on my last day. I remembered stories from the First World War of people being killed in the trenches with just a few hours to go before the armistice. I decided to go ahead. We made it to the northern district but we just couldn't find the clinic. There were no street names and few people around to ask. We tried for perhaps an hour until my two-way radio came to life. It was one of the pilots back at the airport. He said there was artillery shelling on the horizon to the south and if the tanks advanced into Mogadishu the airport was right in their path. He said he'd give me thirty minutes and no more to get back to the plane. Ali turned the car round and headed south very fast. No time now to change our political allegiance with the paint pot. We headed for the town centre, but one street was completely blocked by rubble from a destroyed house. Then as we turned down another street we drove into the middle of a gun battle with people running into buildings for shelter. Ali reversed back down the street very fast with the engine screaming. We tried another route. For a moment Ali lost his way. The pilot radioed again. He sounded anxious as the shelling was getting closer. He couldn't keep the plane on the airfield for much longer and was going to leave in fifteen minutes: if I wasn't there they would have to take off without me. I was determined not to spend the night or possibly even several days alone in Mogadishu. Ali sped down the streets, then announced that he didn't think he had enough petrol to get all the way to the airport. I was really sweating now. There were, I knew, no petrol stations functioning in Mogadishu, but Ali said he had an idea. He took a small detour to a round-about near the harbour. Some men were sitting on the kerb with Coca-Cola bottles at their feet – full of petrol. Ali said they were selling the bottles for US$20 each. I got out some dollars but Ali told me not to show the money yet or we'd be mugged. His brother opened the window a little and talked to one of the men who offered him the bottle. I looked at my watch: time was passing too quickly. The brother was cautious – he dipped his finger into the bottle, smelled it, put it on his tongue then spat it out. He nodded to Ali. Yes, it really was petrol. Ali told me to give the man the $20. As we raced off, he explained that a few days ago, another agency, MSF, had driven here and paid $20 for a bottle of urine – it hadn't done the car engine any good. Perhaps I'd greatly underestimated Ali's brother.

We made it to the ruins of the airport. There were guards at the gates but they weren't interested in us and waved us through; there were never any departure formalities here. Ali drove around shell holes in the tarmac to the plane which was still mercifully sitting at the far end of the runway. The pilot told me to hurry as we were leaving right now. Ali asked what he should do with the wooden crate we'd been unable to deliver. I asked him and his brother to get it off the truck; we'd take it with us back to Nairobi – it would be delivered some other day. I could hear artillery fire not far away and see smoke rising. There was a large group of Somalis gathered round the plane; they wanted to be taken to Kenya. But I knew we couldn't do this. I tried to explain to them that without entry visas, the Kenyan authorities at Wilson airport would make us take them all straight back again. There was a loud explosion close to the airfield. We all instinctively ducked. The pilots ordered me into the plane immediately; the crowd scattered to safety. Ali and his brother drove off quickly, I had no chance to thank him and say goodbye. The pilots started the engines.

At that moment a very tall, angry-looking Somali appeared in front of the plane. He had a Kalashnikov rifle and he was pointing it right at the windscreen of the plane and at the pilots.

He was screaming in English, 'Stop, stop, stop!'

I recalled vividly that a few weeks before, some Somali gunmen had hijacked an Italian relief plane while it was still on the runway. They'd ordered all the passengers off the plane, made them lie face down on the tarmac and shot them; then they forced the pilot to fly them to Kenya.

And this was my last day.

One of the pilots turned to me and asked, 'Any ideas?'

I saw that the propellers were turning, remembered we were a humanitarian organization, and wondered aloud if we couldn't just run him down. Not possible, apparently, for unlike a car we didn't have the acceleration. I had a plan. I got all the US dollars out of my pocket and the pilots added theirs to it. We had about $200. I opened the door a fraction and threw the dollars out onto the tarmac. The idea was that while the gunman was picking up the dollars we would taxi away. The gunman didn't move, he just kept shouting 'Stop!' The only thing left was to try to talk to him but we had no interpreter. I opened the door again and called to the gunman. He came round to the side of the plane.

I said, 'Hello, anything we can do for you at all?' It sounded so stupid.

The gunman looked at me aggressively, but he spoke perfect English: 'Do you realize,' he said, 'that you've left a wooden crate right in front of your propeller?'

I stared at him for a moment, 'Is that all?'

'What do you mean, "Is that all?"? You would have caused a bad accident if you'd hit that crate. I used to be a controller at this airport. In the old days I would have reported you!' He picked up the dollars, 'And you people make me so angry, throwing money away like this. It would feed a Somali family for years,' he said, pushing the money back through the door.

We loaded the crate of medicines into the plane, thanked the gunman, shut the door and took off. As we turned and flew over the blessed, brilliant turquoise Indian Ocean, I could see the gunman below waving to us. I could almost hear him saying, 'Have a nice day.'

It was the last I ever saw of Somalia. One of the pilots turned to me and said, 'Bloody good job we didn't try to run him down, isn't it, Doc?'

# PART 5

# A City Besieged by the Mujahideen: Kabul, 1991

*Chapter 19*

# Landmines

When I was offered the medical coordinator job in Kabul, I was warned it was a dangerous mission – Kabul was subject to shell fire, but I knew it couldn't be worse than Somalia. I flew straight from one mission to the next – from Nairobi via Delhi to Kabul. After the heat and stress of Somalia, I stepped into the fresh, cool air of an April morning at Kabul airport to a warm welcome by some of the medical delegates, many of whom I'd worked with before, and I felt a great sense of relief – with a friendly team I could put up with anything.

The bloody ten-year occupation of Afghanistan by the Soviet army had come to an end two years before in 1989; but the violence continued as the communist Afghan government was left on its own to continue fighting the mujahideen, the 'warriors of Islam'. At the time of my arrival, in 1991, Najibullah's government was losing the war. Government-controlled territory was continually shrinking following mujahideen successes, squeezed into just three main centres – the city of Kabul and the towns of Mazar-i-Sharif in the far north and Herat in the west (see map on page 50). The Russians had left behind a few military advisers and diplomatic staff. The rest of the country was controlled by the numerous factions of the mujahideen who were increasingly fighting among themselves.

The ICRC set-up in Kabul was already well established. There was our hospital in Karta Se, one of the suburbs of Kabul, and smaller first-aid posts to the north and south. There were two other ICRC sub-delegations in Afghanistan with first-aid posts at Mazar-i-Sharif and Herat. The expatriate medical staff of the ICRC hospital lived in rented private houses in Kabul near the hospital. I shared a house with three others. Compared to other missions, there was a difference in the accommodation this time: ICRC had made it shellproof. ICRC engineers had fitted all the windows with huge metal shutters. They were formidable, made of quarter-inch steel plate welded into a box-like structure as big as library bookshelves on big hinges. It took quite an effort to close them against the windows. The ceiling was reinforced with steel plate as well, good protection against shrapnel but it wouldn't have made much difference in a direct hit. Our main fear was a hit on the hospital – it was impossible to protect such a large complex, and the obligatory red cross on the main roof was of no use here.

Most days there was shell fire from mujahideen positions outside Kabul. On the first day I saw the smoke trail of a shell crossing overhead, high up, then the dull thud as it exploded on the ground. Familiar territory. I was disturbed at first with the memories of Somalia still fresh, but it's surprising how quickly you can get used to it. Kabul is a big place and we weren't a military or strategic target and none of the ICRC staff seemed particularly worried so I presumed the risk was less than I imagined. But we always kept the steel shutters closed – it gave a very gloomy atmosphere to the house but it was so much effort to open and close them and one never had any warning when missiles were going to come.

We had the usual three expatriate surgical teams and supporting staff. The equipment and pharmaceuticals were standard and had hardly changed from the Khao-i-Dang days. It was a saying in ICRC medical circles that if you were suddenly whisked away on a mission to an ICRC operating theatre you would have little idea where in the world you were: they were almost all identical. Even the theatre temperature would give no clue: they were all air-conditioned, probably at 22°C. The work was the same as well, but the vast majority of cases were shrapnel injuries from shell fire. So ketamine and spinals again were the usual techniques for the anaesthetists.

We saw some terrible injuries, but because they mostly came from nearby, after a shelling incident in the city, the wounds were fresh and so was the distress. We might hear a shell landing far away then half an hour later the screaming victims were brought into our emergency reception room. I was always aware that after working in an ICRC war-zone hospital for a year or so, one could become immune to the suffering, almost isolated from the personal side of a severe injury and concentrate purely on the surgical problems involved.

One morning, I was in the emergency room. I still had the BBC tape recorder from Simon Elmes and I'd got used to just letting it run. I'd forgotten all about it when some shell victims were brought in. One was a boy of about 7 or 8 years old. He was lying on the floor on a canvas stretcher. Both his legs had been blown away at the knees. He'd been given morphine but it was taking time to take effect. He was shouting 'Dah-kay!'– the word for pain – over and over. I was busy trying to find a decent vein to set up a drip – he'd lost a lot of blood and his veins were shut down; I was asking for intravenous fluids; getting a dressing pack and a pair of forceps to get a clamp on a fast-bleeding artery among the ragged tissue where his leg had once been. It was all routine emergency surgery. I got on with it unemotionally. Months later, when the mission was over, I was in a BBC Radio 4 studio at Broadcasting House in London, with Simon Elmes. He was editing the tapes, getting me to do some voice-overs, and we were listening to the tape I'd recorded that morning in the emergency room in Kabul. Simon was playing one section over and over to get the cutting right. It was the boy shouting '*Dah-kay!*' Maybe it was the fact that the incident was now so far away, but here in the comfort and safety of a London studio, it suddenly hit me: the awful memory of that small boy with legs blown off, suffering and bleeding on the dusty floor. My throat tightened up and I had to make some excuse to go out for a while. It was some time before I could go back in and continue recording.

As part of our mandatory security briefings in Kabul, we were sent one afternoon for a talk on landmine awareness. It was here that I met for the first time Guy Willoughby, the director of the Halo Trust who was working in Kabul at that time. This independent British charity specializes in the 'removal of the hazardous debris of war', especially landmine removal. It is a very hazardous business. To date they've destroyed over 1.3 million landmines in the world. On the lawn in the garden of the Halo Trust house we were shown a range of mines we might encounter. I'd seen the effects of mines in the field, but, apart from a butterfly mine, I'd never seen the mines themselves close up. There were small anti-personnel mines no bigger than a small tin of baked beans, larger anti-tank mines almost as big as a car wheel – and all sizes in between. There were fragmentation mines which have large amounts of ferrous metal in their construction. This is ripped apart into jagged pieces of shrapnel that can disable even armoured vehicles. 'Stake' mines are above ground, maybe hidden in vegetation, triggered by trip wires. Some of these, like the Claymore mine, are directional, sending all the force one way – along a path or road for instance.

'Bounding' mines have a small charge which throws the mine up into the air to about an adult's chest height before the main charge explodes and does the real damage. It also happens to be about the same height as the head of a child. I saw an ingenious mine meant to be dropped from the air, which spins and sends out dozens of near-invisible nylon threads with hooks on the end, like fishing lines. These surround the mine for many metres with a tangle of ready-made trip wires. Someone in an office somewhere must have spent hours designing that one. There were blast mines meant to injure people; pure explosive, the effect of which is to send an intense shock wave upwards that will traumatically amputate a foot or leg and also to violently project whatever is buried with the mine – rocks, stones or gravel – upwards into the air to do even more damage as shrapnel. What remains of the victim's boot and even pieces of his own bone will even act as grisly shrapnel further up his body. I was reminded of Cambodia and the bamboo splinters, or worse, that we'd taken out of patients.

I've never ceased to be shocked at the scientific effort and macabre research, much of it in Europe, that goes into making landmines as lethal as they are.

Perhaps lethal isn't the correct word because landmines are not specifically made to kill people. They are far more effective if they severely maim. If someone dies immediately as a result of a mine, the body is either left there or buried by the victim's comrades. And that is the end. However, the most efficient effect is, for example, to blow someone's heel bone off. This means the victim will be incapacitated and in severe pain. The screaming will lower the morale of his fellow combatants. It will take them time and transport to get the victim to first-aid help. It will use up valuable medical facilities and personnel operating on him and nursing him. Similarly his rehabilitation and mobilization will use up resources. As a handicapped person his country or society might have to look after him for the rest of his life. It would be extremely unlikely that he would be able to fight again. I can hardly imagine some scientist in a smart office somewhere in the civilized world calculating all these effects to produce a better landmine. Of course, to an innocent woman or child triggering a mine while merely looking for something to eat, these calculations are irrelevant.

The fragmentation mine can be detected by metal detectors, but some mines are made of wood and glass. The more modern plastic mines have no metal in them, or perhaps just a tiny metal firing pin and are more or less invisible to metal detectors, so they have to be cleared very laboriously and carefully by simply prodding into the earth on hands and knees. I heard of some devious mine-layers planting a small metal anti-personnel mine then surrounding it with half a dozen plastic mines. The mine-clearer will detect the metal mine and when he kneels down to defuse it, he will kneel on the plastic mines. I learned that the firing pins are very easy to make or adapt – the top of a simple clicking ballpoint pen can be used. When I heard this, I had a flashback and felt a shiver. Back in Cambodia, in Tap Prik hospital, two boxes of ballpoint pens brought for the school had inexplicably gone missing.

In Afghanistan, as in most of the world, people don't make maps or remember where they've planted mines. They may simply be escaping up an unknown mountain track throwing mines over their shoulder. A landmine might cost £2 to buy and plant – but it will cost anywhere between £200 and £600 to take it out. There are well over a hundred million landmines in the ground worldwide. After I worked in Kabul, in 1994, it was estimated that 100,000 mines had been cleared but in the same period another two million had been laid. If no more were laid it would take 1,100 years to clear the world of mines. The average mine lasts a very long time; no one has an exact figure but some have been found still active after over fifty years. Landmines are almost perfect soldiers: they are always ready, they never sleep, they never desert. At the same time they don't distinguish whom they injure and they are still there and still active after all the other soldiers have gone home and the war has long been forgotten. It has been described as mass destruction in slow motion.

There were also some injuries which were purely accidental. When aircraft, especially Russian, were leaving Kabul and were in danger of being brought down by mujahideen heat-seeking missiles, they would send out magnesium flares from the rear of the plane to fool and deflect the missiles. We would sometimes see this from the ground and I would look up and feel for the anxious, sweating crew and passengers up there and vulnerable. Sometimes the flares would fail to ignite, fall to the ground, and be collected by children. They had the habit of taking them home and putting them in the fire to see what would happen. I saw several children at the hospital with very severe burns and subsequent deaths.

## *Chapter 20*

# Into the Field

K abul was the first mission where I'd worked with both sides of a conflict. I'd met the mujahideen and their families when I'd worked in
Quetta, I'd listened to their side of the story, heard the atrocities. Now
I was doing the same with the other side. It's almost impossible not to sympa-
thize with the people you help on an ICRC mission, and I now found myself
sympathizing with the other side. There was in fact so little difference between
the two. The Kabul mission was also unique for me because from Kabul we
were actually giving medical aid to both sides at the same time.

The ICRC field delegates had achieved an extraordinary feat in getting
the Kabul government to give us permission to drive out of Kabul, cross no
man's land into mujahideen territory, supply their village hospitals, treat their
wounded, and remarkably even bring the serious cases back into Kabul to our
hospital – under Red Cross protection – and then return them back across the
front line to their villages. It was not a safe enterprise. These villages were in the
artillery firing line, whether they were military targets or not. In most areas the
Red Cross were welcome but as in all war zones it's dangerous to be a stranger
in an area of nervous, armed combatants. Soon after I had finished the mission,
one of our expatriate male nurses was shot dead while making one such trip to
the south of Kabul.

The first time I made one of these journeys was to the village of Mir Bacha
Kot with Claire Bertschinger, an experienced Swiss/British nurse who made the
journey almost daily. The village is about fourteen miles to the north of Kabul
and the journey felt hazardous. Before setting out each day, Claire used to check
with the Kabul authorities that they weren't planning any shelling, but it was
no guarantee. With a large red cross flying from the radio aerial, we passed the
last government checkpoint on the outskirts of Kabul – the guards there were
friendly but I had the impression they thought we were mad going out into no
man's land. Here, driving the mile or so along the bare, dusty road, we were in
limbo – under the protection of neither side. We suddenly heard a rapid series of
rockets coming over from Kabul and saw their trails right above us, fortunately
high up and well out of our way. They came from a Russian-made Katyusha
multiple rocket launcher. These were nicknamed 'Stalin's organ' presumably

from the musical whooshing sound the rockets made, or maybe it was because, mounted on the back of a truck, the rows of metal pipes looked like an organ, or as our Afghan driver preferred, it was a reference to Stalin's anatomy. We passed another checkpoint and were now in mujahideen territory. The guards and the villagers of Mir Bacha Kot knew Claire well and welcomed us. The village had a very small hospital hut, room for only a handful of wounded. They would be brought in from the countryside from miles around – almost exclusively mine and rocket injuries.

We sat down in the hospital office with the Afghan nurse and the head of the village and as many others who could fit into the tiny room for the obligatory tea and informal chat. I learned that one of the men had returned the previous day from operating a piece of artillery in the hills which was used against Kabul. I asked him how accurate it was, thinking about all the civilians in the city. He seemed puzzled; it appeared that he couldn't actually see Kabul – but he knew it was somewhere over there – and he waved his hand vaguely to the south and that was where he sort of aimed. Despite the apprehension of this trip, I realized I was probably safer here than back in the city – armour-plated windows or not. The talk of armaments continued and the head man told us there had been an incident in a nearby village recently. Two Afghans had procured a US-made FIM-92 stinger missile – heaven knows where they'd got it from. The intention was to fire it at an aircraft leaving from Kabul airport. They weren't sure how it worked so they'd taken it indoors, laid it on the kitchen table and had a go with a screwdriver. The missile fired. Imagine their surprise: one minute the missile was on the table, then there was the most tremendous bang and it set off across the room, demolished the kitchen wall, crossed the street, went straight through another house ... and another, fortunately both empty, before heading off into the countryside, leaving the two men staring at the empty table.

Well before dusk and it was time to leave. We took two wounded patients with us in the Land Cruiser whom Claire had decided should be treated back at our hospital in Kabul. One was a woman with shrapnel injuries to her leg. The other was a boy of seven. He had been outside his village collecting firewood and had come across a butterfly mine in the grass. He had picked it up and it had exploded, blowing his hand away.

These butterfly mines caused many injuries in children. They are small and light, made of plastic, just twelve centimetres across with two wings like a butterfly; one wing contains liquid explosive. They can be dropped in their hundreds from helicopters and were very common in Afghanistan. Some are a dull green or brown for camouflage, others are bright green and children think they are toys and call them 'green parrots'. If they haven't detonated after dropping, or

Tap Prik Hospital, Cambodia.

A ward at Tap Prik Hospital.

The bridge at Tap Prik.

A ward round
with author
at Nong Pru
Hospital.

Theatre audience at Nong Pru.

The road to Nong Pru.

Intravenous drip team at
Nong Pru.

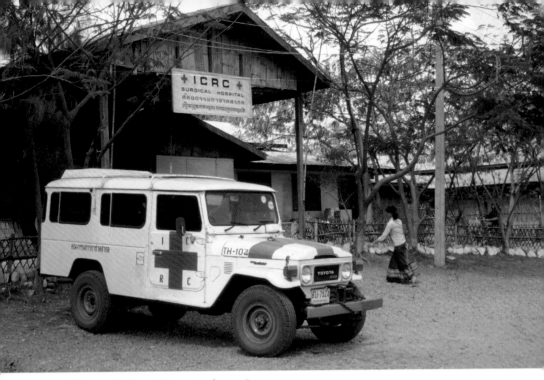

ICRC Hospital. Khao-i-Dang Refugee Camp.

Intensive Care Ward, Khao-i-Dang Hospital.

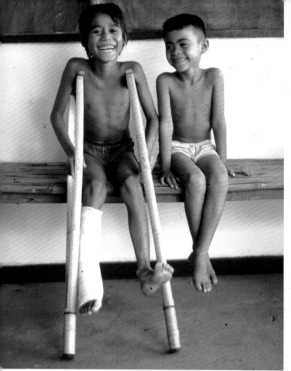

Patients, Khao-i-Dang Hospital.

Kru Khmer doctor, Khao-i-Dang.

Quetta street.

Afghan patients
with author, ICRC
Hospital, Peshawar.

Extracting a
machine-gun bullet
from an arm.

A 180°-bending
prosthetic leg.

Burnt-out tank in a Mogadishu street.

Looted and burned ICRC refugee-tracing office,
Mogadishu.

Operating theatre, Martini
Hospital, Mogadishu, with
bazooka shell damage to wall.

Ali, the author's driver in
Mogadishu.

The author with armed guards outside the Martini Hospital, Mogadishu.

ICRC Kabul, visit to the Kabul Zoo by young patients.

The author with young patients from the ICRC hospital, Kabul.

The author in Grozny, shelled tower block behind.

The ruins of Grozny.

Warning 'Landmines inside' at the main entrance to Grozny Hospital No. 4.

Pleading sign outside a civilian house: 'People are living here'.

Delivery of an ophthalmic microscope to Grozny Hospital No. 4.

A donated oxygen concentrator being used for anaesthesia at Shali Hospital.

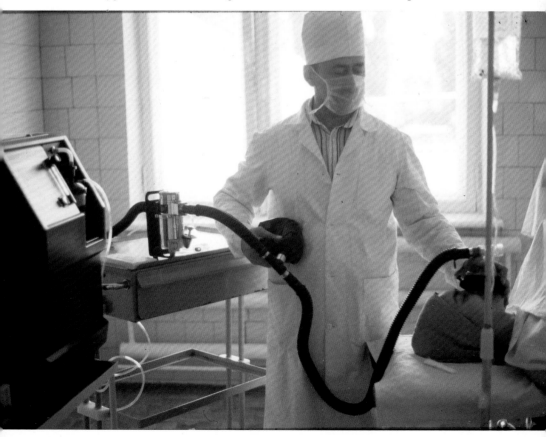

Dry riverbed next to the ICRC Hospital, Lokichokio.

The author with the child, Panda, a lion-attack victim, Lokichokio.

The author inserting a spinal anaesthetic, Lokichokio.

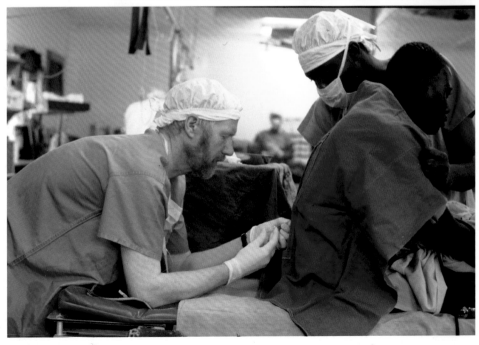

ICRC field hospital in the cricket stadium, Muzaffarabad, Pakistan.

Refugee camp, Muzaffarabad.

Earthquake damage in Muzaffarabad.

The author, right, with ICRC surgical team Sarah and Harald, Muzaffarabad.

Old Fangak, South Sudan.

Boat from airstrip to Old Fangak.

Old Fangak hospital.

A sweltering operating theatre, Old Fangak hospital.

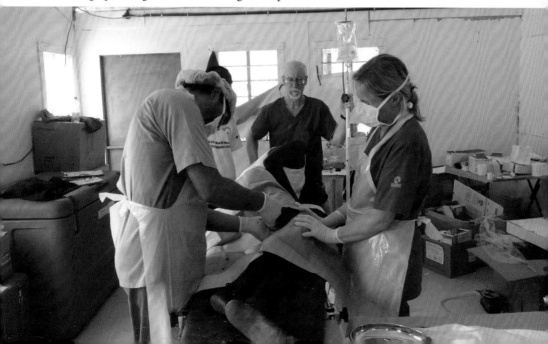

Sleeping arrangements, Old Fangak hospital.

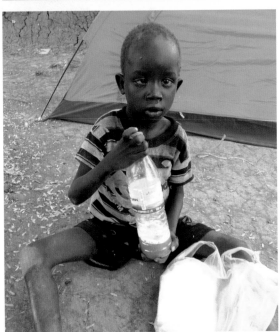

Dwolle making a tamarind drink.

Refugees fleeing along the River Zaraf, Old Fangak.

in some models self-destructing after twenty-four hours, they can be set off by pressure on the plastic wing. This can be cumulative, so a child may press it, bend it, even take it to show to his friends or take it home before one more squeeze and it explodes. I once saw an Afghan child with half a dozen butterfly mines tied all round his belt as souvenirs – still active I supposed as they can't easily be disarmed. We very carefully took them away from him. Don't sit down, kid!

Transfers of patients were not always straightforward. The ICRC delegation in Mazar-i-Sharif had received word of a wounded mujahideen commander out in the field. He had a bad reputation for killing captured government troops, and even civilians – he was known as the 'Butcher of Mazar'. It was rumoured that slitting throats was his preferred method. But now he had a problem. The only medical aid available was at the ICRC first-aid post at Mazar which was in government territory and he would certainly be taken prisoner and shot if he showed his face in Mazar. It took some very intense negotiations by ICRC delegates in Kabul to get permission to fly him from Mazar to our hospital in Kabul in an ICRC plane, under ICRC protection under the Geneva Convention and subsequently back home again. To the credit of the government they eventually agreed. The problem we envisaged was not the transfer but when he was a patient in the hospital. There were other patients there who might have good reason to take their revenge on him. After the operation, we placed him in a separate room well away from the rest while he recuperated. He recovered well for the next few days. One day when we went to see him on the ward round he was missing. He was found walking through the wards, greeting old friends. The other patients, including ones from the opposition didn't seem to mind – they must have known who he was. The next day the Butcher of Mazar was helping with the tea trolley, serving people who a few weeks before would have killed him. I later caught him reading some ICRC dissemination material which was scattered about the wards. I half expected him to ask if he could join the Afghan Red Crescent before he left to go back home. But perhaps that was too much to hope for.

When we eventually flew him back to Mazar, one of his commander friends thanked me and said he would like to present me with a gift. He gave me a pen. I thanked him. It felt a bit heavy. He explained that it wasn't just a pen, although it did actually write. He said that one of his colleagues had got it from the village of Darra Adam Khel in the North West Frontier province of Pakistan. The name rang a bell. There was an unusual cottage industry there. They made firearms. It was said they could reproduce any gun presented to them. They were known for making fake but just as deadly Kalashnikov rifles. The commander explained the pen to me: the tip came off, the body unscrewed, and a .22 bullet was inserted. The pen clip retracted and became a trigger. He'd presented me with a perfectly disguised gun, tiny but lethal. He told me that he'd taken the pen to a peace conference with a rival mujahideen group. He'd signed the peace treaty with this pen, but before he put it back in his pocket, he'd shot dead the rival commander sitting on the other side of the table. He thought I might like to have it as a token of thanks. I said I'd rather not.

While the mujahideen were indiscriminately shelling Kabul, the national army was doing the same thing to the mujahideen. We once had a visit to the hospital from a high-ranking government army officer. He was visiting one of his soldiers who was a patient. The officer was in charge of all the rocket launchers in Kabul that fired out of the city into mujahideen territory. We were asked to treat him as a VIP. I couldn't resist the opportunity. After tea, I gave him a guided tour of the hospital but specifically took him to the children's ward. There had been several admissions of wounded children in the previous few days brought from mujahideen areas to the south. He heard the crying, he saw the bandages covering the stumps of missing arms and legs, he saw the disfigured face of a now blinded five-year-old girl. He asked the nurse in charge what had caused all this. The nurse replied that they were all injuries caused by rockets fired from Kabul. The officer went visibly white and could say nothing. He stared at them for a long time then apologized and hurriedly left. But he gave me a hundred dollars to buy something for the children. His hand was shaking.

We treated the children to a trip to the zoo. I was surprised to find that Kabul still had a zoo in 1991. It was rather a sad, meagre affair, but we imagined that to most of the children who'd maybe spent their whole life in one village it would be special. The main attraction was not a lion or tiger but a pig. It was probably the only pig in Afghanistan – in a Muslim country pork is not eaten. We labelled all the children with Red Cross badges and set off, a few in wheelchairs, two on stretchers. We had to cross the main road to get to the entrance but had to wait while a long train of thirty or more heavily laden camels made their way ponderously past us. It seemed ironic that we had to wait for what to me were exotic camels to pass before we could go and see a pig. Inside the zoo, we faced an unexpected problem: the children didn't know what to do. I imagined children in the UK running off excitedly to see all the animals. Here they just stood and looked at us. The concept of being taken on a trip and simply enjoying themselves didn't seem to occur to them. We had to take them to the pens and show them the animals. Like all children they soon got the hang of it and they got an ice-cream at the end, but I had the feeling afterwards that they still couldn't understand what it was all about.

I made several trips to the only other government enclaves – Herat and Mazar. The only way to get there was by the small ICRC plane. The main circular road route around Afghanistan linking these towns to Kabul was far too dangerous for routine trips. It felt as if these towns were almost under siege. Herat was once a tourist destination, with its famous, beautiful Blue Mosque but the tourists had long since gone. The road from the airstrip into Herat was hazardous in itself; there had been several incidences of landmines being placed on the road during the night by mujahideen. It also wasn't uncommon for the town to receive the odd artillery attack. There was always the fear that the muja-hideen would one day make a final assault on the towns. I had a spare afternoon waiting for the delayed plane to take me back to Kabul, so I took a walk through the almost empty main street. I wandered into the famous but deserted Blue Mosque but was reprimanded because I'd forgotten to take my shoes off. Across the road was a forlorn antique shop whose owner hadn't seen a customer for months. He couldn't sell me a carpet or some of the famous Herat blue glass-ware, but I bought a small bronze oil lamp in terrible condition, full of holes that he told me he'd found buried nearby. I later found out it was Greek from the 3rd century BC presumably when Alexander the Great had come through this region with his armies. It seemed there had hardly ever been peace here.

Later I heard another delegate bought an old blunderbuss from this shop and at Kabul airport on his way home at the end of mission he had been chal-lenged by security: he couldn't take a gun as hand luggage onto the plane. He argued that the ancient piece had probably not been used for 200 years and to prove it he pulled the trigger. It went off, the assortment of metal shot missing other passengers but making a hole in the plaster of the ceiling. It went cargo.

The Russian Army had withdrawn from Afghanistan over two years previ-ous, in early 1989, but there were still Russian diplomats and advisers in Kabul cooperating with the Najibullah government. I met a few in the course of the next few months – I found expatriates of different nationalities tended to mix readily in a difficult country like this. One of the Russians, Gregor, used to invite a few of us over to his house every couple of weeks to play bridge. His official title was Cultural Adviser, but one of our field delegates told me that was a common pseudonym for the Soviet secret police – Gregor was a KGB colonel. I'd read John le Carré. This was the real thing. I was only a beginner at bridge and Gregor claimed he was a beginner too. But when I was partnered with him I always seemed to do better than I deserved. Beginner's luck, but I began to wonder if he had spy cameras over our opponents' shoulders. He was fascinated with the history of Russia as interpreted by the West. I had brought just such a book with me. He loved it, especially our view of Stalin. He didn't say whether he thought our version or his country's was the more correct. I gave him the book. When he'd had a few vodkas he would open up and become more expansive, more indiscreet as he put it. He would regale us with apocryphal KGB stories and played a so-called spy training tape. I'd always imagined the KGB as sombre, serious, humourless people. But this was a spoof tape or as he termed it, a spook-spoof: I presumed he was just having a joke with me but with Gregor I never knew.

'When arriving as a Soviet agent at Heathrow airport, the customs officer discovers you have a second passport in your luggage:

"Why the second passport?"

"Because I do a lot of travelling."

"It is a woman's passport."

"I am having a gender identity crisis."

"What is in this tube?"

"It is toothpaste."

'No, it seems it is Semtex explosive."

"I have a lot of trouble with plaque."'

He explained that he would retire in a few months, he hated the political changes in the Soviet Union – Gorbachov was in power – and before he left Afghanistan he was going to burn his KGB uniform. I said that was a shame. So he gave me his impressive blue KGB dress uniform, which I still have. But he surprised me one day when he told me he had been one of the KGB 'runners' in the UK. One of his 'moles' was Kim Philby. He showed me a copy of Philby's autobiography with a note scribbled on the first page: 'To my friend Gregor.'

'I didn't like him at all,' said Gregor.

After three months, my Kabul mission came to an end. The normal route home would have been a scheduled flight from Kabul to Delhi then to Geneva. I was wondering if there might be a more interesting route and one of the Russian diplomatic staff suggested I fly via Moscow; there was even an Aeroflot office in Kabul still open. So I enquired there and they said yes, they could organize my flight out to Tashkent in neighbouring Uzbekistan then onwards to Moscow. It sounded great. I checked with the head of delegation and he said that any scheduled civilian flight was fine. I went back to Aeroflot and bought my ticket. I asked if it was possible to reserve a seat next to the window.

The official said, 'No seats.'

I should have begun to suspect something was not quite right. I explained that I just wanted to sit next to the window.

'No windows,' he said.

It was leaving day and a rather emotional goodbye at the airport with the expatriates and locals I'd been working with. Through the terminal building I walked out to the waiting aircraft. It was a huge Antonov transport plane – the size of a Boeing 747. Inside the aircraft I had a shock: where I had expected the passenger compartment was a Russian tank. It was true: there were no seats and the only windows were like small portholes high up. There were only five other passengers and the female flight attendant showed us where to sit – on wooden crates. They contained bullets. This was no civilian flight, it was a military aircraft. As a delegate of the Red Cross, careful of our neutrality, I shouldn't have been on this aircraft. I suppose I should have insisted they let me off, but I'd paid for the ticket and didn't want to make a fuss. The heavy plane took off like an overfed goose but it couldn't fly in a straight line because just a few miles outside Kabul it would be above mujahideen territory and a target for any artillery on the ground. It had to turn in tight circles trying to stay in safe Kabul airspace, straining to gain height until it could fly off north. Another passenger was one of the Russian diplomats I'd met in Kabul. He travelled regularly on this flight. We chatted until the flight attendant appeared from the front of the aircraft with a tray. Ah, refreshments?

'No,' said the diplomat, 'they are flares. It appears that someone is trying to fire at us with missiles, so they like to send flares out of the back of the plane to deflect them.'

The attendant busied herself calmly inserting the flare canisters into the bazooka-like tubes at the stern. I soon saw the eerie orange glow of the flares reflecting through the porthole windows, casting their light on the cabin ceiling as they arched away downwards. I was definitely on the wrong plane. I had my ICRC badge to prove I was not Russian, but this was little use at 10,000 feet. I had the absurd idea of waving it at the porthole. I remembered I also had a KGB dress uniform in my luggage. I wondered how long it would be before we were safely over Soviet territory. The diplomat, with typically laconic Russian humour, told me to watch the pilot – we could see him clearly, there was no door to the cockpit – when he stops sweating, you know we've crossed the border. We didn't get shot down, but when we landed at Tashkent on a beautifully cool fresh afternoon I almost kissed the tarmac.

The history of Afghanistan since then has been far from peaceful. The communist Najibullah regime fell a year later, in 1992. The country was then governed by a coalition of the victorious mujahideen groups but the violence continued as they quarrelled among themselves and Kabul descended into chaos. In 1994, the Taliban, a movement originating from Islamic religious schools for Afghan refugees in Pakistan, developed as a political/religious force and took power in several provinces in southern and central Afghanistan. The Taliban seized Kabul on 27 September 1996, and established the Islamic Emirate of Afghanistan until the fall of Kabul to US and British troops in November 2001.

# PART 6

## INTERLUDES:
## AID TO ARMENIA AND SIBERIA

## Chapter 21

# Armenian Earthquake

I'm often amazed by the ingenuity of people struggling to recover from war or disaster. Following the earthquake in Armenia in 1988, I went over there several times for the British Red Cross who had decided to build a children's clinic in Gjumri, Armenia's second city, which had suffered heavily from the damage. As part of the assessment, I travelled widely in the earthquake region finding out what medical facilities were left intact and functioning.

Most hospitals were struggling, especially the smaller provincial ones. Electricity supplies to many villages had been cut off. The alternative for these hospitals was a generator, but diesel fuel was in short supply and deliveries erratic as the transport system had been severely disrupted and many of the roads, especially in the mountains, were now impassable. So the hospitals were trying to manage without electricity, with the result that the health care they could deliver was very limited. Except at one hospital. It was in a small town difficult to get to by road but had a small railway station on the main line to Gjumri. Two friendly and enthusiastic nurses showed me round the hospital. They had a few patients but no electric lights working, just candles in some of the darker rooms. I saw an old X-ray machine in one room. They usually need a lot of power.

'I suppose you can't do any X-rays now?' I asked.

'Yes, we can do X-rays; in fact one of the patients needs a chest X-ray. Would you like to see it working?

I said I'd love to, wondering how they were going to power it up. 'I haven't seen a generator.'

'No, we don't have one.'

I was thinking wind turbine, solar panels, treadmill …

The other nurse looked at her watch. 'I don't think we have enough time; better wait until after the 3 o'clock train.'

I was intrigued.

We had tea and biscuits and the first nurse explained: the railway ran along-side the hospital grounds. It had overhead electrical wires and her husband was an electrical engineer. When they wanted power, he would take two huge metal hooks connected to thick cables and throw them up over the overhead wires and plug the hospital into the railway's supply. The reason we had to wait until after 3 o'clock was that the Gjumri express came through then and her husband had to make sure there was nothing on the wires at that time. I had nightmare visions of a train coming early one day and speeding away, dragging an X-ray machine behind it.

Implementing earthquake relief can involve unexpected difficulties. During the aftermath of the Armenian earthquake, many relief agencies including the Red Cross were trying to get through the usual bureaucracy while plane loads of aid were coming into the airport at Yerevan. On a very busy day, a certain famous singer and actress flew independently into Yerevan to see for herself all the damage. But because the Armenian officials were all keen to meet her and offer her their hospitality, all our meetings with them were cancelled for that day and the planes sat on the tarmac waiting to clear customs. It also didn't go down well with us that the singer was then photographed standing in front of one of our Red Cross planes while crates of *our* aid were being unloaded. But I suppose the publicity value of her visit was a factor in her favour. I couldn't quite see how her personal donation was relevant though: a gift of a thousand Hollywood Barbie dolls.

*Chapter 22*

# Siberia

In 1992 I took on a project for the British Red Cross to deliver medical aid to the Russian Federation. It was a relaxing change not to be going out to another war zone. Russia was in a financial crisis after the break-up of the Former Soviet Union. Boris Yeltsin had had talks with John Major, the British prime minister of the time, who had agreed to send £10 million of medical supplies to the neediest parts of the Federation. Instead of him handing the money over to Boris in used fivers, the British Red Cross was asked to assess where the supplies should go, the Crown Agents would deliver it and the British Red Cross would monitor it and then assess what effect it had had.

I spent a month travelling across the western parts of Siberia visiting hospitals around Tiumen, Ekaterinberg and Novokusnetsk, finding out which medicines were in short supply. Then large wooden crates of supplies were airlifted to Siberia and delivered, all efficiently labelled. A few of us were seriously concerned that much of it would go astray due to theft and corruption.

One of the hospital directors said we needn't have worried, 'East of the Urals, we are all honest – to the west they're all bandits!'

Each of the thirty or so hospitals, in typical Russian fashion, had kept minutely detailed records of exactly where each tablet, each injection and each bandage had gone. Only one small box of asthma inhalers had gone missing: it was said to have *actually* fallen off the back of a lorry.

When I went back to visit Siberia to make an after-delivery assessment, I asked the staff at one hospital which of the items we'd delivered had they found most useful. I expected it to be antibiotics or surgical instruments.

'The wooden crates were wonderful to make furniture,' said the head nurse. 'You're sitting on one.'

# PART 7

# THE RUIN AND DESOLATION OF GROZNY: CHECHNYA, 1995

THE CAUCASUS

CHECHNYA

*Chapter 23*

# The Terrible City

After a couple of years with the NHS, I was ready for another mission. I'd felt the need to practise more anaesthetics in the UK to keep up with latest professional developments, but at the same time keeping my contacts with the British Red Cross. I'd also got myself into a busy lecture circuit and after-dinner speaking on the work of the Red Cross in war zones. I remember giving a talk about Somalia at a theatre in Southport and it struck me that I was spending my days in the theatre keeping people asleep and the evenings in the theatre trying to keep people awake.

In April 1995, I was asked to take up the post of Medical Coordinator for Chechnya. Chechnya is a country just smaller than Wales between Russia in the north and the High Caucasus mountains to the south. It nestles with other republics between the Black Sea to the west and the Caspian Sea to the east. It has its own ethnic population, the Chechens, a fiercely independent people who have had a troubled and often violent history. It became part of the Russian empire in the 1830s when Tsar Nicholas I invaded, facing some bitter resistance. After a brief six years of independence after the 1917 Russian Revolution, it became, together with neighbouring Ingushetia, an autonomous Soviet Socialist Republic. In 1944 Stalin suspected the Chechens of collaborating with the advancing German army and deported thousands of them to Siberia and Kazakhstan. Khrushchev allowed them to return in 1957.

The recent trouble started in 1991 after the collapse of the Soviet Union. Following the example of fourteen other Soviet republics, Chechnya declared independence, with Dzhokhar Dudayev elected president. Russian president Boris Yeltsin refused to accept this and sent in troops. They didn't get much further than the airport of the capital, Grozny, as they were surrounded by Chechen Nationalists and forced to withdraw. By 1994 the situation had deteriorated and violence increased. Tens of thousands of people of non-Chechen ethnicity left the country, including Russian engineers and technicians. Chechen industry began to fail. Paramilitary groups were accused of widespread kidnapping for ransom. Russia tried to invade again and a bloody war followed.

But it was from January to March 1995 that the horror really began. The Russian invasion intensified as thousands of refugees tried to flee to the neighbouring republics of Dagestan and Ingushetia. Many were left behind.

After a continuous five-day Russian artillery bombardment, with accompanying air raids, on the centre of Grozny, the destruction of the city was apocalyptic with an estimated 50,000 civilians, including 5,000 children, killed. Ten thousand Russian troops occupied Grozny as the Chechen rebel groups took to the southern mountains to continue a guerrilla war from there. Half a million refugees fled to neighbouring republics.

I joined the Red Cross team a few weeks after the invasion. It was as yet a small ICRC operation; there were five expatriate nurses already there, but no surgical teams. The job would involve assessing what few hospitals and clinics were still functioning, supplying them with medical aid and helping with reconstruction. Most of them were in Grozny but there were also a few medical facilities, large and small, in outlying towns and villages. There were also some in the mountainous areas under Chechen control. I was told it would involve a lot of travelling which might not be easy as there was a tense, vindictive stand-off between the two sides, the Russian military and Chechen rebels. In addition there were thousands of refugees in temporary camps in the adjacent republics.

I flew by ICRC's small plane from Moscow to the town of Nalchik, the largest city of the Russian federal republic of Kabardino Balkaria where the main ICRC delegation had been established. It was west of Chechnya with just small parts of the republics of Ossetia and Ingushetia in between. It was safe but it was 200 kilometres from Grozny and the aim was gradually to move all operations into Grozny itself as the situation stabilized and became safe.

As we flew into Nalchik airport I was surprised how green it was; I had somehow expected dreary, brown desert. The suburbs seemed to be pleasantly full of trees. It was quite an affluent city by provincial Russian standards; it had been developed as a spa town, particularly a holiday resort for retired or convalescent military personnel. Its heyday had probably been in the 1950s and 1960s but now, at close quarters, it had a rather sleepy, jaded, old-fashioned and slightly neglected air about it.

The medical operation had started with five expatriate nurses in place and they had already begun distributing the aid inside Chechnya. I met two of them, Nellie, a German, and Tamara, an Australian who was married to one of the Swiss field delegates. All the aid – medical, food, blankets, tents, reconstruction supplies – came into Nalchik and was then transported by convoys of ICRC articulated trucks into Chechnya and the adjacent refugee areas. But the main action was in Chechnya, so I set off next day with Tamara in an ICRC Land

Cruiser towards the half-way point, the town of Nazran in Ingushetia. ICRC had a large warehouse there and was supplying mostly food to the refugees who had fled west from the fighting in neighbouring Chechnya. Ingushetia itself had hardly recovered from the Ingushetia–Ossetia conflict of 1992. It was said that for each Ingushetian citizen there was one displaced refugee. During late Sunday afternoon Tamara's husband and his Ingushetian field officer took me for a drive into the countryside. It was a beautiful country; many of the traditional houses had a curious feature, the top roof ridges were decorated not with ridge tiles but with lengths of highly ornate aluminium strips which caught the orange glint of the afternoon sun. But a group of burnt-out buildings showed the signs of recent conflict. The roads were largely deserted. The country stands at the junction between the flat Russian plains and the foothills of the High Caucasus mountains and it didn't take long driving south to enter ever-deepening, heavily wooded valleys.

The field officer wound down his window and looked up. 'There's a helicopter up there. It's Russian military.'

We drove further up the valley. 'It's following us.'

Our Land Cruiser had large red crosses on the roof and bonnet, but the helicopter kept with us, directly above. We were probably only a few miles from the Chechen border; it was my first experience of how tense the situation was in this part of the world. The field officer became nervous and wanted to turn back: from experience I've learned always to listen to the locals especially where security is concerned. We turned the Land Cruiser round and headed back. The helicopter followed us all the way back to Nazran.

The next day I drove with Tamara to Grozny. She knew the place and the situation very well as she and her husband had been there from the beginning of the ICRC action making exhausting and dangerous sorties every day into Chechnya from Dagestan in the middle of winter. First we made a small detour to the nearby town of Beslan in north Ossetia to take some medical supplies to the hospital and clinics there struggling with the influx of refugees. Beslan is a quiet industrial town near the city of Vladikavkaz and it was largely unknown, even within Russia. Ten years later, with the Chechen conflict still raging, I heard the name again – it made world news in 2004, infamous for the Beslan Massacre when a group of armed Chechen and Ingush militants took 1,100 people hostage, including 777 children in the main school in Beslan. Russian security forces stormed the building with tanks, artillery and incendiary rockets. In the chaotic gun battle and fire which engulfed the building 148 adults and 186 children were killed with many more injured and missing.

We continued along the largely deserted road towards Chechnya. The countryside was now gently rolling hills with featureless swathes of green grassland. Occasionally there was an almost deserted village with nothing more than perhaps an old lady, a babushka, crossing the road or a dog scratching itself. Occasionally there was a huge collective farm with gigantic barns but I saw no activity. Many people had left – this was too near a war zone for safety. In the middle of nowhere we passed a small farm set back from the road at the end of a long track with a group of poplar trees to break the monotony. At the roadside a small child, a girl of about 5, waved excitedly at us. I wondered how long it had been since the last vehicle had passed. There was a checkpoint marking the border of Chechnya. I would get used to checkpoints in the next six months. Tamara was driving and she slowed right down well before reaching it.

'Never drive fast towards a checkpoint. If they're in any doubt that you're going to stop, they'll shoot,' she said.

This one presented no problems; the guards were used to ICRC vehicles passing to and fro and they waved us on. Approaching Grozny, we passed what appeared to be large gasometers painted white with the ICRC logo on the sides. There were ICRC water tanker trucks alongside. This was the nearest fresh water supply to Grozny – clean spring water which the tankers were taking in by the thousands of gallons every day.

We arrived at the delegation. It was in the small village of Pobedinskaya – I loved some of the Russian place names – on the main road about twelve miles short of Grozny so considered relatively safe. ICRC had rented and taken over a large bungalow complex. It was crowded and very busy. I put my suitcase in the hallway out of the way with some other luggage. There was a very small medical office where a hassled expatriate nurse was frantically trying to sort out a delivery of medicines that had just arrived. I recognized her from Thailand: it was Hanna, a Finnish nurse. We had a warm reunion but no time to reminisce. She told me, in her familiar, eager way with continuous staccato accent that seems to be common in Finns and with hardly taking a breath, that the crates of medical supplies were standing in the forecourt and they should never have been dropped there and I would have to complain to the ICRC truck drivers and the other drivers were complaining that the crates were blocking the way and they would have to be put in the medical warehouse up the road as soon as possible and anyway it looked like rain and the dressings mustn't get wet and the warehouse wasn't very secure and the locks could easily be broken and anyway it was too small and we should see if we could hire a bigger one … *deep breath* … and people were taking medicines out without signing for them … I was feeling breathless myself now. I helped her shift all the crates in her station wagon. Some children were playing nearby. They helped us carry in the smaller boxes and we gave them chocolate and a few roubles. We would sort out all the problems tomorrow.

I went back to the delegation to collect my suitcase. It was gone. Apparently all the luggage in the hall had been loaded onto the ICRC shuttle bus back to Nalchik and mine had joined it. It took an hour of phone calls to arrange for it to be sent back the next day.

From experience I've concluded that the relationship with the head of delegation is critical and will go a long way in determining whether it will be a good mission or not. So I had my first meeting with Yves, the head of the Chechnya delegation. Within a few minutes I knew it would be fine. Straight down to business: the medical team had been busy but the morale was now low and there needed to be a bit more overall coordination and direction. I'll see what I can do.

The Chechnya operation was in a state of flux – the centre was gradually moving from Nalchik to Grozny itself as the security situation seemed to be slowly improving. So more personnel were moving in and accommodation was in short supply. I was put up overnight in a house owned and lived in by a Chechen family. They had some spare rooms which they rented out, three delegates to a room. Chechen families in that village were making a fortune from ICRC. The loo was a primitive affair a long way down the end of the garden. A small box-like shed boasted a shallow trench inside covered by a wooden board with a hole in it for squatting on. The smell was dreadful. There were no showers or baths, so a bowl of water in the laundry room at the back of the house would have to do. I went upstairs to my room even though I had no suitcase yet to unpack. It would be crowded but it was clean. It was on the side away from the traffic so it was quiet. It had gone dark and I switched on the light. The Chechen lady of the house was in the yard at the back, She rushed upstairs with her son who spoke some English and told me crossly to close the curtains after dark as some weeks before Chechen rebels up in the hills had fired at an illuminated window one night and wounded a friend of hers. Better not to have the light on at all. I suddenly felt tired and a bit depressed. At least the Chechen food that the woman cooked was good though I couldn't recognize what it was.

The next morning enthusiasm returned. Hanna and Tamara took me into Grozny city to see some of the hospitals and the work started in earnest. We drove to the outskirts past a grand sculpture that looked like a mixture of 1950s' Soviet kitsch and Salvador Dali but it was just a sign announcing the entry to 'Grozny, population 387,000' (that's about the size of Bristol, I thought). Then we passed long stretches of industrial plant of grey, ugly breeze block with rows of huge pipes half covered in silver-coloured insulation that ran alongside the

road then occasionally up and over the road to another factory; they were probably petrochemical works. There was no activity at the plants which had a derelict air about them with grass growing through the tarmac as though it had been
several years since they had functioned. We passed by a collection of houses
where on the roadside were scores of glass flagons of amber liquid for sale. The
sun was directly behind them and lit them up so that they glowed and sparkled.
I thought it was apple juice – Tamara told me it was petrol. Here the oil was
literally seeping out of the ground, and people were crudely refining it in their
garden sheds, a very dangerous hobby.

She added, 'Don't be tempted to buy it, it will wreck your engine.'

In fact at one point we saw a black puddle in a field and it was on fire. The
oil reserves in Chechnya are huge and I could see why this part of the world has
been so keenly fought over. We drove into the suburbs proper and I started to
see shell damage to the houses – pieces of masonry missing, bullet holes in the
concrete walls.

'Wait till you see the city centre,' said Tamara.

We passed what might have been a small park or children's playground. It
had red tape all around it and stakes in the ground with red warning notices
stating in Russian, 'МИН' – I looked it up in the dictionary – 'landmine'. But
these suburbs on the western side had largely escaped the shelling of Grozny.
We drove in to the city centre.

In the past fifteen years with the Red Cross I had seen destruction. But
this surpassed everything, even Mogadishu, and I was profoundly shocked
at the sight. I was reminded of those photographs of Ypres during the First
World War and Berlin in May 1945. Then I remembered a quote I'd read, that
'the artillery bombardment of Grozny was the heaviest bombing campaign in
Europe since the destruction of Dresden in 1945'. It seemed that every building
had been shelled. The Presidential Palace was so pock-marked with shell holes
that it looked almost like a skeleton. All around it rubble blocked the streets.
Rows of buildings had walls missing, balconies hanging off. If a giant foot had
stamped on Grozny, the effect would have been the same. The foot was the
Russian army. Above each empty window the concrete wall was blackened with
soot from the fires that had raged inside. Of a group of half a dozen high-rise
apartment blocks only one was still standing but there was a vast gaping hole
where maybe eight or nine apartments had been taken out in one shell blast. The
rest of the blocks had been flattened and lay in piles of rubble except for the
central lift shafts of three of the blocks that for some reason were still standing
like a spinal column. I was aware that all those apartments had been occupied by
civilian families when they were shelled.

Whole areas of the city had simply disappeared. The rubble had been cleared from some leaving just the roads and pavements and perhaps the odd misshapen lamppost.

The central boulevard, once the pride of Grozny and reminiscent of its Parisian equivalents, was a ruin. The once-thriving avenues of green trees running down each side of the road were now black stumps with just the odd charred branch coming off the side. Where there had been cafés were empty shells of buildings. One café less damaged than the rest had re-opened – the only one I saw. People were sitting at tables on the pavement because the café had been gutted and contained only a temporary wood-burning oven and an electric samovar powered by a generator. Above the shop the sign 'Ресторан' – 'restaurant' – was hanging by a hinge, half-blackened with smoke. Around it was a small market, car-boot sale almost, where people were buying and selling food or anything else they had to offer. Leaning against a burnt wall was an old lady in a white headscarf, a crutch by her side, head bowed, holding up a single bottle of perhaps shampoo – hoping to sell it.

The tram terminus had been hit. The tram lines were twisted like spaghetti and all ten trams there had been burned out and the metal had started to rust. They would never run again. I remembered that the Russian word 'grozny' actually translates as 'terrible'.

It was hazardous driving because of all the deep shell holes in the roads. They were neither marked nor cordoned off. Tamara advised me to remember all the holes. I asked about seeing them at night?

'We never ever come into the city after dark,' she said, 'It's far too dangerous.'

On one street a large manhole cover was missing. All the traffic was driving around the hole.

'Be careful if there's heavy rain,' she advised, 'This street gets flooded because the drains have all been wrecked and you can't see where the hole is.'

A few weeks later, it did rain heavily and a car hit the hole and couldn't get out. It was never removed so at least the hazard was gone.

There were Russian tanks and military vehicles everywhere. I was advised to drive right onto the side of the road when one was coming.

'They stop for no one and make no attempt to avoid you,' I was told.

We came to a large roundabout. The centre was sunk below street level and had contained shops round a circular pedestrian way in the middle. Now it contained a Russian T-80 tank which had driven straight over the roundabout, gone head first down into the middle and was now resting on its huge gun barrel, the back end sticking obscenely up in the air above the road. The tank driver, almost paralytically drunk on vodka, hadn't seen the roundabout. It seems that most of the Russian soldiers were drunk most of the time which is what made them so dangerous, both on foot or in charge of a 42.5 ton tank armed with 125mm shells. Hence keep out of their way. It was not unusual in the weeks ahead for tanks to pass us in the street, see the red crosses on our vehicles, lean out of the turret and shake their fist at us, or worse – the other hand was likely to be holding a vodka bottle – and shout something in Russian which I assumed was not complimentary. They were generally antagonistic because they'd heard we were aiding not just the population of Grozny but the Chechen rebels as well. Difficult to argue the neutrality principle of the Red Cross movement with a soldier off his head from alcohol.

The task in front of us seemed impossibly enormous. The long war and the recent blitz had largely destroyed the city infrastructure. No hospital had remained unscathed, some were totally destroyed. Clinics were hardly functioning. The water supply had been destroyed, pumping stations damaged, the sewerage system had been disrupted with all the consequent health hazards. But work had already started and various other aid agencies had arrived to help. I could see that the problem here was different from other missions. This was not in an undeveloped country where people were used to fending for themselves to some extent. This was part of a modern first-world civilization and a city used to being run with sophisticated technology.

## Chapter 24

# Hospital No. 4

I had my first visit to Hospital No. 4, one of the largest in the city and to a certain extent functioning. Luckily, it was far enough from the city centre to have escaped a direct hit from the shelling although some houses around had been destroyed and the roads outside had shell craters that made access difficult. It was also fortunate that when a new modern hospital block was constructed in the 1980s, the old block, although in bad condition and almost derelict, had been left standing to be used for storage. It was this block that was being recommissioned as a functioning hospital, and some old beds were being brought out of storage. The local surgeons had cleared a room for an operating theatre and we gave them a portable electricity generator. The ICRC water and sanitation people had already installed a water tank outside – a hospital can't function without water. The tank was impressive. It was made of blue plastic and curved corrugated iron sections like a very large plastic paddling pool with a roof. It could be ingeniously expanded as it was filled with water and when deflated it was easy to transport. It reminded me of a bouncy castle. It was also used by the people living in nearby houses.

I met Jacques, the water engineer. He was fanatical about water. A Russian woman was filling a large plastic jerry can from a valve in the side as Jacques was inspecting the tank that was now almost full. He put his hand in the stream of water coming from the valve to see if it was cold. The woman glared at him, said something under her breath then emptied the jerry can and started again. She wasn't having someone putting their dirty hands in her drinking water!

There was an impressively large kitchen in an old outhouse with four massive ovens. They were ancient and long neglected but still functioning because they were wood-burning rather than electrical. A group of Russian Hare Krishna members was in there, constantly cooking vegan meals of bread and dhal for anyone who needed it. I met the hospital director who wanted them out so that ICRC could take over and supply food for the hospital patients.

'They need a better diet with more protein,' he said.

I wasn't keen on the idea – they were there first and in fact they had been around from the very beginning, even cooking while the city was being shelled with fighting all around. We reached a satisfactory compromise – they would happily give us two of the cookers if we would erect a partition wall across the middle of the kitchen so they wouldn't be contaminated by our meat, eggs, milk and female kitchen staff. And they could continue to have all the cookers during the night for sleeping on – it was still cold after dark in April.

I was curious about the new hospital block next door. Why wasn't it being used? The hospital director said he would show me. He took me round to the main entrance. The door had a large sign on it – 'МИН' – I didn't need to have it translated. The hospital had been mined. The director told me that Russian troops had been into the hospital when they overran Grozny. He took me inside the foyer. A de-mining team had started work clearing the hospital but there were still unsafe areas. He told me to follow him closely and not open any closed doors. On the main staircase he showed me a slender copper tripwire originally fastened a few inches high across the first step and connected to a grenade. He gave me the tripwire as a souvenir. I could imagine after the fighting, perhaps a mother trying to get help for a wounded child, the first one into the hospital, carrying him into the building and up the stairs …

They had found several more tripwires and primed grenades fastened to door handles on the inside of wards and clinics. Not all the doors had been checked yet. The director said this wasn't the only reason the hospital wasn't being used and he would show me. I followed up the stairs and into the wards and laboratories and theatres. It had all been utterly vandalized. This was not random, drunken destruction. I could see it was systematic, logical, almost careful. It was done to make sure the hospital couldn't be used again. Every single window in the huge five-storey building had been broken – from the inside. They had been careful not to leave one pane unbroken. The lifts on each floor had bullet holes in the doors and in the control panels. Some mattresses had been ripped open, others had been dragged to the centre of the room and set on fire. Everything breakable had been smashed. Even a sewing machine in the ward office had been broken. The operating theatres were the same. Each bulb in the operating theatre lights had been smashed, the surgical instruments were gone. In the eye theatre, the large complex operating microscope, essential for operating on eye injuries, had been made useless: someone had smashed every single lens in it, I suspect with a rifle butt. When they had finished, the soldiers had mined the hospital on their way out. The director had been there and had asked one of the soldiers why he was doing this, why destroy a hospital?

The soldier had said: 'Because the Chechens won't be needing it anymore when we've destroyed the whole country.'

'But I'm not a Chechen,' said the director, 'I'm a Russian.'

'I don't care,' said the soldier.

This was a First World army, in a Second World economy, with Third World chaos.

So Hospital No. 4 was taken on as our first priority. It had to be diplomatically done, of course – we were not trying to take over. The Russians had a lot of pride. The director told me he'd been a communist party member during the glory days of the Soviet Union. It must have been strange for him to be talking to a member of a not-so-long-ago Cold War enemy country. He asked about eventually some of his doctors coming over to the UK as observers. I said the right thing, that I admired Russian medical practice – it's true, they just didn't have the equipment to back it up – and that it should be an exchange trip, as some of us could come over and learn from them. From then on we got on very well. So, if we could have a room in the old hospital as an ICRC office we could start replacing the surgical instruments. Our Finnish constructor Ansi would help get materials to improve the old hospital and find a bigger generator for them. The director was particularly concerned about the loss of the eye operating microscope, I promised him I'd get him one before I realized I had no idea how to go about it.

I planned to visit all the other hospitals in Grozny, all the ones that still existed. And then look at some of the other hospitals and clinics in Chechnya right up the mountains and valleys in the south and into Chechen rebel-held territory – we would aid both sides of the conflict as equally as we could. In fact, the five expatriate nurses had been already getting on with this before I arrived. Two of them, Anne and Ankie, were in the next republic to the east, in the town of Khasavyurt in Dagestan, where most of the refugees had fled, and from where it was easier to get into the southern valleys.

After a few days I drove back to the main delegation in Nalchik, knowing that I was working with a good team. I could feel the enthusiasm and it was contagious. It was good to get away for the weekend, not just because of the rest, the hot shower, decent loo and comfortable bed, but to get away from the devastation, to stand back and take stock and think about priorities because at first sight it seemed overwhelming. ICRC had taken over the top two floors of a large ten-storey apartment block in the suburbs of Nalchik. Surrounded by trees, it had a beautiful view of the Caucasus mountains. Up on the hillside was a funicular that worked irregularly; the plastic chairs were all of garish-coloured kitsch

The apartment block was home to about thirty ICRC delegates, including the UK truck drivers who were shipping large amounts of food and material aid into Chechnya. The block was noisy, mostly people playing loud music until the early hours. One of our Swiss radio operators was the main culprit; he had a large 'ghetto blaster'. It was loud most of the time, but he would turn up the volume, leave his door open and go to the kitchen at the end of the corridor to cook elaborate meals. It didn't bother me too much – I had to compare it to the ruined apartment blocks in Grozny. But the truck drivers, always exhausted and short of sleep, had had enough. When the music was particularly loud one evening, one of them knocked on the radio operator's door, walked in with a very polite 'Excuse me', took hold of the ghetto blaster, walked onto the balcony and dropped it over the side. Ten floors up, there wasn't much left when it hit the ground.

During the Saturday afternoon, together with the head of the ICRC Nalchik delegation and four other coordinators, I went to the opening of an ICRC exhibition of our activities. The Minister of Health for Nalchik was there; he'd brought a group of reporters with him. After a fulsome speech in front of a TV camera, the minister then changed his tone and asked the head of delegation why all this aid was going into Chechnya and not into Kabardino Balkaria – they had economic problems in Nalchik too. The head of delegation handled it very diplomatically but I still had a feeling we'd been journalistically mugged.

On the Saturday evening I was taken to dinner by some of the other delegates. It was known as the 'Mafia Restaurant' but of course the sign over the door didn't say that. There was a hired soldier outside standing guard. We walked in but had to leave our coats in the cloakroom – mandatory in case we were toting a Kalashnikov. It was crowded except for two empty tables at the front next to the window. I headed for them, but was gently drawn away and we all sat squashed right at the back. Apparently it was dangerous to sit near to the window, in case rival Russian mafia gangs decided to shoot the place up. It had actually happened a few weeks before when a car had sped past spraying bullets through the window, Chicago style.

I learned to recognise the mafia cars: they ignored all the red lights – they had the police in their pockets. It was still a favourite restaurant with ICRC personnel though, and later I found out why – all the other decent restaurants had a habit of playing music so loud that conversation was impossible. Not just loud but actually painful on the ears. Even if you shout at the person across the table you can't be heard. One of the noisiest restaurants had a dancer on a small stage with rotating, very bright, flashing lights to add to the discomfort. She subscribed to the 'lethargic' school of dancing, and she chewed gum. In fact we didn't know she was a dancer until she bowed for applause – we thought she'd been waiting for a table.

It was back to Grozny early on Monday morning. Almost immediately I was offered a lift to Khasavyurt in the next-door republic of Dagestan with Yves, the head of delegation and two field delegates. Khasavyurt, with its high numbers of refugees from the fighting – over 60,000 had fled into Dagestan from Chechnya – is just over the border to the east and normally a journey of about seventy kilometres via the Chechen towns of Argun and Gudermes. But our security delegates advised us not to take that route. There had been military activity, reports of artillery bombardment and the road wasn't safe. So we had to take a much longer route north into safer areas following the Terek river to the Dagestan city of Kizlyar and then southwards to Khasavyurt. It was a 200-kilometre and a four-hour journey. On our way we passed along a line of hills with a clear view back to Grozny in the distance. Yves pointed out that this was the place where the mass of heavy Russian artillery had continuously pounded Grozny for five days non-stop with all they had. There were still tanks there and a military presence as though they were ready to do it again if necessary. Some of the tanks were flying the hammer and sickle flag of the now defunct Soviet Union. But it was a pleasant journey through hills and woodland and well out of the conflict areas. In fact it took longer than four hours because of all the checkpoints; there seemed to be one every ten kilometres or so. The Russian guards were not to be hurried and we had to be totally polite and smile. They were obviously bored and I learned that the worse thing we wanted to hear from a guard was, 'I am learning English.' That could add another fifteen minutes to the delay while he engaged us in phrasebook-like conversation.

Yves thought we could take a shortcut at Grebenskaya – another delightful Russian place name – and save us eighty kilometres. But a short way along this minor road we suddenly came across a bridge with something in the middle of the road. The driver was good and stopped short with squealing tyres. One of the field delegates got out and inspected it with binoculars from a distance. It was a mortar rocket. We reversed the car, did a fast three-point turn and headed back. I thought it sensible as it looked like it was unexploded, but the delegate added that it was probably booby-trapped with a tripwire or there could be Chechen rebels in the woods at the roadside waiting to detonate it remotely. Even the red crosses on our car wouldn't cause them to hesitate.

So it was all the way to Kizlyar before we could head south. This area is very near the Caspian Sea and, by now very hungry, we looked for somewhere to eat. Outside the small town of Babayurt, an elderly woman had set up her own simple *al fresco* truck-stop café at the side of the road. It consisted of half an old blackened and rusty oil drum cut lengthways to make a barbecue and she was grilling sturgeon steaks, liberally pouring vodka over them and stepping back as the flames whooshed up at her. With the steak came a bowl full of black caviar that she scooped out of a huge plastic bag. We sat on breeze blocks at a wooden crate for a table with plastic forks. The only thing she could offer to drink was

Russian champagne in plastic cups. I can honestly say it was one of the most appreciated meals I've ever had.

We reached Khasavyurt in the late afternoon; it was good to meet the two other nurses, Ankie from Sweden and Anne from the UK. I soon realized that together with the other three nurses, I'd got the dream medical team. The rest of the sub-delegation in Khasavyurt wasn't so lucky. I could feel the tension as I walked into the office. The field officers were arguing with the food-aid officers, and the Swiss translator seemed to be undergoing some sort of mild psychiatric breakdown and wanted to go home ASAP. I was given a room in the house next door run by a virago of a Russian woman who kept the rooms intensely hot and had screwed shut the windows: it was said she was having a running competition with her neighbour, whom she hated, to see who could get their house the hottest and show off their affluence. The delegation referred to it as the sauna. As I walked in she shouted at me to take my shoes off.

I met Ankie and Anne the next morning and remembered a large parcel addressed to Anne given to me in London by the British Red Cross. I'd faithfully and carefully carried it to Geneva then Moscow then Nalchik then Grozny to Khasavyurt. Anne excitedly took it then saw the handwriting of the address. This was one of many parcels she'd received from a man called Colin from north London whom she'd never met. He'd seen a newspaper article about her when she'd come back from a hair-raising mission to Angola and sort of adopted her and kept obsessively sending letters and parcels. She opened the package to find a bright red woolly hat, a thermal vest (he thought it was probably very cold here) and a Comic Relief red nose to cheer up the refugees. He was wondering if they ought to get married.

I went with Ankie to visit two villages to the south. The refugees were not altogether welcome here as they were a strain on resources but the two villages were close-knit and ethnically Chechen as the border had been moved after the Second World War. We had to get permission from the authorities before we could travel into that sensitive area but then at the first police checkpoint they hadn't been informed so it meant an hour on the radio getting the security man to remind the Khasavyurt police, who had forgotten to tell the checkpoints we were coming. Ankie said this was quite a regular occurrence.

We drove up into the hills, up stunningly beautiful wooded valleys and through hamlets perched high on the slopes until we reached Leninaul village where we stopped to unload medical supplies at the ambulatory clinic and have tea and chat with the friendly staff. They loved ICRC visiting: they said they could talk freely to us. We went on to the nearby village of Kalininaul and had a late lunch with the local doctor – tea and kebab-like shashlik. His surname was Dudayev which had got him into a lot of trouble with the Russians – the Chechen president had the same name – no relation.

Another day in Khasavyurt, and we'd been asked to visit a group of refugees. They had been housed in a grim warehouse that had been turned into flats, but these were just empty rooms separated by thin wooden partitions, two to three families per room, the only furniture being mattresses on the floor. There were no windows and the floors were damp. Most of the children had scabies. Nappies were hanging in all the rooms. They had to cook in the street and there was no nearby water supply. Something had to be done. There was some resistance in the delegation to providing a water supply. Once we started to supply them, it was argued, it would have to continue until heaven knows when. The water delegate, Pierre, was as fanatical as his counterpart in Grozny so we agreed that as water and sanitation came under the medical division, I would give him permission then return to Grozny *fait accompli*.

*Chapter 25*

# Meat Paste and Car Washes

T he next few days were spent going round the other hospitals in Grozny assessing them. More accurately spent trying to find them. The hospitals, in the Russian fashion, were numbered. In the case of Grozny it seemed to go up to Hospital No. 9. We struggled for days trying to find Hospital No. 5. Perhaps it had been completely destroyed or maybe it never existed. Some hospitals were starting to function again by themselves and would just need deliveries of supplies. Others had been deserted. Hospital No. 8 was a dark, miserable block with a bored guard/caretaker sitting on a chair outside the door, elbows on his knees, smoking a cigarette, bottle at his feet. But he had nothing to guard because when he let us in we found the hospital was completely empty, just bare rooms. The caretaker said the Russian authorities were going to turn it into an infectious diseases hospital as they were expecting another epidemic of cholera in the summer (I made a note of another potential problem to come). I later mentioned the plans for Hospital No. 8 to the director of Hospital No. 4. With Russian cynicism he told me not to hold my breath, the place had never functioned even before the present conflict.

Tamara and I visited the Russian Army Military Hospital which had been set up in tents next to the main camp near the airport. It was a dull, rainy day as we drove through the mud into the crowded camp between rows of heavy artillery and tanks. Serious-faced armed soldiers turned and looked at our ICRC Land Cruiser as we passed; the walk to the hospital marquee felt like walking the gauntlet. I've never seen such a tough, mean, dangerous-looking bunch of people in my life before or since. With gaunt, scowling faces and cropped hair, they looked like thugs with an extra attitude problem. There was only one colour – khaki. Tamara is an attractive woman but there wasn't the expected wolf-whistling or suggestive comments or even a 'hello' – just silent, glaring, unsmiling faces. Russian soldiers seemed to us to be of two sorts: young nervous conscripts who just wanted to go back home and crack troops, the elite Spetznaz, some of whom were said to be pure mercenaries who couldn't wait to get in and kill people.

The army medical officer was much friendlier and showed us round his hospital. There was a distinctive but elusive smell, which can only be called 'Odour of Russian Army' – a mixture of carbolic, cheap aftershave and sweat would get close. In his tented ward we saw among all the wounded soldiers a couple of civilians – a 12-year-old boy with a broken lower leg and an 8-year-old girl with shrapnel wounds to the chest. We couldn't tell if they were ethnically Russian or Chechen but they both looked as though they wanted to be somewhere else. We sat down to lunch with the medical officer. Tea and bread with an inch of butter on it and paste from a tin – we had the choice of meat paste or processed cheese but they tasted exactly the same. They had this for every meal. He said he was short of bandages and we said we'd do what we could. I was glad to get out.

I had a meeting with the Water and Sanitation team to discuss strategy. The intense shelling of Grozny had disrupted all the piped water supply underground and the sewerage system. The team were so enthusiastic and efficient that they were now transporting in half a million litres of fresh water per day from the tanks at Chernorechy outside Grozny. I asked why they didn't try pumping water into the existing pipes, see where it leaked out and repair the damage as they found it. I didn't know much about water and sanitation but they were patient and explained that if you did this the water would indeed leak out but then when you stopped pumping the now-dirty water would re-enter the pipes and contaminate the whole system. And if, as was likely, there were broken sewer pipes anywhere near the water pipes, raw sewage would seep back into the water pipes and that would be the end of the water system. The immediate problem though was that the team were so efficient with the water tankers that people were taking it for granted and using it not only for drinking but also washing their cars. A Russian soldier had been seen washing his tank. We thought about this for some time. With ICRC water tanks all over the city, we couldn't realistically monitor them all, and we had no powers to stop the misuse anyway, and the Grozny authorities had other things to worry about. A few days later one of the team came up with the solution. He put up notices in Russian at every water tank and vehicle washing stopped immediately. Translated it said: 'This water contains chlorine so be careful as it will readily take the paint off any car washed with it.' Brilliant.

There were many other aid agencies, NGOs large and small, working in Chechnya and the cooperation was excellent – we were never in competition. In fact quite the opposite: some of the load was taken from us. We had joint meetings every fortnight at one or other of the delegations. I enjoyed these – it was a time for getting problems solved. At a typical meeting, MSF France was supporting Hospital No. 3, MSF Belgium had adopted Hospital No. 9 which was the trauma hospital but they were short of plaster of Paris bandage for fractures. Yes, ICRC had crates of them – they're yours. And would MSF like to take on a Grozny TB hospital that ICRC hadn't got the resources for? It's a deal. Merlin was also putting water tanks into the city so could we coordinate to avoid duplication and would you like Merlin to look at the sanitation problem? Yes. A small NGO was looking to provide psychological help to post-traumatic stress disorder victims. Would we bear them in mind? Certainly.

There were several very small medical charities with small budgets who had decided to undertake vaccination programmes. Good idea, except that all of them seemed to have picked the same valley, the safest one, and had headed there vaccinating all the children against measles, tetanus, polio etc. The next group would do the same. The children in the villages at the lower end of the valley were getting vaccinated for the same thing every few weeks or even days and getting very sore arms. The parents assumed that the more injections the children got the healthier they'd be. We invited all these charities to subsequent meetings to sort it out.

The meetings also avoided any friction. We had a new constructor in from Geneva who had been rather too keen and had marched into Hospital No. 9 armed with a concrete mixer and two-foot ruler and announced he'd start a programme to repair the damage the following day. I had to tell him that MSF Belgium had got it all in hand and this would appear a bit rude to them. At the next NGO meeting I could explain it to MSF and there was no offence taken.

There were other hospitals in Chechnya to assess. Two of them – at Argun and Gudermes on the road east to Dagestan – were not easy to get to as the road outside Grozny and nearby military airfield were prime targets for the rebels. We tried for three consecutive days. Anne and I and two field delegates with a local driver got to the outskirts of the city as far as the last checkpoint but then we heard rapid gunfire and the sound of a rocket launcher. We stopped. The driver asked some locals what was happening. They dismissed it – it was just the army on a training exercise. More gunfire. I was sat in the back of the car between the two field delegates. The one on my right was sweating and physically shaking, eyes wide. He was in acute stress.

The one on my left was totally calm, almost bored, and said, 'What's the problem. Just drive on otherwise we'll never get there. If you turn round every time you hear gunfire we'll never get any work done here.'

It was my decision. But in fact it was made for me. An armoured personnel carrier came the other way towards us, very fast. An officer leaned out and frantically waved us back. We turned around. The next day we didn't even get past the same checkpoint, the guards had closed the road and there were helicopters ahead. The stressed field officer was in the same state: I learned he'd had a bad mission in Angola. I made a note to recommend he be transferred to the safety of Nalchik or even go home to recover. On the third day we made it – Anne and I followed by a truck of supplies. It all seemed calmer. The checkpoint guards were relaxed, checked our papers as usual and waved us through.

Argun was a small town of 25,000 people before the conflict. The hospital was in reasonable condition and working as well as it could, although the adjacent children's hospital had been severely shelled and was disused. The hospital director was pleased to see us and told us they had lost most of their equipment, taken by Dudayev's Chechen forces when they retreated. We left them fifty mattresses and blankets from the truck and made a list of equipment we should bring next time. As we were leaving, an officious man stopped us and angrily harangued us about why ICRC wasn't doing more to help them. We should be ashamed. I told him we were doing our best but inside I felt suddenly piqued and almost added, 'Why don't you ask the Russians the same question!' The hospital director interrupted, drew me aside and said the man was the mayor of Argun and he was stupid and was shouting at everybody because he was useless himself.

We drove on, with a slight obstacle just outside Argun. A railway branch line to Shali crosses the main road at a level crossing here. A long train of tanker wagons had been crossing during the early days of the fighting. The engine and the rails ahead of it had been hit and now the tanker wagons were stuck right across the road. It took some careful and intricate driving to get round them and onto the road again.

We drove on to Gudermes, larger than Argun and about thirty-six kilometres from Grozny. Hospital No. 2 was the main hospital, in fact the only one and it was largely deserted. There was just one maternity nurse and she had no patients. The supplies had been looted and the surgical unit was out of action because during the fighting, hundreds of bullets had come through the windows and had hit most of the equipment – sterilizers and anaesthetic machine. Even the operating table had bullet holes in it. It would be a good hospital to support and the constructor could patch the place up. Outside there was another member of staff, the gardener, who amidst all the concrete and brick debris was patiently tending the flowerbeds.

The truck headed home and I thought it was getting late but Anne wanted to check out a hospital in Shali, thirty kilometres to the south. Just before the town we saw a hospital sign but it was a small psychiatric hospital. We stopped to investigate. It was full with a dozen psychiatric patients but no staff to take care of them: they had all fled. They had some food which a few of them cooked for the others, and mattresses on the beds but all very dirty. We unloaded all the blankets we had in the back of the Land Cruiser. Then we heard shelling, quite close ahead of us. Time to go.

We had to work our way through flat featureless countryside on back roads which weren't on the map to try and get back onto the main road to Argun. We thought we were doing well until the road became ominously narrower and rougher and then after a few kilometres stopped at a farm. So back the way we had come. More sounds of shelling. This was getting serious and it was getting late. Chechnya is not the place to be outside after dark and responsible ICRC delegates do not get stuck in the field. We eventually found a blessed main road and with relief Anne put her foot down. I don't know what was more dangerous: the shelling or the speed we were going – straight over potholes, creating clouds of dust so we could hardly see the road, through villages without slowing, scattering dogs and chickens (please don't hit a child!). There was some major military activity going on because just before Grozny we saw a huge explosion and fireball behind us. At the outskirts, the soldiers at the checkpoint were all crouching behind their bunkers and waving us frantically through to get out of the way. We made it to the delegation just as night fell and in time for us to walk calmly into the evening security meeting.

One day I met Bashir, head of the Chechen Red Cross which we were supporting with supplies. He introduced me to two Chechen women who ran the Red Cross Home Nurses Programme and who looked after people having difficulty taking care of themselves. I went with them on two home visits. The first was a 40-year-old woman, Irina, who had severe fragilitas ossians, a disease of fragile bones which had caused severe disability: her spine was affected and she was literally doubled up and could only walk with difficulty using crutches. She lived alone with only a neighbour's cat for company. She had no electricity, no radio, no TV. She had stayed during the Russian offensive: there was no one to help her escape. There had been a lot of shelling around but her house had escaped. When the Russian soldiers stormed through the area shooting and looting, they broke into her house but when they saw her there, deformed and disabled, they had a sudden epiphany of pity and gave her some food. In fact one solder had returned later with more food. She chatted with us for quite a while; she was remarkably cheerful and smiled a lot, but occasionally gave out a sigh. She said her aim was to try to move to Moscow; she had friends there but not their address. I investigated the possibility in the weeks ahead but trying to trace her friends and getting permission from the authorities proved impossible (people's movements were still restricted and needed an internal passport for Moscow). I failed and regretted it.

The second visit was quite different, almost bizarre. It was to a house with three very elderly women living alone; the youngest was 92 the oldest a hundred and four. They were all very deaf and had bad eyesight. That area too had suffered severe shelling but they didn't seem to know anything about it. Most of the houses around them had been destroyed and were now rubble, but theirs was remarkably still standing, sticking out of the devastation as though it had some sort of divine protection. I asked them about the present civil war – one of them said they never liked Lenin, never trusted Stalin and had always been loyal to the Tsar.

'No, I mean the recent war?' I asked.

Ah, that. Well, it wasn't true that they weren't patriotic. They had never sided with the Germans. And as for Hitler …

They really didn't know about the present conflict. While the battle was raging and the whole infrastructure of the city destroyed, they only knew something was not quite right when the man from up the road didn't appear with their regular milk and the postman had stopped calling. They noticed some of the plaster had come off the kitchen ceiling and the electric kettle wouldn't boil. The only help they were now getting was from the Chechen Red Cross who were supporting them totally.

While we sat and drank tea, one of the women was persuaded to tell us about her childhood before the 1917 revolution. She told us a story of a woman she knew just after the Second World War. Her elderly grandmother was a devout Christian living a long way away in Moscow who insisted on hanging a picture of St Cyril on her wall despite the persecution against Christians under Stalin. The granddaughter was so worried about this as it was only a matter of time before someone spotted the picture and grandmother would be arrested. She managed to get to Moscow to visit her and persuade her to remove the offending picture. But the old grandmother, who had very bad vision, had made a mistake. The framed picture with candles and incense burning in front of it was in fact a picture of Stalin not St Cyril. The granddaughter said not a word.

I got involved in what are called detention activities. It has always been an important role of ICRC to look after the welfare of prisoners of war and to inform opposing forces in any conflict of the Geneva Convention regarding them. It can be a daunting and often thankless task and the detention delegates need infinite persistence and patience to gain access to prisoners. They liked to have a medical delegate with them when they did their visits to assess their health and to provide medicines direct to the prisoner that hopefully wouldn't go astray. Dogged persistence was certainly needed in this conflict. It seemed that when the delegates eventually got a meeting with the highest-ranking officer in Grozny, they would be told that unfortunately he wasn't able to give them permission to visit prisoners; that could only be given by some department in Moscow. So the detention delegates would go to Moscow and spend an inordinate amount of time trying to find the right person and then more time trying to get a meeting, often to be told that our information was incorrect and that it was the army command in Grozny who had the authority. Back to Grozny. No, back to Moscow. If I were a cynical sort of person I could imagine the man in Moscow waving them goodbye then phoning his counterpart in Grozny: 'They're on their way back!'

There were in fact fewer prisoners than might be imagined because many of the captured soldiers never survived – on either side. But we eventually got access to a prison in Grozny and were able to register them. I was sitting in the car with a detention delegate one day waiting for access to the prison – it took three hours before we were told our permit had been cancelled. I asked him how he could be so patient. He was about to extend his mission another three months but what had he actually achieved since being here? He told me he had persistently asked for better conditions for the prisoners. In this particular prison twenty of them were all crowded into one small cell; summer had arrived and it was impossibly hot and stifling inside the cell. He pestered the prison chief who eventually took out a brick from the cell wall to provide a miniscule amount of ventilation. I said I thought it was a ridiculously small benefit for such a lot of effort.

'Not if you're a prisoner sitting next to the hole.' he said.

One day I went on a prison visit with Tamara and Maria, a detention delegate, and our interpreters, to the town of Mosdok, a hundred kilometres north-west of Grozny in the next republic, North Ossetia. We were trying to trace a couple of Chechen prisoners who we heard had died in custody. We were directed to the hospital but met with a hostile director,

'Why are you wasting your time with a couple of criminals?'

We didn't get any information but the journey wasn't completely wasted. We had permission to visit a Russian prison train a few miles out of Mosdok. The train was kept in a large but deserted railway siding overgrown with weeds and guarded by five tough but bored Russian soldiers. But they were cooperative and friendly enough, probably because of the two women in our group. There were three prisoners on the train but in fact they weren't prisoners of war; they were Russian soldiers arrested by their own military police, so they didn't officially come under the Geneva Convention. They were awaiting transfer to a military prison. The train consisted of two dull-green corridor coaches; normally each would have had several separate compartments of six to eight seats, like the old British Rail carriages, but these had been adapted to make each compartment a jail cell. The seats remained but they were bare wood without the upholstery. The windows on each side were completely blacked out as was the door. It was impossible to see anything outside. The only light inside was a dim electric light. The prisoners were in solitary confinement. We each visited one of the prisoners. They were all young conscripts, arrested for desertion. The one I talked to had been conscripted from his home town outside Moscow. He was eager to talk to us. His name was Nikolai and he had worked as a filing clerk in one of the government departments there. He was frail-looking, about 17 years old, thin and slightly built – a complete contrast to the well-built older guards outside who were professional soldiers. He had been in the train cell for six weeks and was very pale. I wondered when he had last seen daylight. He was shaking slightly and looked scared with staring eyes. I could see the sheen of sweat on his waxen face – all the signs of stress. He told me the younger conscripts were bullied by the professional soldiers and he had been scared from the moment he had been sent to Chechnya. He had been posted as a checkpoint guard to the south of Grozny but he could hear shell- and gunfire almost every day. He had been terrified of being captured by the rebels; he'd heard stories of what they did to their prisoners – tortured and even castrated. He just wanted to get back home to Moscow so he'd left his post and started walking north. He had only gone about fifty kilometres before he was caught by the military police. There was not much I could do for him but I was allowed to take messages back to his family through our tracing agency and the Russian Red Cross. I gave him some chocolate bars and some reading material but it seemed very inadequate. I'm not sure he knew why we were there and I hoped we hadn't given him any false hope of being released. But he thanked me for shaking his hand and being friendly and calling him by his first name and treating him with dignity.

Afterwards we had tea with the guards who chatted up the two women. They told us that nothing much happened here. Every two weeks an engine would take the train up the tracks into Mosdok to get supplies and fill the water tanks then bring them back again. For a prisoner it must have been like being a commuter in hell. I asked what would happen to the prisoners like the one I'd seen. They told us their future was very bad. Nikolai would probably never survive the next five years in a military prison: he was too frail and weedy-looking to withstand the brutality from the guards or other prisoners. Even if he did, he would still have to serve perhaps another five years in a 'punishment squad' to be used as front line troops, cannon fodder. I remembered reading somewhere of a conversation between Eisenhower and the Russian general Zhukov during the Second Wold War when they were discussing how to get rid of landmines.

Zhukov had said, 'The best way to get rid of landmines is to march a penal battalion over it.'

The guard said that little had changed. Punishment squads were the first to be sent in if there was a risk of mines. It was unusual for them to survive to ever be discharged from the army.

## Chapter 26

# Chechen Checkpoints

Checkpoints were a fact of life in Chechnya as in many military-controlled areas. There is a certain art to dealing with them. The ICRC truck drivers particularly used to get frustrated with them. On a bad day, the guards would order them to unload all their heavy crates, have them checked against the manifest then load them up again. Then they'd drive ten to twenty kilometres to the next checkpoint and have to do it all over again. The secret was not to show irritation or anger. After a few trips the guards would get bored and wave them through. I used to carry a packet of cigarettes in the Land Cruiser. I'm a non-smoker but handing a guard a cigarette and even a Red Cross 'souvenir' lighter could make things much easier.

I had a potential problem with a checkpoint between the delegation at Pobedinskaya and Grozny itself which we passed every morning. One day a guard asked me for painkillers for a headache. This could have been the thin end of the wedge – the back of the truck was usually packed with medicines – so I said that all I had was some paracetamol of my own and gave him two tablets. They found out from my visa that I was a doctor. Previously they'd asked an MSF doctor to look at one of the guards who was ill with a stomach upset. The next time I passed, they had two more soldiers with medical complaints for me to look at. I could see this developing into a regular GP surgery every morning. I had to be ruthless and stop it. I told them that I was a specialist and could only diagnose certain complaints.

'What sort of doctor are you then?'

'Gynaecologist.'

They waved me through.

The new recruits were often put in charge of checkpoints. We were wary of them; they were often scared, nervous and unpredictable. It's often been said by ICRC people that we'd rather be faced with a professional soldier than a young inexperienced one. The professional is calmer, more logical and when he shoots he tends to hit the one he is aiming at, not bystanders. There was a story of a young guard at a checkpoint in charge of a machine gun. They'd stopped a coachload of Russian officials as a matter of routine. The young guard was bored and playing idly with the gun, finger on the trigger. It went off and sprayed the coach with machine-gun fire. He was so surprised he couldn't take his finger off the trigger, the gun got hot and it started firing by itself in all directions until it was out of rounds. Everyone dived for cover. Fortunately the officials were high enough up to escape injury but the suitcases in the luggage compartment at the side below them were a mess.

I was travelling to Gudermes one day with a Swiss field officer. The checkpoint outside Argun was manned by some new nervous guards, raw recruits. They all looked very young. One of them, obviously in charge, was sitting at a table outside the bunker. A guard motioned us out of the car to the table. The one in charge asked us for our documents in heavily accented English. I got the impression he was showing off to his watching colleagues.

'You. Where your papers?'

We showed him our passports.

'Where your passports?'

This was puzzling; he had them in his hands. We showed him our Russian permits. He hesitated, then: 'Where your papers?'

There was nothing else to show him except our international driving licences. He didn't want these. He was getting agitated and the situation was getting tense. It seemed to me he'd got himself into a quandary here. It didn't help that he didn't know any other English words and certainly didn't know anything but the Russian Cyrillic alphabet. It occurred to us that it had become a matter of his losing face with his colleagues. We looked in our bags to see what we could offer him. The Swiss delegate had an expensive box of chocolates sent from home. But bribery could get us arrested. Inside were the chocolates and on top of them a piece of glossy paper with one side describing which were the coffee creams and which were the hazelnut clusters. On the other side was an elegant, gold-embossed coat of arms of the chocolate company and fine italic writing stating that if these chocolates failed to satisfy then the customer should return them for a full refund.

In a moment of sheer genius, we nodded in recognition, gave the glossy paper, coat of arms side up, to the guard in charge and said, 'Ah, you want papers (and *please*, don't turn it over and see pictures of chocolates)!'

The guard solemnly took it, scrutinized it carefully, picked up a rubber stamp and inkpad, and stamped it very hard several times, gave it back and stiffly waved us through. He had saved face. We ate all the chocolates in relief.

It was important for us to help the population on the other side of the conflict but it was not easy to get into these areas to the south up into the Caucasus mountains. It was certainly not safe crossing no man's land. Also, as the front line had continuously fluctuated north or south as each side in turn had advanced, the retreating army had the habit of laying landmines for protection. This middle ground would be unsafe for many generations to come. However, we set out for Shatoi, a strategic town sixty kilometres south of Grozny which we had been told was in Chechen rebel-held territory, on what appeared to be a quiet day. We took two Land Cruisers and a Chechen interpreter. I left my Russian interpreter Alexander behind; if there was any trouble and we were stopped by Chechen troops or indeed bandits, it was not the place to be a Russian.

We put the large Red Cross flags up on the radio aerials and headed south through the villages of Novi Atagi, Chiri-Yurt and Duba-Yurt into dramatic and beautiful mountainous countryside with the huge lofty chain of the snow-covered Caucasus peaks beyond. At the frequent military checkpoints, the guards looked at all our maps to make sure there were no marks on them.

We were ordered: 'Don't mark the position of Russian troops or checkpoints on them.'

We passed through Zoni village, completely flattened, nothing left standing, before the valley became very steep and narrow; the tortuous single-track road had sheer rock walls up on our left and steep drops down to the ravine below on our right. We came across a derelict tank, damaged and rusty, half blocking the road. Then there was another tank hanging over the edge of the ravine. It looked as though it had been gutted by fire. On the rusty turret was a bouquet of flowers. There were many more tanks, at the side of the road, all damaged, all burned out, most with flowers placed on the turrets. The interpreter told us that a few weeks ago, a convoy of fourteen Russian tanks had unwisely charged up the valley in an assault on Shatoi. The Chechen rebels had been sitting waiting up on top of the mountainside above the road. They had fired bazookas at the first and the last tanks in the convoy and immobilized them. The tanks in between couldn't advance or reverse past them along the narrow track and couldn't fire their guns up the steep cliffs. They were sitting ducks. The Chechens had taken their time and leisurely picked off each tank in turn, finally throwing incendiaries into the tanks, burning the soldiers still inside alive. There were no survivors. It was a massacre. The flowers had been placed there later by Russian soldiers as a memorial.

We emerged from this gorge of death and were stopped at another checkpoint five kilometres short of Shatoi together with a couple of other civilian cars. The guards said that there had been shooting ahead, and we had also heard shell fire; they thought Shatoi was in Russian hands again but they weren't sure and we had to wait until the all clear. It was a hot day and we got out of the cars into the fresh air. One of the female interpreters started picking wild flowers at the side of the road. A guard rushed over and told her to get back to the car, there were landmines on the roadside.

'Stupid woman!' he muttered.

After an hour we were let through. The officer in charge of the checkpoint said he would give us an armed escort into Shatoi. We politely declined. The last thing we wanted in an unstable situation like this was to be seen associated with a Russian military vehicle.

We arrived at the outskirts of Shatoi and found the house of the hospital director. There was the sound of distant shelling from the other side of Shatoi. We asked the director if he knew who was now in control of the town.

'Who knows, probably no one,' he said.

I suspected we were in no man's land between the two forces. We were shown round the small hospital. What a mess! It looked as though it had been burnt out, there were large shell holes in the roof, lots of fire damage inside and puddles on the floor where the rain had come in. Then we heard very close shell fire. The director was calm and told us not to worry: it was all outgoing. We were getting nervous – who was firing? He didn't know and added rather obviously – either the Russians or the Chechens. Yes, but if there's outgoing shelling, whoever's being fired on will most likely fire back.

'Why not stay for tea?' he offered.

We refused and said we had to get back. Being Chechen, he must have thought us very rude. We offered to supply large polythene sheeting for the holes in the roof, our constructor would help replace the electrics and the plumbing and we gave him all the medical supplies we were carrying.

'What about a new roof?' said the director.

I declined. Firstly, with all this shelling there was a high chance the roof wouldn't last very long and also the authorities in charge would have no incentive to do something for the hospital themselves, from whichever side they were from. This was a problem that was getting more significant as the weeks passed.

We left in a hurry, back down the narrow gorge. Near the end were more tanks, new ones this time, but one of them had a damaged track and soldiers were hurriedly trying to repair it. It had been hit by a shell when the gorge had come under fire while we were in Shatoi. It seemed like the Russians weren't learning any lessons here. And it seemed we'd been very lucky. This was not the place for us to linger either. We drove fast towards Grozny.

It was a relief to get out of the mountains and we made a relaxed detour via the town of Urus-Martan to the west. It was a relatively safe area and there had not been as much damage here as it was pro-Russian and anti-Dudayev. We found the hospital and the director showed us round; it was in a poor state – there were many tiles missing from the roof, plaster off the walls. Inside were dark, dank, almost-empty rooms with no electricity, no equipment, and just one patient. The floor was wet and we could see that the basement was completely flooded up to ground level. The director asked us to completely renovate it. I sympathized with him and said it must be heart-breaking to have his hospital come under fire like this and then be looted. He looked surprised and offended. I had made a *faux pas*.

'But we've never been attacked, or looted. The hospital was like this before the war started.'

He said he'd never received any help at all from the NGOs. I knew for a fact that one of our field delegates had given them a crate of medical supplies when she'd passed through recently.

'What about ICRC's donation?' I said.

'Oh, they're useless. They never stop here. We'd much rather have you lot – MSF.' His turn to make a *faux pas*.

We offered to provide a pump to clear out the basement and unblock the sewerage pipes. We couldn't realistically renovate the hospital. This was economic neglect not war damage and we couldn't start restoring every rundown hospital in the whole of the Russian Federation.

We had weekly general meetings in the delegation every Saturday morning. It was the time to sort out problems, major and minor.

Meeting of 3 June 1995:

Item 1: Some Russian had peeled off the large plastic ICRC logo from the door of Hanna's Land Cruiser and stuck it on his own van. This is taken seriously. Anything he does would be attributed to the Red Cross. It has to be found.

Item 2: Two drunk Russian soldiers have broken into Hospital No. 4 and stolen our constructor's tools and all the polythene sheeting.

Item 3: The laundry in Hospital No. 4 Maternity Unit has been supplied with industrial washing machines but they haven't been used yet. Why not? Because they said the generator wasn't big enough to cope with them. We have supplied a bigger generator. Still not in use. Why? Because they don't have any washing powder. Washing powder donated. Still not in use because they don't have any nappies to wash. Okay, buy them some ****** nappies!

Item 4: One of the expatriates has been injured. People sit up and take notice. No, nothing serious. One of the female delegates living with one of the Chechen families had gone to the loo down the garden in the middle of the night in pitch darkness and accidentally stepped down into the hole. Grazes to the leg, strained hip and couldn't get rid of the smell from her shoe.

Item 5: Why don't we just offer to build proper inside toilets in the Chechen houses? Because the Chechen landladies think that inside loos are a filthy and unhygienic idea. And anyway it's a big investment when we don't know how long ICRC is going to be here.

Item 6: The temporary toilets at the delegation, a couple of huts over holes in the ground, are unbearably smelly especially with the warm summer weather. What is being done? The job had been given to a local Chechen builder to upgrade them. Apparently all he'd done was to paint the huts brilliant red. The smell remains the same despite this.

Item 7: Something has to be done about the overflow accommodation. We had rented a derelict technical school in Pobedinskaya. It was newly painted but none of the rooms has windows, there is no hot water and there is only one electric ring for cooking for up to 12 people. There are other problems: the Russian caretaker has the habit of turning off the water supply and blackmailing us for a higher and higher rent. Rather ironic that we were pouring more than enough water into Grozny yet we were experiencing local droughts. The caretaker is also in charge of the generator. Someone had brought a video machine with films to while away the evenings. But after the caretaker has drunk his vodka and wants an early night, he simply switches off the generator without warning. We've lost count of the number of half videos we've watched.

Item 8: The field delegates are taking boxes of medicines into the field to use as gifts when visiting difficult areas looking for prisoners or information-gathering. No complaints about giving medical aid but field officers aren't medics and don't explain what the medicines are for – and they don't sign them out of the warehouse and stocktaking is getting impossible.

Item 9: This leads into something more important and some friction between the Detention and Medical divisions. The detention delegates have identified the valleys up in the mountains where they want access and the medics should concentrate on supplying these valleys – as a sort of passport to access. The medical delegates respond that they thought the magic words in ICRC were 'needs-led'. In other words, we supply medical aid to where it's most needed. Simple as that. The argument rumbles on.

Item 10: There is a rumour that the Russian authorities have a huge warehouse full of medicines and medical equipment in Grozny but they're not distributing any of it because the NGO's are donating enough supplies of their own, thank you very much.

Item 11: This applies also to rebuilding/restoring all the hospitals. There's another rumour that the Russian authorities have a list of hospitals that need rebuilding and funds have been allocated but they're holding back because, again, the NGOs are doing the work for them. The head of the Russian Health Authority in Chechnya has explained that as the fighting hasn't finished yet it is no use restoring a hospital which is just going to get damaged again at the next attack – NGOs are wasting their time. I could see his point but what happens to all the wounded patients in the meantime. It would be sensible for us to undertake temporary repairs to hospitals to enable them to function but not start expensive rebuilding schemes. Let the Russians do that, but don't hold your breath.

As medical coordinator I had a lot of meetings to attend, from daily delegation meetings to major decision-making meetings with staff from Geneva coming every six months or so. I felt I really wasn't needed at some of them – where there was no connection at all to medical activities – but I was flattered that I was invited. I mentioned this once to Yves, head of delegation. He apologized rather sheepishly and said he invited me automatically as it was a long-held rule in ICRC that if just one person at a meeting didn't speak good French then the meeting had to be conducted in English. So if I was present, the others couldn't ramble on as long in English as they could in their native Swiss/French so meetings were considerably shorter. Nice to know I was contributing something, then.

I did try to speak French at one of the bigger meetings when the VIPs came down from Geneva. My bad accent didn't seem to matter until the end of my presentation on our work with the other NGOs in Chechnya. I described them all and was doing fine until the last moment when I announced that we welcomed the arrival of the French branch of Action against Hunger – *Agence Contre la Faim*. I couldn't understand the laughter that went round until someone confided to me afterwards – because of my bad pronunciation of *la faim*, it sounded like *la femme*, the Agency against Women. I kept to English after that.

I had two trips outside the Caucasus region. The first was to Moscow to buy medical instruments and equipment especially for eye surgery in Hospital No. 4. The Russians have an excellent reputation in this field and I was pleased to meet the famous and well-respected eye surgeon Svyatoslav Fyodorov from the

Moscow Research Institute of Eye Microsurgery. He advised me on surgical instruments and pointed me in the direction of the best optical manufacturers in St Petersburg and in Zagorsk, seventy kilometres outside Moscow.

In Zagorsk, it was a good shopping trip even though it took all day trying to buy an eye examination slit-lamp. It was well made and at a bargain price but the waiting around was truly Russian in its duration. Everything came to a stop at lunchtime, so I went outside to look around. The town has now been given its old name, Sergiev Possad. It's famous for its Trinity Lavra Church of St. Sergei together with a cluster of smaller churches and a monastery. It was a hot day so I went into the church. It was dark and cool, very narrow but very high with a strong smell of incense. A small choir was singing unaccompanied orthodox Russian chants – soaring female sopranos and very deep black-bearded basses. There were no seats but I stood enthralled and deeply moved for an hour. It seemed a long way from the brutality, distress, destruction and death of Chechnya but in a way it reflected the sadness and fatalism of the Russian soul.

On to St Petersburg where I bought an operating microscope from an optical instrument factory. It was less than a quarter of the price than in Europe. It was of excellent quality too. The only problem was, like a lot of Russian equipment, it was very bulky and heavy. Still that might not be a bad thing in a war zone. I almost felt it was robust enough to drop by parachute. When crated up there was no way I could get it in the car let alone into the ICRC aircraft to get it to Nalchik. The sales lady said she would send it by rail, it would take nine weeks. There was nothing else I could do, but I realistically knew it would never get there. Two and a half thousand kilometres by Russian railways? No chance.

I was wrong. Nine weeks later I was told the operating microscope was waiting for collection at Nalchik station. When I delivered it to Hospital No. 4, the director cried and gave me a hug. I felt like Father Christmas.

*Chapter 27*

# Budennovsk

The next trip wasn't so relaxed. On 14 June we heard that Chechen separatists had attacked the town of Budennovsk in the *oblast*, or province, of Stavropol on the western Russian steppes, about 200 kilometres north-west of Grozny. This was the first time the war had been brought outside Chechnya and into Russia itself and it was a shock to the Russian public and the government in Moscow. Chechen rebels, led by Shamil Basayev, a man who two weeks before had lost his wife, his child and nine of his close relatives in a Russian air raid, crossed into Stavropol disguised as a column of military trucks purporting to be carrying coffins of Russian soldiers killed in Chechnya. They attacked the Budennovsk town hall and police station causing civilian deaths. They then retreated to the town hospital where they took about 1,800 hostages, including 150 children and some women with newborn babies. The Russian army was brought in to lay siege to the hospital. The next day, when the authorities were slow to negotiate, the Chechens killed six hostages.

Yves, the head of delegation, suggested that Tamara and I, with field delegates and Russian interpreters, take two Land Cruisers full of medical supplies to Budennovsk and offer help to the other hospitals there. The journey was rather fraught. Before we were halfway there, the roadblocks started to get serious. The army had commandeered trucks and large agricultural vehicles to block the roads. They were letting very few people through and everyone was thoroughly searched. At the first checkpoint four men from the car ahead of us had been ordered out of the car while a soldier ripped the seats with a knife, throwing the stuffing into the road. Our Russian interpreter said they were looking for guns. The men were ordered to open their shirts. While one soldier examined them, two others had guns trained on them. I asked the interpreter what was going on.

'They're checking to see if they're fighters.'

'How can they tell?'

'Someone who's been using a gun a lot will have bruising at the front of the shoulder where the rifle butt kicks back.'

They were still being searched as we were waved past: the checkpoints had been notified to let us through. At one of the checkpoints the guard said we were mad to go anywhere near Budennovsk.

Within twenty kilometres of the town, about the size of Tunbridge Wells, the roads were eerily empty of traffic. As we entered the suburbs we could see a plume of black smoke ahead. The problem was that we were approaching the town from the south; we knew the hospital under siege was also in the south and we had no street map. We didn't want to drive straight into a battle zone.

We were advised by radio from Nalchik to take extreme care – the first storming of the hospital had taken place at 5.30 that morning with many more civilian casualties in the streets. There was said to be a group of Chechen fighters roaming loose somewhere in the town. Through deserted streets we suddenly came across an official-looking building, part of which had recently been on fire and was still smoking. We heard gunshots and we thought for a moment we'd had the supreme bad luck to drive straight to the hospital itself. But this was where one of the earlier attacks had taken place. We heard more gunshots, now closer, and quickly retreated. It took an inordinate amount of time to approach the town from the other side via side roads which weren't on any map. But we found a Polyclinic, a four-storey casualty and outpatient clinic where the wounded were being brought. They said they'd had sixty-four wounded and thirty-one dead since the morning's attack and the siege at the hospital was still continuing. The clinic was a mass of activity and confusion, doctors from all the nearby towns were there. Anxious people were crowded around the front of the Polyclinic and Russian troops were everywhere guarding the clinic. We delivered the medical supplies and the clinic staff were particularly glad to see suture material and dressings. In all this confusion, the staff insisted, in true Russian style, of checking every item against the list we'd brought and laboriously entering it into their stores register by hand.

We visited another clinic nearby, curiously named the Cement Factory Health Centre, to donate supplies as wounded were also being brought there. Back at the Polyclinic we were given a large physiotherapy room on the top floor to stay overnight and use as a base. From there we could see the siege hospital about a kilometre away. At about 2 p.m. the second assault by Russian troops on that hospital began. We could see huge clouds of black smoke curling up and an interminable two-hour barrage of machine-gun fire, artillery and stun grenades. I could feel for the hostages caught up in it all.

It was difficult to find out what was happening and strange that we had to listen to the BBC World Service broadcasts to find out what was going on before our eyes. We heard that the attack had failed. More casualties were brought in and this time I was invited to come down to the A&E admissions room to help out. The first patient I dealt with was a colonel with gunshot wounds to the shoulder who had been part of the assault force. The seriously wounded, including him, were airlifted to other towns for surgical treatment. It was very hot in A&E and exhausting with nothing to drink but very strong black Russian tea. I went outside for a breath of air. The hospital had given me a tabard to wear with the Russian word for 'doctor' on the back. The event had attracted the world's media and a reporter with a UK camera crew asked me very slowly and deliberately if I spoke English.

'Yes.'

Could I give them any information? I told them that we'd had another fifty wounded brought in and more were arriving. He thanked me and as he walked away I heard him say to his crew, 'They speak damned good English here. Hardly any trace of an accent.'

Our relationships with the media weren't always harmonious. I was later interviewed by another UK camera crew who'd come up from Grozny. The reporter turned the conversation round to Chechnya itself and he was quite aggressive. They'd come across a small psychiatric hospital in one of the south-ern towns in Chechnya with no one looking after the patients, rather like the one we'd come across in Shali. In confrontational style he asked me why ICRC hadn't found this hospital and, now that we'd been informed, what were we going to do about it. I became quite aggressive myself and explained that we couldn't be expected to cover the whole of Chechnya; we were a charity without an infinite budget and we weren't the National Health Service for the whole damned country and if he was so concerned, why didn't he write me a cheque right now and we'd use it to improve their conditions. He declined and as far as I knew the interview was never broadcast.

We spent an uncomfortable, hot, mosquito-ridden night sleeping on hard examination couches in the therapy room. We were joined by a dozen Russian Spetsnaz soldiers who were grabbing some sleep on army camp beds. There was that Russian army smell again. Their commander ordered them to keep their boots on in case they had to move out quickly, but as soon as he left, off came the boots and the smell of Russian army feet added to the ambience together with their snoring.

There was further gunfire in the early morning but that attack also failed and it soon became very quiet. The two sides had started negotiating and the number of wounded coming in decreased then stopped altogether. Everything seemed 'paused', waiting for the next event. There was an intense anti-Chechen feeling everywhere. A story was going around that the Chechen fighters had intended to reach Moscow, bribing the checkpoint guards on the way, but they'd run out of money at Budennovsk.

'Good heavens!' said the director of the Polyclinic. 'I would have given them money just to get them to move on to somewhere else.'

A compromise was reached in the negotiations: the hostages were released, the Chechen fighters were granted safe conduct back to Chechnya and Russia agreed to end military activity and conduct more negotiations in Chechnya. In fact the military ceasefire, if it ever happened, was very brief. But it was seen as a turning point in the war. It 'boosted morale among Chechen separatists, shocked the Russian public, and discredited the Russian government', quoted a Russian journalist. Officially, in the three days of the Budennovsk siege, 129 civilians and thirty-six military were killed including 105 hostages; over 400 people were wounded.

The convoy of Chechen militants slowly made its way under safe conduct back to Chechnya via Dagestan with the world's media following every move.

Anne, one of our nurses, was in Dagestan and saw the convoy passing. She later told me that one of the militants leaned out of a truck. He recognized her from when she'd delivered medical supplies to one of the villages in the south of Chechnya. He'd been present when she'd had tea with the villagers.

He shouted, 'Hey, Anne! ICRC Anne! When you coming to have tea with us again?'

Not exactly the sort of publicity ICRC was keen on. Anne quickly melted back into the crowd. Fortunately a following TV crew just missed the exchange.

When it was all over we met the director of the siege hospital. She showed us round what was left. It looked all too familiar, as though it was in the centre of Grozny. There were shell holes in the walls and black smoke marks above many of the glassless windows where there had been fire inside. Three burnt-out ambulances were standing outside. We went inside two of the hospital blocks. It was a mess; equipment had been piled up against the windows to act as shields or barricades so most of it was damaged by bullets and shells – it was expensive stuff too. There were mattresses and rubbish strewn over the floor as though someone had had a wild party in a squat. The floor crunched underfoot, not just from broken glass but from thousands of spent bullet cases. There was what looked like a shell impact on a wall making a gaping hole. Next to it was a chair, covered with blood.

In the theatre, the operating table had obviously been used during the siege and below it was a pile of blood-soaked dressings. In a corridor, a metal trapdoor in the floor was open and below were rows of utility pipes in the basement; it looked as though someone had desperately tried to hide from the violence. The children's ward was completely gutted by fire; the director thought it had been purposely set alight. Three women and a man, members of the medical staff, were listlessly clearing up. They had been hostages together and seemed to want each other's company. One of the women told us about their three days under siege – she said they'd not been treated badly. When I asked, I was told there was no plan for stress counselling. As the woman talked she would occasionally stop and cry.

Budennovsk was only the first of such sieges: in 1996 in Kizlyar-Pervomayskoye, forty-one civilians, thirty-seven Russian servicemen and ninety Chechen militants died; in 2002, in the Moscow theatre hostage crisis, 129 civilians including nine foreigners died; in 2004, in Beslan, 334 people were killed including 186 children. Shamil Basayev, the leader of the Budennovsk siege, was killed by Russian security services in 2006.

It seemed to be quieter in Chechnya for a precious few days afterwards so I took advantage and made as many visits as possible while I could. As I drove with my Russian interpreter Alexander, we passed the outskirts of Grozny through an area which looked rather like a huge chaotic reclamation centre, with acres and acres of bits of old reinforced concrete, bricks, tiles, rusting metal girders being piled high by busy bulldozers. I asked Alexander about it. He said it was the ghost of Grozny. All the remains of shell-damaged buildings, all the rubble from the streets was being brought here to be dumped.

First we drove to the town of Shali to deliver a promised oxygen concentrator to the hospital. I loved these machines and they were priceless for anaesthetics. About the size of a small suitcase, you plug it into the mains – air goes in at one side and almost pure oxygen comes out at the other. Magic! I'd bought three of them in Moscow at US$2,000 each; but as life-savers they were worth every cent and half the price we'd pay in the West. Distributing them to infinitely grateful hospitals gave me a huge frisson of satisfaction. Such a small thing but a highlight of the whole mission. Oxygen concentrators were especially useful here. It was very difficult for the hospitals to get supplies of oxygen, the cylinders of compressed oxygen were heavy and in a war environment could explode violently if hit and set the whole place ablaze. I'd also learned from experience that the cylinders are not easy to transport through checkpoints as soldiers sometimes mistake them for artillery shells. But the concentrators are rather like vacuum cleaners – with a few years' supply of paper filters they'll go on for a very long time and, most importantly, long after ICRC has left.

It seemed safe to travel south for once and when we arrived at Shali hospital we started to unload boxes of much-needed medical supplies and the oxygen concentrator. But then the director of the hospital appeared. We'd never seen him before. He was quite irate and said we couldn't just arrive with supplies like this. We'd have to come back another day when we'd made an appointment.

Now take all these boxes away. Fair enough, but it's not easy to make appointments in a war zone.

As soon as he'd gone a group of nurses rushed out. 'We'll have them, we'll have them!' they shouted, and one of them pointed to where the director had disappeared and said, '*Gloopie starry doorak!*' which I think meant, 'Stupid old fool'. We delivered the concentrator to the operating theatre where the anaesthetist was overjoyed. He seemed to want to go and find someone to anaesthetize – anyone.

While I was demonstrating it, the director had sidled in and was watching us. 'Right,' he said, 'we'll have five of them'.

Dream on, I thought.

On to Argun where things were in good shape; there had been some shelling but away from the hospital. We passed the familiar stuck railway train then to Gudermes, where they'd started operating again. It was beginning to be a good day, the sun was out but not too hot. The road was still quiet so we decided to press on to Khasavyurt in Dagestan; it would save the otherwise very long detour some other day. There was an MSF car ahead of us so we followed it on the long, straight, easy road – safety in numbers. It stopped inexplicably and let us pass, then carried on behind us. Before the border we reached the wide, shallow Aksay river but the bridge over it had been hit by shelling, one of the supports had gone and there was a ten-metre-wide gap in the road. We saw a car coming the other way; it had driven down the bank across the shingle flats, negotiated the river and successfully come up at the other side. We decided to give it a try. But down at the river it looked fast-flowing and deep. It would only need the Land Cruiser to start floating and we'd end up miles downstream. There was already an abandoned car further down stuck among the rocks. The MSF car was behind us. I got out and asked them,

'Would you like to go ahead and show us the way across?'

'No, we thought you'd done this before, that's why we're following you.'

We both waited for another car to come along and successfully followed it across. The day continued well. In Khasavyurt, I revisited the refugee warehouse. It had now been supplied with water, toilets and even showers thanks to the enthusiasm of Pierre, the water delegate. I thought I'd better rein him in a bit now or he'd be building jacuzzis. We drove on, with a slight detour because the police had closed a checkpoint after arresting two men smuggling arms. Eventually we could go no further because there in front of us was the Caspian Sea, deep shimmering blue, sparkling in the sun, the largest enclosed body of water in the world. We'd reached the town of Makhachkala where I'd heard there was an orthopaedic centre making limb prostheses. We were warmly welcomed by a constantly smiling woman, Sabira, the director, who showed us round. I was the first English person she'd seen and we got on very well. There was a busy workshop and a rehabilitation ward with a boy of 12 being fitted with bilateral below-knee prostheses after a bus accident. They were simple but very good prostheses. I was impressed. It had been a constant problem how to deal with amputations in Chechnya – the workshop in Grozny had been largely destroyed and I'd been looking for such a place for ICRC to sponsor until a new one might be built. This was ideal, it was out of the conflict zone and much safer. Sabira was delighted with the idea, they just needed a few improvements and raw materials. To celebrate, even if rather prematurely, Sabira took us to the beach – I'd told her I'd always wanted to paddle in the Caspian Sea – where we bought ice-creams, took our shoes and socks off and paddled.

It was a long way back after a long day, but it had been one of those days when I felt we'd achieved something. It was also still relaxingly quiet on the road.

Alexander had become my permanent interpreter by now. Importantly, he could guide me when it came to difficult negotiations with officials. He knew the Russian way of doing things and knew how to read personalities: this man needs to be flattered; this one is good and you can do honest business with him; this one is a crook. He was also excellent at negotiating difficult checkpoints. He had been to one of the best foreign language schools in Moscow. His friend and fellow student there had gone on to become Mikhail Gorbachev's interpreter. Alexander shared the driving and was good company on long trips. He told me he had only once been outside the Russian Federation and that was in the days of the Soviet Union. He had been posted to Egypt with his wife, which was unusual. The political commissar, who was supposed to keep a close check on all the Russian staff and spoil their fun, was permanently drunk so they had had a wonderfully free time seeing the sights. In Moscow we had a young driver who was boasting about an expensive police speed trap detector he'd just bought. Alexander produced a bottle of vodka from his briefcase and said that this was just as effective at police checkpoints at a tenth of the price.

*Chapter 28*

# Bugs and Bandits

G ood days were becoming rare. There was a new fear as the summer progressed of a cholera epidemic. It had happened often in past years. Now it would be aggravated by a half-destroyed city and very limited medical facilities. We stockpiled thousands of intravenous drip sets, saline infusions, oral rehydration fluids and antibiotics. In the event, nothing happened, only a handful of cases. Cholera is spread by faecal-contaminated water and I wondered if it had been avoided by the millions of gallons of fresh drinking water we had brought into Grozny and the other towns. Then we heard of a case of bubonic plague. This induced a sense of panic and dread among all the medical delegates, myself included – visions of the mediaeval Black Death. But when we contacted the experts in Geneva, they told us not to worry – it's easily treated with a course of tetracycline, one of the simplest and cheapest of the antibiotics. Times change.

As the health scares decreased, the hassles with the authorities increased. I once invited the Russian director of health for Chechnya to one of the inter-NGO meetings to show him what we were all trying to do, a sort of PR exercise. It was a mistake.

He was dismissive to the point of rudeness and told us: 'Look, why are you all wasting your time here. You should just give me all the money, I'll decide what needs to be done, and you can all go home.' I wasn't popular with the other NGOs for a while.

I was also looking into the possibility of reviving the defunct blood transfusion service in Grozny. The existing building was damaged but easily repairable. The problem was with the local administration. They had always paid blood donors and they had also charged recipients for every unit of blood given. This was something that ICRC could never agree to and we had reached deadlock.

As the weeks went by we met other obstacles. We were informed that the water supplied to Grozny by the NGOs, almost exclusively by ICRC and the UK-based charity Merlin, would have to be tested by the Ministry of Agriculture which for some odd reason was in charge of water supplies, and that we would have to obtain a certificate before we were allowed to continue. That proved very difficult. One would be forgiven for thinking they didn't want

us there. Then we were informed that our radios were illegal and we would have
to apply for a special permit to use them. It was impossible to continue working
if we didn't have them, for security reasons alone.

Then the attacks started. We had moved our medical stores from Pobedinskaya
to a huge warehouse nearby which was once used to store engineering parts for
the petroleum factories. It was more secure and inside there was somewhere for
a guard to sleep at night. We arrived one morning to find it had been looted.
All the terrified guard could tell us was that the robbers were heavily armed
with machine guns and bazookas and had made light work of all the locks. I
could think of only two groups, one on each side of the conflict, both military,
that had access to such weaponry. It certainly wasn't the Grozny branch of the
Women's Institute. The local police were not interested. Their view was that
if we were going to donate it all to Chechnya anyway, then the robbers were
simply doing the distribution for us and saving us the trouble. Then we could
all go home. A moment of *déjà vu* there. Fortunately we had not transferred all
our supplies to the warehouse yet. Most of it was in Nalchik. So we decided to
move small quantities at a time, only enough for us to distribute immediately. It
was a wise decision. Two weeks later the warehouse was broken into again. We
had had enough of the warehouse and the supplies were then put into several
smaller locations which no one else knew about, not even the authorities.

It became more serious. Two of our female staff, one expatriate and one local,
who shared a house, were woken at 3 a.m. by what appeared to be Chechen soldiers. The two were roughly treated at gunpoint and robbed of US$400. It was
difficult to apportion blame: we were told that either side were very proficient
at imitating the other.

MSF had a bad time, they were robbed at gunpoint of US$30,000 from their
safe. Then it happened again some days later and we heard that one of their
logistics delegates had lost his front teeth from a rifle butt. MSF withdrew from
Chechnya to consider their position.

I came towards the end of my six months. Geneva offered me an extension of
contract. It was tempting but the job had been tiring and the prospect of going
home to hot showers, clean toilets, temperate climate and no violence was over-
whelmingly desirable. I was offered a good rest at home then maybe a return for
a longer-term contract, maybe a year or even two. I thought about how reward-
ing it could be in setting up an orthopaedic workshop, sorting out the problems
of the blood bank and getting a blood transfusion service running. There was
also the prospect of setting up our own ICRC hospital with expatriate surgical
teams. I thought hard about it and reluctantly decided against it. I felt I'd made
the wrong decision and it bothered me for months afterwards.

However another contract would have meant I would probably have been in Chechnya in December 1996. I was shocked to read a news report: ICRC had opened a new hospital with expatriate surgical teams in September 1996 at Novye Atagi south of Grozny and had already treated 300 war-wounded. One night in December 1996 six expatriate hospital medical staff were shot dead in their beds by gunmen. Could have been me. All ICRC personnel were subsequently withdrawn from Chechnya.

After I left, the war continued. In December 1995, Russian artillery and rocket attacks killed at least 267 civilians after a Chechen militant raid on Gudermes. The hospital was badly damaged for a second time. In March 1996, over 1,500 Chechen fighters infiltrated Grozny and launched a three-day attack, capturing much of the city and large caches of weapons and ammunition. In April 1996, Russian troops massacred over a hundred civilians in the town of Samashki. That same month there was a repeat of the Shatoi massacre, whose aftermath I had witnessed, when another Russian armoured column was ambushed and destroyed in the gorge with between fifty and a hundred Russian soldiers killed.

What is described as The Second Chechen War occurred in August 1999. In response to a Chechen militant invasion of Dagestan, large numbers of Russian forces were again sent into Chechnya and seized Grozny after a winter siege lasting over three months. The Russians made extensive use of air attacks, artillery bombardment and long-distance weaponry. Many Chechen towns and villages were destroyed. Civilian deaths during this time are estimated between 25,000 and 50,000. At least 14,000 Chechen rebels and 4,400–7,500 Russian troops were killed. I often wondered what happened to those three elderly ladies and to the disabled woman. Since then there has been an uneasy peace, broken occasionally by sporadic terrorist attacks and kidnappings, but rebuilding has begun in Grozny to such an extent that I would probably find the place unrecognizable.

# PART 8

# LANDMINE INTERLUDE

*Chapter 29*

# Cause and Effect

As I did more missions for the Red Cross, I felt niggling concerns that we were looking after the victims of war but not doing anything to stop those wars or at least to stop some of the horrendous methods used to propagate those wars. Of course this was not the mandate of the Red Cross movement. Its fundamental aim is to promote the principles of the Geneva Convention and relieve suffering that results from war.

However, in the 1990s, at the same time that I was having these concerns, the Red Cross took an active stand in this direction. For the first time in its history the Red Cross started lobbying politicians, against the manufacture and use of landmines. On every mission I had seen and treated countless landmine victims. From the jungles of Cambodia to the deserts of Afghanistan and Somalia and the streets of Chechnya. Banning landmines was a cause I felt passionate about and I became involved in the campaign and was asked to join in the publicity activities of the British Red Cross. Between missions, I met Princess Diana who had taken the anti-landmine cause to heart and who, in January 1997, just months before her death, had visited a mine-clearing programme in Angola with British Red Cross officials. It was valuable publicity. I was invited to her funeral in September 1997 as a member of the British Red Cross. I sat in the transept of Westminster Abbey just a few yards from the flag-draped coffin. The parallel of violent death – hers from a car accident and in the wider world from landmines – was not lost on me.

The government announced a complete ban on the manufacture, transfer, import and export of anti-personnel landmines in May 1997. The anti-landmine publicity campaign was interesting, satisfying and I have to say enjoyable, not least because of the people I met. In 1997, there was a campaign fundraising event which involved a breakfast trip on the Orient Express from London's Victoria Station to Southampton, and lunch on board the *QE2*. I was having breakfast on the train, going over a speech I was to make on the *QE2* when it was suggested I confer with the other speaker who was sitting in the next carriage so we could coordinate the two speeches. I walked through and found to my surprise that it was Lord Richard Attenborough. I hesitated to disturb him at his breakfast but I needn't have worried.

'My dear chap,' he said warmly grasping my hand, 'come and sit down. Waiter! A glass of champagne for my friend here. Have you had breakfast?'

I've always cherished the moment. After the speeches, I was sitting at one of the lunch tables with Terry Waite and Elizabeth Dole, President of the American Red Cross and wife of Senator Robert Dole. The fourth one at our table was a serious grey-suited man who was rumoured to be Mrs Dole's FBI security agent. He told me that I was sitting at the same table as someone who would probably become the first female President of the United States. Throughout the meal he had his right hand tucked into the inside pocket of his jacket. Terry Waite thought it must be a gun, I thought it was his wallet. We were all taken back to London by coach. The FBI man asked for him and Mrs Dole to be let off at their hotel. It was also my stop so the three of us got off and the coach drove away and disappeared. It was only then that the FBI man realized it wasn't the right hotel, that they were miles away from it. Security alert! I frantically tried to get them a taxi but these had all disappeared while a possible future president of the US was standing vulnerably on the streets of London with a very anxious FBI man armed only with a wallet. A taxi was eventually and thankfully found.

I'd been invited the next day to Brighton as the guest speaker at the 1998 Labour Party Conference. Every year they have an independent non-party affiliated speaker to talk about a current topic and that year it was landmines. The only slight problem I had was getting through the very tight security barrier to the conference hotel where I was staying. I had brought a deactivated empty plastic butterfly mine, given to me by Guy Willoughby of the Halo Trust in Kabul, to use in the speech. British Red Cross had let security know about this well in advance but they still had to satisfy themselves by borrowing my penknife and pushing it into the landmine. For one unfounded moment I had this awful image of it going off. There's publicity and there's *publicity*. The security man was happy. But he said, 'I can let you in with the landmine but not the penknife.' Not a phrase you hear every day.

I'd carefully prepared the speech and had a long list of statistics on a sheet of paper. Number of people killed by mines, number of injured, number of children, percentage of lower limbs lost, upper limbs lost. Halfway through the speech I realized that to me it wasn't a matter of numbers and percentages, it was an image in my memory of some poor child lying broken and bleeding on a dirt floor in the middle of some godforsaken corner of the world. I put the paper away and just told it as it was, adding that during the hour of the speech, three more people would have become victims of mines.

I was happy that the speech was well received. I was even more satisfied later that afternoon when it was announced that UK funding for landmine clearance would be doubled to £10 million, and would be used to support and train local people to do their own clearance.

There was a rather unexpected consequence to my involvement with land-mines. The British Red Cross headquarters had a request from a UK company who were running a joint operation abroad with Tajikistan. They were looking for a doctor who was an expert in mines. BRC thought of me and I knew that Tajikistan was recovering from civil war at the time so I went along to a meeting with the company officials. It turned out they were a gold mining company extracting ore up a remote valley in the north of the country. I explained there'd been a slight error here with the word 'mines' but they offered me a month's post in Tajikistan anyway as their medical officer. In fact I wasn't as unqualified as I thought as the CBM mining company were very generous and funded a project to upgrade the local hospital in Taror and establish health clinics in the poor villages up the Magdian valley where there had been virtually nothing before. Right up my street.

# PART 9

## SUDAN, 2000

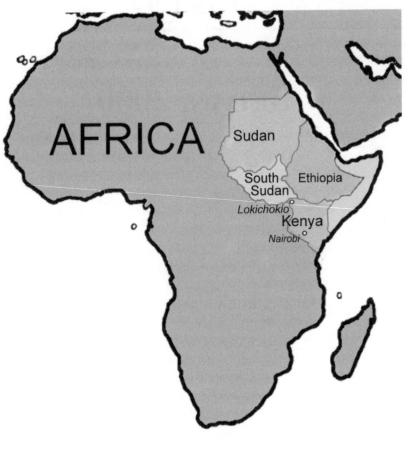

SUDAN

*Chapter 30*

# The Hospital in Lokichokio, Northern Kenya

The year was 2000, and in the new millennium I was missing the excitement of working with the Red Cross and so I accepted a post as anaesthetist for a few months at the ICRC hospital at Lokichokio in northern Kenya treating war-wounded from the conflict in the Sudan.

The civil war in the Sudan began in 1983. It polarized into north versus south Sudan. The north was Middle East-orientated and Islamic. The south was more traditionally African, Christian or Animist. In the south the Sudan People's Liberation Movement (SPLM), which later split into rival factions had rebelled against the government of Sudan in Khartoum in the north. The south wanted more influence in government and protested against Islamization. Civilian casualties and famine followed in the wake of this civil war and, in 1989, Operation Lifeline Sudan (OLS) began. A consortium of five UN agencies and forty-one NGOs including ICRC was created to provide emergency relief in the aftermath of the deaths of more than 300,000 people. The base for this operation was the insignificant town of Lokichokio. It was in Kenya up against the border with south Sudan and it was on one of the few highways into the Sudan. The condition of the road was poor, liable to flooding during the rains, heavily mined, and attracted bandits. But it had an airstrip from which aid could be flown into Sudan and the injured could be accepted or evacuated from the conflict areas.

This was the second time I'd been in Lokichokio. Memories were still depressingly fresh from the last time I'd visited the town during my time as medical coordinator for Somalia nine years previously. I flew into Nairobi and headed for the main ICRC delegation. The place looked the same, just some extra offices. I recognized some of the old faces among the local employees. Somewhat thankfully I noticed the expatriate ICRC personnel on the Somalia desk had all long since changed.

I had a day there for briefing and found time to relax for a few hours. I sat on a bench reading all the information I'd been given – ICRC were always thorough, even with details of where you could buy toothpaste or the type of electricity socket in each sub-delegation – I suddenly smelled the sweet familiar scent of bougainvillea, the bright red flowers on the bush right behind me, and it took me back vividly, as only smells can, to the time I had worked from here into Somalia. Time had mellowed the bad memories. It took me back even further to the delegation in Wattana on the Thai–Cambodian border. I made the most of it. Lokichokio with its dry parched earth would be very different.

Next morning I was taken to Wilson airport for the flight up to Lokichokio. The first thing I noticed was that the plane was much bigger than the Beechcraft I'd travelled in nine years ago; in fact it was a scheduled passenger flight of Kenyan Airways. The second thing I noticed was that we flew much higher. No stunning views of the Rift Valley this time and no flamingos on the lake; we were flying above the clouds. When we landed at Lokichokio I was astonished. It was no longer an airstrip, it was an airport – now the second largest in Kenya with a hundred flights taking off per day. There was no longer a small village of a thousand people, it was now a huge town of 12,000. It had all grown out of the aid business. Lokichokio was thriving on the conflict across the border. As aid agencies and relief flights mushroomed, so did the shops and the boutiques and the banks and businesses. So did the smart hotels with swimming pools and the restaurants with international cuisine. You could now get BBC, CNN and Sky by satellite. But it was also reminiscent of a Wild West town, especially after dark. There were black marketeers smuggling goods into Sudan and mafia-style factions running the more lucrative businesses. Surrounding all this there were also what can only be described as slums where the Turkhana tribespeople lived. It wasn't surprising that they'd become town dwellers – the NGOs had provided them with a reliable clean water supply by boring deep wells. This was becoming more important as there had been droughts for the past three years. Schools had also been set up for them and of course with all the NGOs and especially the ICRC hospital present, they had access to some of the best free medical services in Africa. This was done as policy because the NGOs needed the goodwill and cooperation of the local Turkhana to run the relief effort. If the Turkhana saw all this aid and money being poured into Sudan and not getting any benefit themselves, there was going to be some resentment: life for a Turkhana was no bed of roses either. Some NGOs were in fact focused only on the Turkhana in Lokichokio and not the Sudanese. But I couldn't help wondering, from previous experience, what would happen to all this and to the Turkhana if the civil war was resolved and the NGOs, especially ICRC, pulled out. It was just as hot though – that hadn't changed – at a stifling 40°C, hotter than blood heat.

Our delegation and residences had grown; they now had to accommodate two surgical teams together with more delegates and more pilots for the increase in supply flights. But the banana trees had grown tall and most of the compound was blessedly under shade. I also noticed the huts now had verandas and they were thatch-covered rather than corrugated iron and would be much cooler.

The next day I set off for the hospital with the surgical teams in the ever-present Land Cruiser. We passed through the edge of the town, past some shops – these were no more than four walls and roof all made of corrugated iron – with elegant, peculiar names like the 'Half London Fashion House' which sold T-shirts and plastic shoes sparkling with glitter. There was an optimistically named 'Grand Hotel' which was no more than a large garden shed. Turkhana women were walking in a stately procession along the road. Their long necks were covered by enormous numbers of bead necklaces, string after string of them. On their heads they had large sacks or water pots. One woman carried a solitary cola bottle perfectly balanced.

The hospital was about two and a half kilometres from the town on the site of a small encampment called Lopiding, so it had become known as Lopiding Hospital. The road was covered with red-grey dust with sparse, struggling, thorny shrubs dotted on the flat landscape and in the distance, impressive hills soared up on each side. Immediately before the hospital was a wide, dried-up riverbed – vehicles had to negotiate down the bank across the flat and up the other bank to the hospital gates. The riverbed was occupied by a few makeshift dwellings of branches with children playing and a train of four roped camels led by a herdsman in stately procession. The hospital had grown enormously; it now had almost 500 patients. The orthopaedic centre for making and fitting prosthetic limbs was also much larger and very busy. This was now the largest civilian field hospital in the world.

We started the day with one of our weekly staff meetings. One of the three surgeons, André, had returned on the same plane as me. He stood up to announce that he was feeling much better since his sick leave in Nairobi, and that he would now try to get on with everyone and was sorry for his previous bad behaviour. That was rather ominous. I started work immediately: there were on average a hefty fourteen operations a day. The vast majority, over 95 per cent, were gunshot wounds with only the odd mine or shell injury. Less than half of all the trauma cases were actually war wounds, the rest were due to plain lawlessness, mostly from around Lokichokio itself.

The other 5 per cent of trauma seemed to be snakebites. Within the first week I'd seen so many snakebites, I began to think there should be two queues in the admissions room – snakebites and 'others' – although the admission book made interesting reading: 'bitten by crocodile, mauled by lion, spear wound (assegai) through thigh, burns after lightning struck hut'. So the anaesthetic as usual was mostly ketamine for debridement of bullet injuries especially limbs. I was seeing more fresh wounds in Lopiding than in other ICRC hospitals because some were coming from just up the road. This also meant we were having to deal with more difficult cases – abdominal and chest gunshot wounds. In other war zones, these victims usually died before reaching us.

The work, though long and hard, had its compensations – the operating theatre was air-conditioned, walking into the cool of the theatre from the blazing heat was a joy. The hospital wards were huge canvas marquees with hundreds of simple wooden bedsteads. The post-op and intensive care ward was a former warehouse, with wooden walls and tin roof but with gaps high up in the walls all the way round to let any breeze circulate. After a day of ketamine anaesthetics, the post-op ward was full of dozing patients – not having the expected side effect of nightmares, but instead all singing deliriously, unfortunately not the same song, and it was a cacophony. One of the expatriate nurses was very keen to record some of what she assumed was ethnic African music. But a local nurse assured her it wasn't ethnic, it was pure gibberish.

The snakebite injuries were difficult to treat. Many snakebite victims probably died on the long journey to get medical help. It wasn't just a case of giving an antidote – some snakes injected necrotoxins, poisons which chemically kill skin and muscle, slowly spreading away from the site of the bite, killing more and more tissue relentlessly in the days that follow. I saw some horrific snakebite injuries, dead hands and feet with foul-smelling gangrene creeping up legs and arms. The only thing that could be done was to debride the limb well above the level of the dead tissue, almost like cutting down trees ahead of a forest fire. Many of the victims I saw were small children who didn't have the experience to avoid snakes. The Dinka people of southern Sudan, as part of their animist religion, regard some snakes as divine and I heard of some people feeding snakes to appease them and releasing them into the wild, it was considered bad luck to kill them. It made us all very cautious about walking into grass around the villages we visited in Sudan. Some surgeon at the hospital with a sense of humour invented the pseudo-medical term 'retro-arboreal-peri-micturatory-genito-herpeto-mordant injury' which means being 'bitten by a snake in the privates while relieving oneself behind a tree'.

Back at the delegation, I spent a restless night in my hut. I was still tired from the flights and the day's work in a theatre I wasn't accustomed to, but I was kept awake by the loud music coming from the town. There were two open-air nightclubs in Lokichokio with disco music that went on until 2 a.m. twice a week and various bars with their own loud sound systems. Then, at around 3 a.m., there were gunshots. If this had been a first mission I would have dived under the bed, but it was a sign that I was getting used to it that I just lay there blocking my ears with a pillow. I had been warned there might be gunfire, but with memories of Somalia and Chechnya coming to the surface, I started calculating the chances of a bullet coming through the thin walls until I lapsed into a welcome sleep.

There was another disturbance at 5 a.m. This one was less threatening but even more irritating. It was to be a regular nightly occurrence –some large bird had taken up residence in a tree in the compound and it had a very loud and very peculiar, almost human-like mating call. Next morning they told me it was known to the ICRC expatriates as the Orgasm Bird. Some weeks later I heard that some people had had enough of this noise, that they'd managed to capture the bird and took it miles away from Lokichokio before releasing it. I said it would be embarrassing if the noise didn't actually stop after the bird had gone.

The two surgical teams alternated on-call after working hours and there were many times during the following months when we'd be called out in the middle of the night to deal with an emergency admission, inevitably another gunshot wound. The road to the hospital could be particularly dangerous in the dark. There were gunmen around, even bandits and the police would regard any vehicle out on the road at that time as suspect and could readily open fire. So the whole team would travel together in one Land Cruiser, very slowly, with a huge Red Cross flag flying on the radio aerial and a searchlight on top illuminating it and us so everyone knew who we were. Within days I had to make the trip at 3 a.m. to the victims of a road accident. A truck driver, very drunk, had been taking people tightly crowded in the back of the truck over the border after dark. His truck had left the road and overturned. The driver had run away leaving six dead and twenty-six injured, eleven of them seriously.

On a few occasions at night, the security delegates, who had to be called before any journey was made, refused to let us make the short trip to the hospital as the situation was just too dangerous and the police had advised us to stay put. Unfortunately the night nursing staff at the hospital would have to cope with the emergency until it was safe for us to come at dawn. No use having a dead surgical team. Once we heard prolonged gunfire late one night: a police car itself had been ambushed by bandits. One of the policemen had been shot in both knees and elbow. He subsequently lost his arm.

The surgery for gunshot wounds followed the regular pattern – thorough debridement of the wound, prevent infection, and only suture the wound after five days. Because of the large numbers of gunshot wounds at Lokichokio, I was gaining a lot more experience. It is not a simple injury to understand. In the old days of low-velocity guns, the bullet just drilled a hole as it entered and you could see the damage it had caused – 'It's only a scratch, Sheriff,!' But rifles evolved so that even though the bullets were getting smaller, their velocity was increasing until the ubiquitous Kalashnikov AK-47s, for example, were firing a 123-gram bullet at 730 metres per second, more than twice the speed of sound. The physics isn't difficult: the energy that the fired bullet possesses has the formula: mass x velocity squared, so double the speed and you quadruple the energy. And when the bullet hits, all that energy is transferred to human tissue when it stops the bullet. It doesn't just bore a hole, it causes a violent shock wave through the tissue, sometimes more than thirty centimetres distant from the path of the bullet. It's called cavitation, and the result is a huge area of dead tissue. If the bullet doesn't kill instantly there is the problem of pieces of clothing forced into the wound at the same time, plus shattered bone and bleeding arteries and the outcome is a gangrenous-infected wound which would readily kill the patient. There were also rumours that some fighters were dipping their bullets in snake necrotoxin to cause further injury. Some of the wounds we saw were certainly very slow to heal and resistant to surgery, but this was a hot, dirty and dusty place and patients were often malnourished and disease-ridden to start with. We admitted a patient who had trodden on a booby-trap – it was simply a nail hammered through a piece of wood. But I was told the nail had been poisoned, perhaps with snake venom, and it wasn't easy to dismiss this idea. Instead of the small hole in the foot healing quickly, the whole forefoot was gangrenous up as far as the mid-lower leg, the tissue was shrunken and yellow, almost skeletal, as though it belonged to an ancient mummy. It had to be amputated.

*Chapter 31*

# Shape-changer

As in all ICRC hospitals, the training of the locals was major policy. We had an ongoing teaching programme for the 150 local medical staff, specially training some of them to do wound debridements and others to do the anaesthetic. They were very good. Even something as specialized as spinal anaesthetics was possible. It didn't need any particular academic mentality, it needed practical skill, following the rules exactly, obsessive cleanliness and the ability to tell when something was beyond their capability. ICRC was not going to be here forever; the time would come when we would have to leave. Then there would hopefully be a basic but safe continuation of care which we had taught them; the alternative was little or no health care whatsoever. The training extended to physiotherapists, rehabilitation, laboratory technicians and blood transfusion staff.

Some of the local staff were Turkhana. We were invited to the home of one of our theatre nurses. He lived just outside the hospital rather than in the town of Lokichokio and I was surprised to see that his home was an impressive traditional Turka hut, made completely of brushwood and thatch. Around this he had staked his claim to an acre of land which he had fenced with interwoven thorn branches to keep his half dozen cows in. I asked him why he'd kept his herdsman's occupation now that he was working for ICRC and drawing what was a relatively very good wage.

'ICRC won't always be here,' he said, 'but I will.'

In contrast, a ward nurse from Nairobi who was sending all his money back home to his family, showed us where he was living in the town. It was a crude shelter made from old wooden fruit crates stacked to make a single room surrounded by the noise and litter of a hundred or more similar shacks with no sanitation or running water.

A significant part of our week was given up to teaching the local staff. But I had underestimated the power of deep-seated ancient tribal traditions. We had a hut put aside for what we euphemistically called the School of Nursing. One day I was lecturing to a group of six of them about the cardiac and respiratory systems. I described the circulation of the blood, the way the heart works, the way the lungs allow oxygen to perfuse into the blood. I asked questions and they had a good basic medical knowledge and were obviously understanding the physiology very well. We had a small written test. The marks were good. At the end I asked if they had any questions.

A girl put up her hand: 'Can you advise on a medical problem with someone in my village?'

'Of course, please go ahead.'

'Well, he is an *ilimu*.'

'I'm sorry. What is an *ilimu*?'

'He is a shape-changer. Every month he turns into a wolf. What is the treatment?'

They must have thought I had shape-changed into stone.

To the patients, some of our routine techniques probably seemed like magic. We had a lot of small children to anaesthetize. They would be brought to the theatre, carried in by mother, and they were inevitably crying, some even kicking and screaming. The children never liked needles so we used a technique I'd used in Cambodia and Afghanistan. We would keep the syringe of ketamine hidden and as the child entered through the theatre door we would give them a quick intramuscular injection into the bottom with the smallest needle. Even the mother didn't see it. The child hardly seemed to be aware of it but the mother would be amazed as we took the child from her; the screaming would stop within a minute and the child was unconscious almost before reaching the operating table. The mother's look said it all, 'How on earth did you do that?'

Sometimes traditional superstitions can be used to advantage. I heard of one doctor working in Africa who had several patients with depression and psychosomatic illnesses. He had no modern pharmacy to hand, but someone had mentioned that in that part of the world devils were thought to be green. So he'd given his patients a dose of phenolphthalein, a harmless acid/alkali indicator. It goes in as a colourless liquid but in the urine in comes out bright green. The green devil thus left the patients via the urine and they started to feel much better. A unique placebo.

An anaesthetist friend of mine was working in another refugee field hospital. He wasn't doing too well because he had competition from the local witchdoctor who was bad-mouthing western medicine and this anaesthetist in particular – his medicine was weak and useless and the witchdoctor was far ahead when it came to powerful treatment. One day the anaesthetist had a patient for debridement of a leg wound. The patient wasn't happy and it took a long time to persuade him to get up on the operating table. The anaesthetist gave him a spinal anaesthetic: he anaesthetized the skin, then introduced the long spinal needle between the vertebrae of the patient's back. He had just injected a couple of millilitres of anaesthetic into the patient's spinal fluid. It normally takes a minute or two for the anaesthetic to block all the nerve fibres that go through the spinal canal and supply the muscles and sensory nerves from the waist down. The patient didn't wait: he'd had enough and suddenly jumped off the table walked out of the theatre into the hospital compound telling everyone he was going to the witchdoctor instead. The anaesthetist had had enough as well. He simply followed the patient out into the compound, looked at his watch and did a quick estimation for his timing. He called out to the patient and said he was so offended by this behaviour that he would put a curse on the man and take away the power of his legs for – another quick estimation of when the spinal would wear off – the next couple of hours. The patient suddenly found his feet tingling and the power drained away from his legs and he crumpled to the floor. The crowd was impressed to say the least. The apologetic patient was brought back to the theatre, had his operation and was so grateful when his legs came back to life later that he humbly presented the anaesthetist with a basket of eggs. Problem solved. From that day on, the street cred of the anaesthetist was unmatchable and the witchdoctor kept well away from this awesome magician. Quite what the General Medical Council in the UK would have made of it is a different matter.

Sometimes I thought we went too fast and the local staff struggled with scientific principles. We had a small problem with blood transfusions. They were taking the bottles of blood straight from the refrigerator at 4°C and transfusing it cold. This is not good. Not only does it make the veins collapse and slow the transfusion, it doesn't do the physiology any good, can interfere with the blood clotting mechanism and can actually cause hypothermia even at tropical temperatures. I asked the nurses if they could warm the blood a little before infusion. I found later they decided the best method was to wrap the bottle in a blanket. That would warm it up. I was tetchy that day: it was exceptionally hot weather and even after the years in the tropics I still get tetchy when hot.

'Why on earth will wrapping something cold in a blanket warm it up? It will just insulate it and keep it cold,' I asked in exasperation. 'Why didn't you ask one of us expats what to do?'

'The nurse from Finland told us that was the way to do it.'

I apologized with my head in my hands.

Sometimes on missions, when the work was done, we'd be relaxing outside the operating theatre in the hospital compound, and there always seemed to be children around. I used to do the odd magic trick to make them laugh. I have a cousin who performs magic professionally, and he taught me how to make a coin disappear from the palm of my hand; simple stuff but kids used to love it and ask for more tricks then try to work out how it was done. We were sitting outside in Lopiding one evening, having a break from operating and having something to eat. Children were playing around us but they were a little too cautious to approach us as some of us were relatively new faces. So I got them to come nearer with a smile, took out a coin and made it disappear. I then took it out of a kid's ear. Gasps of surprise. Routine children's party stuff. Then I reached into the thatched roof of the veranda above us and retrieved another coin, and another. It's not difficult when you know how. The kids were mesmerized, staring at me with wide eyes. Quite a crowd was gathering. I took the coin and again made it disappear but this time reached inside the bag of fruit we'd brought, took out a banana, handed it to one of the children and got him to peel it and inside the banana was the coin. Believe me, it's a very easy trick, but this was too much for the children. No laughter here – they backed off warily. The concept of a party trick was completely unknown to these youngsters – to them it was very real. For quite a long time afterwards, they avoided me whenever I walked by in the hospital. I heard them whisper '*Maganga!*', 'witchdoctor', more than once. There was another unwanted consequence. Next day someone had to stop children climbing up to the roof of the veranda and pulling the thatch to pieces trying to find more coins there.

A few weeks into the mission, there was an unpleasant incident. One of the Dutch nurses had left her bag in the operating theatre changing room. It had forty dollars in it. At the end of the day the dollars were missing. It was not as one might think an unsafe thing to do to leave money in a bag like that, because the trust and respect we shared with the Turkhana had made it unthinkable that anyone would steal from us. That evening over dinner we discussed what we should do. It was not easy. The money could have been taken by one of the local staff working in theatre, or by a patient, or a patient's relative, or simply some opportunistic thief walking into the hospital off the street. It could have been one of the other expatriates. Someone checked the *Red Cross Handbook*, the bible of how to manage problems in the field. No answer there in the FAQ section. The important thing was not to offend anyone, not to jeopardize the good relations that had been nurtured over the past few years. The best solution we could come up with was to forget all about the money and make sure all valuables were safe in future; but there would always be left that seed of mistrust over the unsolved crime.

The next morning we thought of another idea. I had a quiet word with our chief theatre nurse, Marotso, who was a very clever and sensible man and was held in high regard by other staff in the hospital. He was shocked and disappointed when I explained about the theft. I told him we couldn't think of a diplomatic solution. He nodded then said that he might be able to help – he had a cousin who would provide the answer and get the money returned. It turned out that his cousin was a *maganga*, a real one, and very well respected, in fact he was a greatly feared one. A few weeks before, someone had stolen one of his goats and he had publicly put a curse on the thief. The one who'd stolen the goat had killed and cooked it, but when he took the first mouthful, he had choked – to death. The *maganga*'s reputation was riding very high at that moment. The next day, between operations, Marotso, called us to the door. A large crowd had gathered in the courtyard outside where his cousin was chanting and dancing, shouting at the crowd and drawing in the dirt with his stick. Marotso explained that he was saying that he was disgusted with whoever had stolen the Dutch nurse's money and that he was preparing a curse for the one who'd stolen it which would kill the thief in the middle of the night. By six o'clock in the evening of the same day, the forty dollars had re-appeared in the Dutch nurse's bag. Put that in the Red Cross management guidelines.

We sometimes made assumptions when treating Sudanese from small villages and we didn't make allowances for the fact that they had no health facilities whatsoever and no experience of any sort of modern medical treatments. A father from one such village brought his son to the outpatient clinic. The small boy had a small scalp wound which had got dirty, was slow to heal and had become a little infected. The wound was cleaned well, and as the child said the wound was sore we gave the father a packet of paracetomol with instructions to come back every day for new dressings. We were starting to get concerned after the third day that the wound wasn't healing even after all the cleaning, in fact the wound now had a white discharge coming from it. Some antibiotics were given. A week passed and the wound was still discharging. It was decided to take the child to theatre to have the wound probed and infected tissue removed. But when the surgeon put a pair of forceps into the wound he pulled out a soft white mass that was the cause of the discharge – it was what was left of a paracetomol tablet. The father had quite logically assumed that the tablet should go where the pain was. It had never occurred to any of us to tell him to give it by mouth.

Despite the years of experience in the field, I still made the odd mistake. I drove to the hospital one morning, down into the broad long-dried-up riverbed which was about fifty metres wide. The hospital gates were immediately on the far side but there were a few ambulances standing outside the gates and no room to either get past them or to park. So I stopped the car on the flat sandy surface of the riverbed and walked the few metres to the hospital. An hour later, one of the local hospital security men came to me and advised me to move the car. Why? There were dark clouds far away on the horizon in the direction of the Ethiopian

Highlands. The skies above us were the usual brilliant deep blue without even a wisp of cloud. It hadn't rained in Lokichokio for more than a year. I said I thought he was being far too fussy. I'd move it after we'd finished the morning's operations. He insisted on taking my car keys and hurried to move the car up into the hospital. I looked out of the window and noticed people were moving their tents out of the riverbed. Twenty minutes later, still with blue skies above us, the riverbed was a torrent of brown, wild, frothing water carrying whole trees and debris with it. The flash flood was caused by the heavy rainfall many miles away up in the hills. I heard that often tents, vehicles, cattle and humans had been caught before and never seen again. We couldn't cross the river at the end of the day and the next day the rains came. We were stuck in the hospital for forty-eight hours. African thunderstorms have to be seen to be believed. The rain hits the corrugated roofs like stones and it is almost painful to walk out in it. The sandy ground of the hospital compound turned to slimy mud. The rain was more than overdue and we could hear the Turkhana singing, I suppose, in welcome. And for once it wasn't due to the ketamine. The shooting during the night stopped for a few days, or maybe the sound of the rain was just louder.

I made another mistake in exactly the same place and I should have known better. I'd bought myself a stool. Turkhana tribesmen always seem to take with them two indispensable items – a very long curved stick to control the cattle and a very small stool, called an *ekicholong* like a long, elongated, oval yoyo or diablo, used instead of sitting on hot, stony ground. I was driving to work one day and reached the dry riverbed where I saw a very elderly Turkhana tribesman, stick in hand, sitting on his *ekicholong* stool, I had to have a photograph so I went up to him and asked him in what I thought was good Swahili,

'Can I take your photo?' I asked. He nodded.

There was obviously a misunderstanding because as soon as I took the photo, the irate Turkhana stood up and started throwing stones at me. I made a dash for the hospital gate. At least it brightened up the bored gateman's day. He lectured me to be very careful photographing these people. I know, but I've only been at this game for twenty years. Slow learner. And I should be thankful: at least no one ran over my camera with a tank.

Not everyone held ICRC in high regard. The local pastor at the church in Lokichokio told me about an African evangelical worker who had asked to distribute bibles to patients in Lopiding Hospital a few years ago. He had been refused. So he had widely broadcast his opinion that 'the Red Cross despite its emblem is anti-Christian'. I could take his point. There again, ICRC is very protective of its neutrality, not just politically but religiously, especially in the case of the Sudan conflict where the 'other side' in the north is Islamic. It cannot be seen to even slightly favour one side or its creed. In fact the evangelist soon solved his problem. He came back to Lopiding with a truckload of medical supplies which he was donating to ICRC. While he was delivering the medicines, he left the doors unlocked and let it be known that also in the truck was a large number of bibles. When he returned he was very pleased to see that his truck had been looted.

There was a story of an ICRC feeding programme in the region involving a large number of villages, but one village had been forgotten – these villages weren't on any maps and it was quite easy for any aid agency to simply not know they were there. One of the delegates was journeying along a dusty desert road far from anywhere with his local driver in an ICRC Land Cruiser, all white with prominent red crosses an each side and on the bonnet with a large Red Cross flag flying from the radio aerial. They came across a group of six men standing in the road and it soon became apparent that they were armed. They stopped the ICRC vehicle and the local driver got out to talk to them. He came back and told the delegate, that the armed men were waiting for the first Red Cross car to come along. They said they were very angry that ICRC had not included them in the feeding programme and they were going to shoot every Red Cross person they came across. The delegate broke into a cold sweat, but the driver told him just to keep calm – he would talk to the gunmen and see what he could do. He went back to the gunmen and, after a short conversation, came back to the car, started the engine, told the delegate it was all okay and drove off again down the road. It was a mile or so further on when he knew they were safe that the delegate finally asked the driver what he'd said to the gunmen.

'I told them you are not the Red Cross, you are a Swiss diplomat, with the Swiss flag of a red cross on a white background. The flag they should be looking for is a white cross on a red background.' The gunmen had apologized. It was only another few miles down the road that the relieved delegate suddenly wondered what would happen if some real Swiss diplomats did come down that road. Or Médecins Sans Frontières, come to that.

# Chapter 32

# Into Sudan

I soon did my first of several medical evacuation trips into southern Sudan by plane. It was a long day. The medical delegate who ran these visits was a tough German Swiss nurse called Annelise. Five of us – two medics, a field delegate and two pilots – took off in a small Twin Otter, white with red crosses on both sides and on both wings top and bottom, so there would be no mistaking who we were. These were dangerous skies to fly in.

We took off from Lokichokio airport. It was busy and we were held up in a queue as a series of six transports loaded with food aid took off before us. We flew low, northwards, deep into Sudan. It was a flat landscape, alternating between featureless brown earth dotted with thorn trees and sudden patches of luscious green. We passed over tiny settlements with perhaps three or four thatched *tukul* huts with mud walls. Cattle trails but no roads here. We flew over an incongruous huge, straight concrete canal, now dry, derelict and desolate. There had been many attempts by outside countries to exploit the oil reserves here but it was neither easy nor safe to do so.

We landed at the village of Koic, which was lucky to have a dirt airstrip, to drop off one of the ICRC detention delegates who was visiting some captured government soldiers and was concerned for their welfare. On we flew.

The next stop was the village of Thonyar but the pilots were having difficulty finding it. No radio beacons here and GPS wasn't as widely used as it is now in aircraft. There were no landmarks, no large towns and no motorways or railway tracks to follow. There was occasional low cloud and mist obscuring the ground. We saw a large river. Was that the White Nile? Glancing at the fuel gauge, we found the airstrip and landed at Thonyar. It was chaos. A huge, cheerful, disorganized crowd gathered round the aircraft. They had brought patients, many from miles away, for us to evacuate to Lopiding, but we had to be very selective. The plane was small and our hospital was overcrowded as it was. We could only take those patients back with us who needed serious surgical treatment. Minor injuries could be treated just as easily at the village clinic. While the pilots unloaded boxes of pharmacy supplies, dressings and medicine, Annalise and I examined each patient, lying on their stretchers on the red earth of the runway. No privacy here. The noisy crowd was tightly packed around us, pushing, trying to get a good view of the examination at close quarters, children in the front row. We had to keep asking them to give us some space. We saw thirty patients but only accepted two stretcher cases and three walking wounded. With each patient, Annalise would make a decision, and give a very firm 'No!' – low, disappointed moan from the audience or 'Yes!' – triumphant 'Yow!' from the crowd, as though it was some sort of raffle for a Caribbean cruise.

Then the crowd parted as they brought us another man on a stretcher. They told us he'd been shot in the back some weeks before and now he was paraplegic. The wound had healed well, but if the bullet had damaged his spinal cord, no surgical treatment of ours could help him. Annalise said no, we couldn't treat him at Lopiding. There was an air of tension now. The first-aid people from the village were pushing us to take him. He was some sort of VIP, either a military commander or a headman of a village in the area. We explained that paraplegics were better treated in their own village by their own family.

The tension increased but was broken by another arrival. It was a 28-year-old woman on a stretcher. She was seven months' pregnant and had been bleeding for the past twenty-four hours. She was very weak and looked very, very pale. I struggled to find a pulse. I hadn't done any obstetrics since 1976 as a junior doctor but it's reassuring how it all starts to come back. The placenta was prematurely separating from the uterus and the bleeding would continue until the baby was delivered. I decided to take her back with us to Lopiding for urgent Caesarean section. We got her on the plane but by now it was very overcrowded and I was having to step over patients, stretchers and crates of supplies. I almost tripped over a broken leg to get to the woman's arm to put up a drip and push intravenous fluids into her as fast as I could. But as the pilot started the engine and began taxiing along the airstrip, the woman started to go into rapid labour and I could see the baby being born. It was a breach delivery, bottom first. I got them to stop the plane. It was a quick delivery – the baby was very small and it was obviously dead. Fortunately the placenta followed immediately afterwards and I saw it was all in one piece; the empty uterus tightened up well, as it should, and the bleeding stopped. At least the mother would be fine now. I breathed a sigh of relief, so did Annalise and the pilots. I suddenly noticed one of the other patients, a man on a stretcher, in the crowded cabin; he couldn't really move out of the way and his face had been twelve inches from all this activity and blood and mess and placenta. He looked ashen and was not happy. We took the woman off the plane; she was stable now. We gave the village medics all the intravenous fluids we had on board. They were very competent and would look after her.

There was a last attempt to persuade us to take the VIP paraplegic. Annalise said a very feisty 'No!' and we taxied again to the end of the airstrip. As we took off and passed the wildly waving, cheering crowd, we were astonished to see the paraplegic man stand up and walk away with his stretcher under his arm.

We flew to Nyal to refuel and transfer the patients to an ICRC DHC-5 Buffalo aircraft which would take them directly back to Lokichokio. Time for a very belated lunch. The pilot shut the doors of the Twin Otter and sprayed the inside with pungent fly spray to kill the teeming mass of flies we'd also picked up. I couldn't taste what was in the sandwiches.

We flew on and the country below us changed to mile after mile of bright green swamp and small patches of open water. We landed at the village of Wathzek. This area was in government hands. It was very different, a quietly tense place, very hot with 100 per cent humidity and alive with biting horse flies. Everyone wore khaki fatigues. There was apprehension in the air as there had been fighting here very recently. We'd been asked by radio to come and pick up some wounded soldiers here. But no one seemed to know anything about them. We waited and waited. Then someone came to tell us that the soldiers weren't here. They were many miles away in some village in the swamp which didn't have an airstrip. They said that most of them had already died anyway and the rest would die soon. As we took off, no one waved. It had been a long day.

I did another medevac trip a few days later. There were two ICRC medic planes setting out from Lokichokio that morning. The Buffalo had one of the nurses, Debbie, on board. The other was the Twin Otter with Annalise who said her flight would be the most interesting, as the Buffalo had only one routine stop. So I chose the Twin Otter. We flew to Washjak, a very poor settlement with a dull, miserable atmosphere and the people dressed in rags. A little girl, blind, stumbled in the dirt. There were many cases of tuberculosis but we couldn't take these. We accepted three patients with gunshot wounds. We taxied to the end of the airstrip, but had to wait while the villagers chased off a crocodile slowly ambling along the runway.

On to Benshowa. There were twenty-two detainees here, government soldiers captured by one of the rebel groups. The prisoners were kept huddled together in two huts. On the flight with us was an ICRC detention delegate, Christa. She registered all their names as POWs. I examined them, they were cowed and looked very scared. Some of them had slight wounds, but not enough for surgical treatment. Christa, Annalise and I sat in chairs under the shade of a large tree with the rebel commander in charge and ten of his men. The commander was a large strutting man, dressed in immaculately clean khaki and a bright crimson beret, who looked like a prize fighter with attitude – imagine a cross between Idi Amin and Mike Tyson. He stood rather than sat at the head of the group with a Kalashnikov rifle held nonchalantly against his shoulder. Christa gave a speech about respecting the rights of prisoners according to the Geneva Convention and treating them properly.

The commander nodded and said in a drawl, 'Before, we used to shoot prisoners, now we have to keep them?'

'Yes,' said Christa.

'Then is the Red Cross going to provide extra food for us to feed them?'

'No.'

From the look on his face I could almost hear him thinking, 'Then we'll just shoot them all.'

The commander then told us about one of his own soldiers in another village, shot in the head, still unconscious, and the bullet was thought to be still there. Annalise said that she couldn't take him to Lopiding. There followed a prolonged discussion between the commander and Annalise which was turning into an argument. She called me in as a reinforcement. I explained that there was nothing we could do surgically: our surgeons were not trained in neurosurgery and anyway it was not simply a matter of digging a hole in the brain and taking the bullet out. That would probably cause even more damage. The commander continued to argue. Annalise continued to resist and stare him out with a look like steel. It was a face-off. I could see the commander tapping his finger against the trigger guard. For goodness sake, Annelise, I thought, don't go too far. Back off a bit. This guy could just as easily shoot us all as argue with us. She was a tough cookie. In the end he got bored and wandered off for something to eat. Let's call it a draw, shall we? We got back to the plane while we could.

We tried to land at Alebo but we heard on the radio that rains had washed away the runway. On the way home, we passed over a huge herd of hundreds of gazelle streaming away from the noise of the plane, down into a ravine and up the other side, magnificent against the background of the far off Ethiopian Highlands lit orange by the late afternoon sun. A strange paradox below us of beautiful nature and miserable humanity.

Back at Lokichokio airport I chatted to an ICRC mechanic and mentioned the rather disturbing day we'd had; perhaps I should have gone with the other plane. He disagreed. The Buffalo had come under fire. He told me the aircraft had been parked on the airstrip at Chalcot and had been strafed by a government jet several times. It had been the only plane on the runway, its Red Cross markings clearly visible. The crew and passengers, including our nurse, Debbie, had been standing outside the plane and had managed to run off into the bush and safety. He pointed to the plane at the side of the airfield. It had a gaping hole in the fuselage, where shrapnel had struck, gone right through the cabin and out the other side. It was only extreme good luck that there had been no patients on board at the time. There were more large holes in the wing and the landing gear had been hit. They had got the Buffalo in the air as soon as possible and limped back to Lokichokio and made an emergency landing. It was later declared a write-off and never flew again.

Flying into southern Sudan was always risky for ICRC. Later it had to suspend flights into Sudan after a rebel faction allied with the government seized one of our aircraft and detained three Red Cross delegates for more than five weeks. The year after I worked in Lokichokio, in 2001, a Danish ICRC pilot out of Lokichokio was killed when his plane was shot at on its way to Khartoum.

The state of some of the civilians coming in from Sudan was very poor – poor diet made worse by disease, and intestinal parasites. I saw a woman patient with the most severe anaemia I had ever seen. For her, a normal haemoglobin level, the test for anaemia, in the UK might be 120 grams per litre; 100 would be anaemia. I've seen patients as low as 80. This woman's was 23.

I presumed that by now I was hardened to the sight of any wound or disease that the developing world could possibly present. Nothing could shock me. But I was caught out. One morning, I was called to the out-patient hut to see a mother and child who had come into the hospital after days of walking from Sudan. The child was a 3-year-old girl and she was suffering from a condition called noma or cancrum oris. The cheek and the upper and lower lips on the right side of her face had been eaten away by this creeping disfiguring disease. The raw edges of retreating skin and muscle exposed her teeth and gums and made her face into an awful parody of a sardonic smile. Saliva dripped uncontrollably from her mouth. The child, who had once had a very pretty face, looked up at me with sad eyes. It was pitiful. Totally pitiful. My throat tightened up and I couldn't speak for a while. *Cancrum oris* means cancer of the mouth but it's not a cancer. It occurs particularly in sub-Saharan Africa especially in 2- to 6-year-olds. It seems to happen in malnourished children whose immunity to infection is greatly decreased, giving otherwise harmless bacteria the opportunity to take hold. The eating away of the face is relentless and it is difficult to reverse; it can take many months. Only then can limited attempts be made at some sort of surgical reconstruction of the face. It is estimated there are half a million children in Africa with cancrum oris. The child was too young to be aware of her appearance and the difficulties ahead, as she lay on her mother's lap, listlessly and hopelessly trying to suckle on a shrivelled, empty breast. We admitted her to the children's tent. She would have the open flesh thoroughly cleaned and for several months given a high-protein diet with folic acid and other vitamins to get her into a good physical condition before any surgery was considered. It would be a very, very long stay.

It's difficult not to have favourite patients in a hospital. As well as this child, there was an 18-month-old Sudanese girl called Panda, who spent two months in the ICU after a lion had tried to drag her out of her hut by the head. The mother had courageously thrown a blazing log at the lion who let go of the child. The severe scalp lacerations that resulted needed many operations and skin grafts taken from her legs. The child hardly cried but sat in the ward on her mother's lap with a serious expression. It became a challenge to make her smile at least once a day.

As the weeks went by it became even hotter and tempers frayed in the heat. The expatriate staff at the hospital unfortunately weren't getting on well. One surgeon was taking a keen interest in the surgical treatment of the condition known as vesico-vaginal fistula, usually a consequence of the lack of good obstetric and midwifery services in that part of the world. He was having cases flown in from Sudan. It is very specialized surgery and one of the other surgeons disagreed with him. He pointed out that the long time scale of the multiple operations needed meant that when the first surgeon left at the end of his mission, the other surgeons would be left with a lot of half-completed surgery. Besides, this was getting widely out of the ICRC mandate to treat only victims of war injury.

André had been showing signs of stress again – shouting at expatriate staff, with one of the theatre nurses in tears. He was complaining about the lack of blood for transfusion and threatened to drag donors in off the street. Worse still, he was shouting at local staff and actually pushed one of them out of the way. This was dangerous. At the next meeting we got an abject apology from him but perhaps another stay in Nairobi for him was due. I was rather grateful I wasn't the medical coordinator for this mission.

Halfway through my stay, I started feeling very ill with watery diarrhoea. Stool test showed amoebic dysentery again. By the next day I had become very dehydrated, which gave me a violent headache and I couldn't eat or drink because of vomiting. I sat in the nurses' office feeling dreadful and I decided I needed an intravenous drip. The surgical teams were very busy in theatre, so I put a drip up on myself in the back of my hand – this from someone who as a child hated injections and almost had a needle phobia. The problem was it didn't occur to me that you really need two hands to do it and certainly to fasten it down with a dressing. A nurse eventually walked into the office as I was struggling and helped. I had to apologize for what looked like someone giving themselves a fix in her office. She was impressed: she'd never seen anyone do a self-intravenous-cannulation before. I joked about how I was hopeless with needles at a younger age – I used to kick and scream and bite the doctor's fingers and my mother would say, 'Now stop that! You're forty years old and should know better!' The nurse said that anyone who still had a sense of humour couldn't be that ill. In fact, after rehydration, with two fast litres of saline infusion, it was amazing how well I suddenly felt. There were several other cases of dysentery among the expatriates over the next few days, and immediate intravenous drips were *de rigueur* and worked wonders. It must have just looked a bit odd for patients to come to the hospital and see the doctor operating with a drip in his arm.

For all the work we did, evacuating war wounded from Sudan and the surgery we performed on them, the mission was becoming, to my mind at least, flawed. It was now almost twenty years since I started the first mission in Cambodia and I felt more qualified now to express an opinion on it and advise at a higher level within the organization. It's not difficult to set up a field hospital in or near a war zone but it can be incredibly difficult to take it out again when the situation improves or even when the fighting stops completely. I thought we'd learned the lesson of Khao-i-Dang hospital during the Cambodian conflict. It was twelve years before that hospital could be closed.

As Lokichokio grew in size, the hospital was taking more and more patients from the town itself. We were becoming the permanent health service of a town we had ourselves created. But the number of wounded who were coming out of Sudan or who we were evacuating by air was becoming small by comparison. In fact if one stopped to think of the tiny percentage of war wounded who got to us compared to the thousands dying in Sudan, one would be in danger of becoming disillusioned. The idea was mooted both in Geneva and at Lokichokio that Lopiding could be justified by turning it into a 'training' hospital. Recruited surgical teams would spend some time at Lopiding getting familiar with war-wound surgery before moving on to what I suppose ICRC would have to call 'real war zones'. However, I'd seen the potential problems of this idea elsewhere. While training is necessary and goes on all the time in medicine and surgery in the general population, the idea of practising on a specific group of people doesn't sit easily next to medical ethics. And besides, I still remember when the unfounded accusation was levelled against ICRC in Quetta that we were sending our junior surgeons there to practise on the mujahideen. It was easy propaganda ammunition to fire at ICRC.

After I left Lokichokio at the end of mission, the hospital continued there for several years more, but it was clear that ICRC was keen to leave. In 2005, southern Sudanese rebels and the Khartoum government signed a treaty to end a twenty-one-year conflict that had claimed over two million victims. The following year, ICRC closed Lopiding Hospital and withdrew all its operations from Lokichokio. The orthopaedic workshop which had served more than 4,000 amputees was moved to Juba in Sudan.

The town of Lokichokio began to die when the aid agencies started to move out and into Sudan. They had been by far the main employer of local people. Flights from the airport became fewer and fewer. The town no longer had any purpose. It was becoming a ghost town. Most businesspeople were not local: they were urban Kenyans, primarily Kikuyus, or they were Somalis, and as an economic assessment commented, 'the spending power of the town's traditional inhabitants, the Turkhana, who are nomadic pastoralists, is minimal.' So the businesses started to pack up and move out, some of them taking advantage of the safer conditions in Sudan and the expected burgeoning of the economy there. The hope that Lokichokio would become a truck stop on the now safe and improved road into Sudan was perhaps too optimistic.

The hospital was handed over to the Kenyan Ministry of Health which had plans to keep it open as a regional clinic. The last I heard it lay empty and vandalized in an area which like the town of Lokichokio itself was turning back into desert.

Postscript: The optimism of 2005 about the future of the new nation, South Sudan, didn't last. Tribal rivalry routinely progressed to violence and in December 2013 a split in government forces precipitated South Sudan's own vicious civil war in what is probably the poorest country in the world. In 2014, I was back in South Sudan with a group of ICRC surgical teams working out of Juba, the capital, in very difficult and dangerous conditions. Some of us remembered the relative safety of Lokichokio and began to regret that we'd closed the hospital there.

# PART 10

# AN EARTHQUAKE IN THE FOOTHILLS OF THE HIMALAYAS: PAKISTAN, 2005

MUZAFARRABAD - PAKISTAN

## Chapter 33

# Tremors

*The recent tremors felt by the residents of Karachi's coastal belt should not be construed as a prelude to any major earthquake as such minor seismic activities are a common phenomena to any seismically active region.*

Pakistan Government Statement: 26 September 2005

On 8 October 2005 at 8.50 a.m. a severe earthquake measuring 7.6 on the Richter scale occurred in northern Pakistan with its epicentre nineteen kilometres north-east of the town of Muzaffarabad.

Affected population: 4 million
Seriously affected: 1 million
Homeless: 500,000
Deaths: 75,000
Injured: 100,000

In geological terms, the sub-continent of India/Pakistan has, for the last fifty million years, been colliding against Asia and pushing up rock into what we know as the Himalayas. In the time scale of earth's history, this devastating earthquake was just one of the millions of relatively small and insignificant crunches that have occurred since.

I got the call from the British Red Cross one afternoon a few days after the earthquake and was asked if I could leave for Pakistan the next day to join an ICRC surgical team which was being sent out for about four to six weeks to treat victims of the earthquake. After a hurried call to an understanding anaesthetic secretary at the hospital in Hereford, I was in London the next day for a short briefing, the usual immunizations for cholera, meningitis, rabies but not babies, diphtheria, tetanus and polio. They asked if I could take some of the injections with me – second doses etc (buy yourself a vacuum flask to keep them cool, it will be very hot in Pakistan), and would it be possible to inject them into myself at the correct time? No problem, I said proudly, you're talking to a man who puts intravenous drips up on himself. I can do it with one hand tied behind my back.

By the same evening I was on the overnight flight to Islamabad. My thoughts on the plane were that it was good not to be going into another war-zone for a change. As one gets older, life seems to get more valuable. I also felt I'd had more than my share of luck and didn't want to tempt fate much more.

I arrived after a crowded, tiring seven-and-a-half-hour flight at half past five in the morning. Other medics arrived on other European flights in quick succession. There were one or two old Red Cross friends. Other aid agencies were coming in and I recognized some old faces among them too. The surgeon I would work with was Harald, a Dutchman with previous ICRC experience, and who'd worked at the same hospital as me in Shetland. We medics get around. An ICRC minibus was waiting to take the seven of us into Islamabad to the main ICRC delegation. When we arrived we found it didn't open for another two hours. You could tell even now the ones who were the beginners and those who'd done a few missions before – some got agitated discussing who they should phone, some of us sat on the veranda, feet up in the cool morning sun and waited for someone to turn up. Sarah, a Swiss anaesthetic nurse on her first mission, said she didn't know who her anaesthetist was and she was very wary about meeting him. I told her not to worry – it was me.

The 'welcome service' lady eventually arrived so we welcomed her. She looked hassled – before the earthquake this was a quiet posting. We had another briefing and we were asked if we'd all brought sleeping bags and warm clothing?

'Well, no, we were told it was hot.'

'No, it will be minus five degrees at night. Your national societies should have told you that, and by the way there's no food in the delegation so you'll have to go into town and buy some. You'll leave for Muzaffarabad by helicopter this evening.'

So we took a taxi into town to eat but it was Ramadan so the shops were closed. But eventually we found a small bakery, run by a Hindu, which was selling coconut macaroons. And there was a clothes shop next door run by his brother who could sell us sleeping bags and very garish, almost fluorescent, warm clothes which would certainly never be worn again back home.

We then had a phone call from the delegation asking us to get back there right away. The plans had changed. It had been decided that they would now send four of us by road to the large town of Abbottabad, thirty-five miles south-west of the epicentre. It had a large hospital where many of the injured had been taken. We climbed into the ICRC minibus with our luggage. But then a medical team from the German Red Cross arrived. They were told to come with us in the minibus. There was a lengthy rearrangement of all our luggage so that the enormous amount of theirs could be packed in and we all tried to squash in together. The natural leader of the German team was a frightening large nurse called Heidi who had a feisty attitude. She said we couldn't all fit into one minibus and demanded another one for the German team. No one in the delegation was prepared to argue with her.

Harald and I looked at each other: 'I'll bet she opens glass ampoules with her teeth.'

Actually we grew quite fond of Heidi, she was a superb, ultra-efficient nurse.

All the luggage was taken out of the minibus, the German suitcases and rucksacks were identified, and ours were put back in. We were off, engine started, just driving out of the gates when Heidi reappeared. She stood, legs apart in front of our bus, hands on the bonnet. The second minibus was unavailable: we would all travel together in this minibus and our luggage would follow when the other bus was available. Out came our luggage again.

Tempers were getting frayed, voices were getting raised. Harald and I were relaxed and thought it was quite funny and tried not to smile. I put my sunhat over my eyes and thought I'd have a doze and catch up on my sleep. After all, what was the problem? We'd get there eventually, no one wanted to shoot at us, there weren't likely to be landmines ahead, and I had a bag of coconut macaroons.

In fact the four-hour journey up the Karakorum highway into the hills to Abbottabad was dangerous even without landmines: the roads were very crowded and often narrow, we were travelling very fast but other cars were overtaking us. Coming the other way, cars were overtaking other cars, even on blind bends, and everyone was constantly sounding their horn.

We miraculously reached Abbottabad and our rundown, sparse but very clean hotel which served a decent meal. No suspicion of Osama bin Laden being a resident at that time but he was probably in town. We all went for a short walk down the street; it was a poor area of town and there was little of interest. I suspect it very rarely had European visitors because everyone stared at us. Or perhaps it was the odd clothes we'd just bought.

I went to bed early at half past eight, but was woken suddenly at 2.21 a.m. by an earth tremor. I'd never felt one before and being asleep I couldn't be sure it wasn't a dream. But it was real. The bed shook from side to side for a few seconds. It was an aftershock and I knew they were common after a major quake. I heard the next day that it measured 5.5. The next morning during breakfast up on the roof café we felt another aftershock of 5.8. We decided to take our breakfast and eat it in the open courtyard below.

We were met by the Finnish medical coordinator Pertti, whom I'd worked with in Lokichokio in 2000. He took us to the main hospital in Abbottabad which had also suffered some damage from the quake; we saw half a dozen less well-built houses in rubble and a large petrol station demolished but fortunately the fuel hadn't ignited. We were surprised when we drove into the hospital grounds, every inch of lawn and tarmac was filled with patients on stretchers in the open air, maybe 200 of them with all their relatives milling around, feeding them, shading them from the sun.

Pertii went inside to talk to the hospital staff. He returned to tell us that the hospital building was unsafe, we were shown great earthquake cracks in the walls which is why many of the patients had been moved outside.

It was decided we would join the Finnish and German teams and travel to Muzaffarabad. Four minibuses were procured and after more repacking we all squashed in for the four-hour journey. It was spectacular, the mountains became higher, the views more dramatic as we drove gradually into the foothills of the Himalayas. A flat green valley would end with a steep tortuously winding road up over a mountain ridge and down into another valley with a town laid out before us. Then up again.

The high road suddenly emerged out of the hills to reveal a dramatic panorama of the town of Muzaffarabad below us. A town about the size of Bath, it nestles in the valleys where the Jhelum and Neelum rivers meet coming from the high mountains and adjoining Kashmir. Pertii pointed out a cricket stadium on the far side of the town; we were surprised to hear that was where the ICRC hospital was being erected.

The town looked intact from a distance. It was only as we drove into the streets themselves that we saw the awful devastation. Hardly any building seemed to be undamaged, whole houses had sunk into rubble; a whole apartment block, up against the side of a hill had simply slipped down into the road. Rubble had been partially cleared from the major roads, but many were still blocked.

The hospitals in Muzaffarabad were trying to cope with all the injured from the town, but many clinics and the University hospital itself had been damaged. And it was expected that there would soon be a massive influx of wounded from the outlying districts and up in the mountains. These areas were so remote and the road infrastructure so damaged that the wounded were still painfully making their way in to get help. We stopped at the main ICRC delegation, a large rented private house; it was crowded and bustling with activity – medical, food aid, sanitation, displaced persons, tracing delegates – all overworked, trying to get an ICRC Land Cruiser, trying to get the use of the satellite phone …

'It's no use sending the tents to Abbottabad, I need them here in Muzaffarabad!'

We were supposed to be sleeping here, but all the rooms were used as offices; there were sleeping bags rolled up and piled in the corners of each room. People were simply sleeping on the floor where they worked. We decided we were better trying our luck at the hospital. The hospital was a truly amazing sight. The town's cricket ground was a majestic affair. It was not just a field. Pakistan is devoted to cricket and they had been in the process of improving the site by building a full-size stadium with high concrete terraces all the way round for seats, a grandstand at one end. There was a formal gated entry but the terrace buildings still had scaffolding up and only part of the concrete walls had been faced with marble, yet the cricket matches had continued – until we arrived. But now it was the perfect place for a field hospital. It had a large open area as flat as – well, as flat as a cricket pitch – with no nearby buildings to fall down on us with the aftershocks, but the solid terracing around us made a secure compound and we could control all entry through the one gate. Even though we weren't in a war zone, security was taken very seriously. One of the spectator terraces was covered with half an acre of brightly coloured clothes. They had been donated by some charity who hadn't thought about how they were going to distribute them so they had dumped them here. A few people were picking about among them but the best clothes had already gone and recent rain had made a sodden mess of the rest.

ICRC was building its tent hospital in the middle of this stadium, and even after seeing so many Red Cross field hospitals, this was the most miraculous. It was a race to be ready for when patients arrived and a race against the weather: rain was forecast. Within three days it was complete, accepting patients and fully functioning. It was a famed Norwegian Field Hospital. Everything needed was dropped by helicopter on site. The organization was superb. All the wooden crates were colour-coded and numbered – green was for nursing equipment, yellow for the operating theatre, there were X-ray crates, laboratory crates, electric lighting and cable, steel wash-basins contained in crates which themselves unfolded ingeniously to form their own washstands. All the other crates could become beds or tables. Nothing was wasted. The tents were huge, consisting of rows of aluminium frames bolted together and covered with canvas. When everyone helped with the tent-raising, you could have set it to the music for the film *Witness*. It was all like a gigantic flat-pack from IKEA. It meant hard work from dawn to dusk, no hot water, meals grabbed when you could, sleeping under canvas – morale was sky high. It was one of the most enjoyable things I've done with the Red Cross.

We had local men as guards on the front gate. One of them was an avid cricket fan and this was his home ground. He couldn't believe the damage we were doing to the surface.

'Please not across the pitch!' he shouted, running towards the digger which was making a drainage ditch across the wicket.

Trucks and cranes were leaving deep ruts in the surface. When he saw a JCB digger excavating very deep holes for the latrines, he sat down on what was left of the turf, his head in his hands. You could feel for him. We reassured him it could probably all be put back to its original condition but I believe the idea was to leave this tented hospital where it was after the mission had finished and donate it to the town's health authorities. It's not worth the cost of removing these field hospitals for use elsewhere. It was finished ahead of schedule. Now we were ready for patients but there didn't seem to be any.

It was proposed at a meeting that we should accept any surgical patients, non-quake related, rather than waiting for quake victims. I had to stand up and make a point: shouldn't we just wait a day or two to see if quake victims started to come in rather than fill up beds we might need desperately soon enough. And haven't we learned lessons about exit strategy from previous ICRC missions, I said pointedly. I was also getting bolder with experience. The point was taken. Fortunately, as it turned out, because the next day the wounded started to come in.

# Chapter 34

# Influx

When word got around that we were here, the trickle of patients became a flood. We had three surgical teams working, with an on-call system for the few patients that came in during the night, although in one case a truck full of wounded arrived at two in the morning. Everyone suddenly seemed to have second careers thrust upon them. I was sharing my time between anaesthetics and running the X-ray tent – the expected Japanese radiographer had been delayed. It was a case of trying to work out by trial and error how to get the X-ray machine to work, and even more complicated developing the prints in baths of developer and fixer like the old days of photography. A lesson learned: don't use chlorinated drinking water to make up the developer – it makes terrible prints.

I loved the idea of just getting on with it. Forget your medical specialty, if there's other work to be done and you feel competent, just get on with it.

Two days after the opening we had eighty patients in the wards, twenty-four operations a day, and we would soon be running out of bed space. But having experienced regular bed shortages in UK hospitals, there was something refreshing about saying, 'We'll just erect another tent.' We had an obstetric tent for deliveries, displaced people still have babies, but these were few and far between so that tent became another post-op ward and the obstetric nurses turned their roles into trauma nurses. Versatility – we were on top form and knocking sixes over the boundary! Within a week we had over 200 patients.

There were more women and children patients than we expected. The earthquake had happened in the early morning when they were inside their houses; a lot of the men were outside and escaped injury. The children especially had some horrific injuries where the roofs had collapsed on them. They suffered crush injuries to the limbs, abdominal injuries that needed laparotomies. These types of cases soon became less frequent, I suspect because they were dying before they could reach the hospital.

There were large numbers of fractured legs in children. They were treated conservatively with traction for weeks on end. This meant the legs would be fastened up onto a high bar at the foot end of the bed and the weight of the pelvis just off the surface of the bed would pull down on the fracture site and re-align the ends of the broken bone. There was a whole tent full of small children in two rows, all with legs up in the air. It sounds medieval but in fact it makes the fracture more comfortable and is remarkably effective. The main problem for the children is boredom. But children's entertainer is a good alternative profession and my simple magic tricks go a long way when it comes to children – and adults for that matter.

As anaesthetist, I worked mostly with Sarah, the Swiss assistant. She was very competent with a safe pair of hands and we were using simple ketamine anaesthetic for the most part, but she confided to me she was finding it difficult without the usual equipment. How do you manage without ECG and all the other modern monitoring devices? I showed her how we did it in the old days (I was starting to sound like an anaesthetic antique) – keep your finger on the patient's pulse, feel the condition of the skin, watch the patient instead of the monitor. In other words, use your own senses. I felt I was teaching someone who was used to flying a Boeing 747 how to handle a Sopwith Camel.

'How do you measure respiration?' she asked.

I sellotaped a piece of cotton to the patient's nose to show her.

'That's wonderful, who taught you that?'

'Would you believe a 13-year-old girl from Cambodia?'

A flashback and I hoped the girl had survived. She'd be a 37-year-old woman by now. I wondered if she took up medicine.

Sarah was soon doing spinal anaesthetics, something she wouldn't normally be allowed to do in Switzerland. But she had the skill. It's not an easy procedure and when she started having a bit of difficulty with them and a few failures, she said she was developing a psychological block. I said it was all a matter of confidence and a bit of luck. I used a bit of psychology on her in turn. I said there was a word I'd learned from a Japanese sage. If you fail with a spinal, just chant the mantra 'Shimata' and you'll always succeed next time (thank you Mariko). It worked – like a charm as it were – and she never looked back.

I saw some interesting pathology. There were a lot of goitres in patients here; it's a swelling of the thyroid gland in front of the throat due to lack of iodine in the diet. It's very rare now in the UK, but some of these were huge. They presented a particular anaesthetic hazard. The swelling can actually erode the delicate rings of cartilage that keep the trachea, the windpipe, open. An unsuspecting anaesthetist can give an anaesthetic, the muscles relax, the rings squash and the weight of the goitre closes the tube. Suddenly the patient can't breathe. With experience I was getting very wary of these conditions.

The work got easier as the days passed and we settled into a routine but still there were twenty operations or more per day. Nights in the tents were becoming a problem: nighttime temperatures were dropping well below zero and the sleeping bag I'd bought turned out to be very thin, but I managed to get hold of a Norwegian army bag which could keep anyone cosy at minus 20°C. Nighttime calls to the operating theatre became less frequent but finding the way to the loo in the dark with drainage trenches and tent guy ropes in the way was a challenge. Noise was the main obstacle to sleep. There was a small dog somewhere up on a hillside housing complex outside the stadium. Every night it would start yapping, then other dogs would join in until it sounded like Crufts, then there would be blessed silence for a while then the little dog would have another yap and it all started again. Then the muezzins would make the call to prayer in the early hours from the mosques, but never synchronously and never in the same key. Then the noise of trucks leaving early to drive up into the hills, all constantly sounding fanciful tunes on their horns.

There were soon many wounded and displaced people being brought to Muzaffarabad by helicopter from the more inaccessible areas. It was the only way in for some of them as many of the roads winding along the sides of the ravines had been destroyed by the quake. It was a huge operation. Helicopters were arriving regularly at the town's airstrip and there had to be some triage system of assessing them and deciding their needs: which of them needed emergency accommodation, which of them had minor injuries, which needed surgery. So we had a rota where one member of the surgical teams would spend the day at the airstrip, identify the surgical patients and send them on to the hospital.

I had my first day on the rota, driven through the town, it was good to get out of the stadium for a change, across an impressive mini-suspension bridge spanning a ravine and on to the airstrip. The army was in charge of the airfield and the first-line triage was done in a tiny airport office by four members of the Pakistan Medical Corps in their immaculate uniforms. They would call us in to assess the severely wounded. They were very friendly, and when I happened to mention that I'd forgotten my hat against the strong sun, one of them gave me his crimson beret as a gift – I still have it – but I'm not sure it was within ICRC guidelines to be wearing a military hat at the same time as an ICRC shirt badge. I invited him to visit the ICRC hospital. He did a few days later and was impressed. 'If only I wasn't in the army,' he said, 'this is the place I'd love to work in.'

The helicopters would sometimes land with only a few minutes between the next one bringing bewildered, traumatized hill people from their shattered communities. The helicopters were a motley international collection. As well as Pakistan Air Force ones and private varieties hired ad hoc by aid agencies, two

Chinooks landed with the markings of the US Air Force. The ICRC helicopter I saw had been loaned from Tajikistan. As they landed, their huge blades would stir up large clouds of dust, everyone tried to get into the office whenever there was a landing otherwise the swirling dirt would get into eyes and throats. Vendors sitting in the road outside the airstrip would curse and desperately try to cover up their wares and stop packets of cigarettes from blowing away.

I accepted thirty admissions that day, many fractured limbs, an horrific crushed arm in a 13-year-old girl, gangrene had already set in and she would lose the arm even after extensive surgery. Some had escaped fractures but had extensive skin loss where rock or concrete had stripped it away. One woman had had her arm trapped and the skin had been peeled from mid-forearm to her hand as if it was a glove that had been half-removed. As each group came in I would radio ahead to the hospital warning them what to expect as the ICRC ambulance shuttled back and forth all day with the victims.

A rescue team from South Africa arrived with patients and told us there were still 500 injured people up the distant Shakar valley, fifty of them seriously. There were other aid agencies with smaller field hospitals and we shared the patients between us. Two of the very small aid agencies seemed to feel rather neglected and got into the habit of running out to meet the helicopters to stake their claim. The rest of us didn't feel the need to take part in this rather undignified 'gold rush'. I was irresistibly reminded of the VolAg Archipelago on the Cambodian border. In fact one of these aid agencies later approached ICRC to ask if they could use some of our beds – they could do the surgery but hadn't got the facilities for post-op care. Sorry, but no, we're short of beds as well.

During a lull between landings we had tea with the Pakistan army doctors, one of whom told me that he'd been surprised and impressed that India had sent a convoy of aid trucks to help with the relief efforts. Tensions were still high between India and Pakistan over the long-running Kashmir dispute. We agreed that it's strange how something good can come out of catastrophe. In fact, he said, Pakistan Air Force rescue aircraft flying in the vicinity of the nearby no-fly zone of Kashmir had no trouble from India. The only minor incident was when a UN relief plane got lost and had inadvertently flown into India.

On a quieter day, some of us were taken to the centre of Muzaffarabad to get some idea of the destruction. All around the stadium were flattened houses. Walls collapsed and concrete roof slabs brought down with twisted metal rods pointing in the air, the remains of crumbled reinforced concrete. I had wondered why the deaths from this earthquake had been greater and the injuries more severe than previous equivalent earthquakes in Pakistan. The building methods had changed over the years: instead of brick walls and wooden roofs collapsing, it was now huge concrete slabs. We passed the ruins of the town's largest hotel and what was left of the university then into the old market area. Here the devastation was even more complete – the houses and shops were packed so close together that they had fallen against each other. It was impossible to go any further by vehicle. We had to go on foot. The streets were piled high with rubble and in fact it was a scramble over concrete blocks, heaps of bricks and the odd door or window, to get through most roads. We put on our ICRC badges so that we wouldn't be mistaken for gawping tourists. Piles of electric cable, hopefully not live, had fallen from above and were scattered over the top of the rubble. We occasionally smelled the stench of death – there were still bodies under the rubble. A side of a house had collapsed outwards; the table inside still had a half-eaten meal on it. At the remains of another house, on the pile of debris sat a man, listlessly sifting through what was left of his business.

We entered a ruined pottery shop, now half open to the sky, some of the pottery smashed but the rest miraculously still on display. It was untouched, there had been no looting. Suddenly a heavy electric-light fitting crashed to the floor behind us. These buildings were not safe and we hurriedly left. One half-ruined general store was still open. We chatted to the owner and explained what ICRC was doing. He said he'd lost a lot of his stock in the quake, and perhaps ICRC could replace it. Unfortunately not, but one of our group bought a couple of cheap cricket bats and plastic balls from him to play cricket in the stadium. He was on his first mission. We suggested he hide them away out of sight. An ICRC rescue team carrying cricket bats is not good publicity.

There was another purpose to the trip: we were delivering medical supplies to a small village clinic just a few miles outside town up the Neelum valley. The road wound its way into one of the steep valleys. It was obvious that there had been a huge landslide along here, all bare, newly exposed pieces of rock like a huge scree slope. The road snaked its way over the top of the scree. The traffic hugged the side of the road nearest the mountainside and for once very slowly and carefully; no one was driving near the edge and we knew that it wouldn't take much for this whole slope to slip down into the valley, taking the road and us with it. As we rounded a bend, we saw a hundred metres below us a yellow bus, overturned with multi-coloured clothes, what was left of luggage, scattered around it. At the next bend we could see right down to the river far below us at the bottom of the ravine. There had once been a steel suspension road bridge linking the two sides. It was now a twisted ruin of metal, evidence of the tremendous forces released by the earthquake.

Later I had the chance to fly with one of the rescue helicopters searching for more survivors up in the higher, more remote valleys. It was only from the air that I could see what the earthquake had done geologically to these mountains. The Himalayas are relatively young mountains, only 50 million years old which is recent in geological time. The Grampians by contrast have been there for 500 million years. The rocks in the Himalayas, because they are young, have had little time to settle and solidify. They are naturally still loose and crumbly. Together with the steepness of the mountains, this makes them unstable. Before the quake, they were green, covered with trees and vegetation. Now whole acres of mountainsides had slipped down into the ravines far below, leaving white scars where the underlying rocks were exposed. Many of these mountains had been home to scattered villages and they too had tumbled down the slopes, taking the inhabitants with them.

We made our first stop; flying low we saw someone waving a piece of bright red cloth to attract our attention. The problem was to find a flat piece of ground to land on, not easy for the pilot manoeuvring carefully and watching his rotor blades uncomfortably near the mountainside and scrawny trees appearing out of crevices. The man who had waved us down was a shepherd, and his wife lay injured in the remains of their stone hut. The roof had gone and the man had improvised a makeshift roof of shrub and odd pieces of plastic sheet. She had fractured her pelvis. Their small son had a crushed hand. Nearby was another fresh pile of rocks. It was the grave of their other small son. We took the whole family on board. Before we left, the shepherd took us a few hundred yards to his neighbour a little higher up the ridge. Here a stone hut had been completely destroyed. We were told his wife and children had all been killed as the earth had slipped away and plummeted a hundred metres below. His sheep and goats had gone too. He had nothing left at all. He was sitting on the pile of stones that had been his home and his life. He stared into space, trancelike, simply unable to stir himself. We took him with us and flew further up the valley.

We found another village perched on the mountain. They waved at us to land. This was quite different. Here was an 11-year-old girl with a fractured arm needing evacuation. The houses had suffered damage but they had started to rebuild. They showed us what they'd done – the first building they'd tackled had been the school; they told us it was the most important thing they had. Until it was finished, they were giving lessons to a group of small children sitting hunched up inside a pyramid of salvaged timbers covered with a large sheet of blue plastic.

As we made a third brief stop to take a woman with a shoulder injury, I was reminded how we sometimes take people at face value. We loaded the woman into the helicopter watched by a shepherd carrying a sheep across his shoulder who looked at the helicopter with awe as if this was something of the modern world far outside his primitive experience. The helicopter pilot told me he was trying to warn the hospital that we were on our way in, but he wasn't getting good radio reception here.

The shepherd came forward, nudged me with his elbow, reached inside his jacket pocket and said, 'Would you like to use my mobile phone?'

Apparently he used it to contact his brother way across the valley to save having to climb all the way down the ravine and back up the other side.

The pilot was trying to find out where we were on his map. The shepherd said, 'You can borrow this if you like,' and from his other pocket produced a GPS. On the flight back he said that according to his GPS his village had moved six metres northwards and six metres upwards after the quake.

The optimism we'd seen up in that village in the mountains was reflected in some of the patients in the hospital. During one of the daily ward rounds, I was chatting to a man in one of the wards; he looked very poor. His 10-year-old daughter was a patient with a broken leg. I said how awful it was for him to have lost everything – his house and livelihood had been completely destroyed.

'But I've not lost everything,' he said. 'I have my children and I spent all my money on their education. They still have that and nothing can take it away from them.'

'What do you most need?' I asked.

'Pencils and paper,' he replied

I noticed his daughter was writing on a pad. When I looked at it she was laboriously writing all the English words she was hearing during the ward rounds. Education is highly valued in Pakistan and not taken for granted. I would love to know what eventually became of the man's daughter.

The German Red Cross team was running a clinic just outside the cricket ground in a large house they were renting. It had a few beds inside as a small ward. It seemed that Heidi had taken control. Every evening, we would hear the muezzin calling the faithful to prayer and we would hear Heidi calling out, 'All members of the German team to the 9 p.m. meeting. Now!' We thought she was using a megaphone, in fact she was just talking into her radio. We were always running short of beds even though the constructors were erecting new tent wards as fast as they could. Someone dared to ask Heidi if we could use the German team's ward as a temporary measure. Certainly not. It became quite a contentious issue. One of the Norwegian surgeons asked if I ever watched *Fawlty Towers* then added: 'Whatever you do, don't mention the ward!'

After a month, towards the end of mission, there were fewer admissions. New teams were coming to replace us. Harald, Sarah and I got into the habit before the evening meal of walking round the outside of the stadium. We enjoyed strolling through the middle of one of the displacement camps, 200 or more tents in a jumble of human activity; there would be fires and primus stoves cooking the evening meal, children crying or playing, people carrying plastic water canisters from the standpipes. One evening two young girls approached us, giggling. They offered us pieces of paratha bread. It was the end of Ramadan.

On the day the team left for home, we were driving to the airstrip, to an awaiting helicopter that would fly us directly back to Islamabad rather than going by car on the crazy roads. But on the way, in the centre of Muzaffarabad, was a traffic jam; police appeared, then a couple of gunshots, and crowds began to run past us. A man with a bleeding head was being marched away by the police. Sudden memories of missions in war zones. It was a demonstration that had turned violent. The demonstrators were protesting about the moving of some of the displacement camps out of the town and into the countryside. More gunshots, nearer this time, and the driver of our car did a difficult but fast three-point turn – along with all the other cars in the street and we headed back to the safety of the stadium. It was three hours before it was safe for us to do the journey to the airstrip.

While we were waiting at the hospital, I climbed up the terraces right to the top of the grandstand for a last look around. Outside I could see all the displaced persons camps, acres and acres of rows of white tents, each with a family whose lives had in a moment been dislocated. It was nearing winter and getting colder, it would be impossible for the hill-dwellers to go back up into the mountains now. This was no time for reconstructing their houses and their lives up there. They would have to endure the winter down here in the tents. Would they go back up in spring? It was easy to see how they might stay on in Muzaffarabad and become poor urban dwellers and a traditional way of life would be gone forever.

I looked back into the stadium. The sun was low now in the late afternoon, casting a bright, rich, orange glow on all the rows of ICRC tents that housed the hospital, the wards, the operating theatre and the laboratory, all with large red crosses on the roofs. It was an emotional sight. I felt an unexpected surge of pride. We had operated on perhaps 700 or 800 patients in a month, yet that was a very small proportion of the number injured during that earthquake.

# PART 11

# WAR IN THE POOREST COUNTRY IN THE WORLD: SOUTH SUDAN, 2014

South Sudan

# SOUTH SUDAN

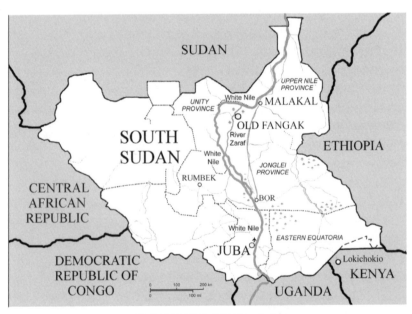

SUDAN

UPPER NILE
PROVINCE

UNITY
PROVINCE

White Nile

MALAKAL

OLD FANGAK

SOUTH
SUDAN

River
Zaraf

ETHIOPIA

White
Nile

JONGLEI
PROVINCE

RUMBEK

CENTRAL
AFRICAN
REPUBLIC

BOR

White Nile

EASTERN EQUATORIA

JUBA

DEMOCRATIC
REPUBLIC OF
CONGO

Lokichokio

KENYA

0    100    200 km
0    100 mi

UGANDA

# SOUTH SUDAN

# Chapter 35

# Security Level 'Extreme'

By 2014 I'd semi-retired from the NHS, my working week was a leisurely two or three days of easy anaesthetics in a small peripheral hospital away from the main hub of a very busy, fraught district hospital, away from long hours, missed lunches and the tiring nights on call. I had time to enjoy my spare time and enjoy an awakening spring of the Herefordshire countryside.

I'd assumed my time with the Red Cross in the field had now ended. Then a phone call came from the British Red Cross in April of that year asking me to help with the ICRC mission in Southern Sudan. They were having trouble recruiting experienced anaesthetists and needed someone for a short period to bridge a gap until they found one. I rather surprised myself by agreeing to do six weeks.

I'd always followed the news and progress about the countries I'd worked in. Sometimes the outcome was good. The Cambodia that I remember as a dangerous, blood-soaked, and hopeless place was now as peaceful as it ever was and a popular tourist spot. Other countries like the Sudan had gone the other way. After leaving Sudan in 2000, I was optimistic that the civil war would be resolved. It wasn't. Southern Sudan got its independence from Sudan in July 2011 and became a separate country with its capital Juba, but the violence continued and by 2013 the new country was at war with itself – the South Sudanese Civil War. Over 300,000 civilians have been killed in this war and over a million displaced. South Sudan is regarded as the poorest country in the world.

I was used to the routine. There was a preliminary series of briefings at the British Red Cross headquarters in Moorfields in London. I was told there was not much information from the ICRC headquarters in Geneva but I'd be a member of one of the three surgical teams. *However*, the country was unstable. Recently a team had hurriedly had to leave the town of Malakal in the north because of the fighting. These northern states, Jonglei, Upper Nile and Unity, were reported as unsafe. The security delegate told me their security situation was now classed as 'extreme'. I was getting a sense of *déjà vu*, very familiar from previous missions – the feeling of 'what have I let myself in for here?'

*But*, this was not really a problem, I was told, as I'd be working in the far south, in the capital, Juba. Good.

*However*, Juba was tense. The government was in control but there were constant threats from opposition forces outside.

*But*, I'd be safe as I'd be working in an ICRC hospital inside the main ICRC compound with high walls and good security. The hospital was clean and pleasant with air-conditioning, they said. That's nice.

*However*, Juba had been attacked by the opposition three months previously and all the ICRC staff had to leave in a hurry via UN planes – most having to leave all their luggage behind. I had a flashback to Somalia.

*But*, the Sudanese are very friendly and welcoming. Good to know. Have I used up my nine lives yet, I asked myself?

I flew via Addis Ababa with a six-hour stopover. It was pleasantly warm and I mistakenly thought the climate in South Sudan would be similar. Ethiopia is at a high altitude, South Sudan is not. As I sat in the scheduled Ethiopian Airlines plane to Juba, I had the feeling that I was now used to – flying into a war zone.

I could make out a large, winding river glistening on the dull greyish-green ground. It was the White Nile. We descended towards the light brown smear on the western side of the river that was Juba. It felt very, very hot: 36°C when we landed at Juba airport. And it would get hotter.

The immigration and baggage hall was a small bungalow a long, hot walk from the runway – no airport bus was available. The hall was crowded and disorderly. I stood in the immigration queue. It took twenty minutes to get to the desk to be told I was in the wrong queue. Two more queues and thirty minutes later I had a precious visa stamp in my passport that had cost US$100 precious cash. Another queue for baggage claim and miraculously my luggage had arrived straight through from Heathrow – I was amazed. But there was no one to meet me. I sat on my case outside the airport with my Red Cross badge prominently displayed trying to keep in the shade – near the equator at midday shadows are diminutive here. A local Sudanese ICRC driver arrived after another thirty minutes. He'd assumed the plane would be an hour late as usual. Today it wasn't. He drove me to the delegation. The airport road into town was wide and well surfaced but I could see the roads leading off were mostly hard, irregular dried mud, lined with untidy shacks and primitive stalls. It all seemed run-down, untidy, littered, sand-blown and depressing. There was not much sign of any new investment or anything modern. Juba is small for a capital city – just over 300,000 people, about the size of, say, Coventry or Nottingham.

The ICRC delegation was a large compound occupying a whole block surrounded by a solid three-metre-high wall with a serious steel gate with a barred peephole so the guards could see who it was before letting us in. It was reassuringly pleasant inside, with tidy bungalow offices and several *tukuls* – the traditional mud huts with conical thatch roofs. Shelter from the blazing sun was provided by some brilliantly flowered trees. A local worker was hosing green plants in pots and the spray made a rainbow. My spirits lifted a little – this wasn't such a bad place to work. I had a briefing with the medical coordinator, Yves, a pleasant and friendly Belgian who seemed to be efficient and knowledgeable. He was impressed that this was my thirteenth Red Cross mission – he'd never known any medic who'd done so many – he seemed slightly embarrassed that I'd also done more medical coordinator jobs than he had but diplomatically suggested I might be able to help him out if necessary. He was classically well-read and said he would regard me as his Nestor. The briefing turned up a few surprises. ICRC didn't have a hospital in the compound after all, or anywhere else in Juba.

*However*, ICRC had an arrangement to help out at the Juba Military Hospital where they had few doctors and were overwhelmed with wounded patients brought in from the surrounding country. As military installations are generally the first to be targeted in an attack, I found this a bit worrying.

*But*, some surgical teams were being sent to outlying areas where the need was greater, mostly in the northern states of Jonglei, Upper Nile and Unity. Those names were familiar to me – security level 'extreme'.

The ICRC personnel were accommodated at three of the better hotels in the town. I was taken to the Imperial, a mile away from the delegation. It was small and simple, only half a dozen rooms around a bar and restaurant but it was pleasant enough. It was clean and each room had blessed air-conditioning. I was tired and this was luxury. I wandered through the bar – it was dark but from the glare of a large TV I could make out the faces of locals watching football – to the empty restaurant where I ordered the first thing on the menu – a hamburger. I should have gone vegetarian.

Next day I had more briefings. Security was tight. We were absolutely forbidden to take photos in Juba – people are arrested for that. We were not allowed to walk anywhere outside the compound, we should always travel in an ICRC car, minibus or Land Cruiser, and be in constant radio contact; departures and arrivals should always be logged and journeys after 9 p.m. were strictly forbidden. The administration briefing took hours, filling in a myriad of forms, health records, next of kin details, a convoluted application for a *per diem* allowance to cover the cost of food etc., a work permit application form, travel permit, ad infinitum. I filled them all in and was told I had to do it all again, this time in blue ink. I resigned myself: it was too hot to argue.

Lunch was taken in the delegation dining room in a large, elaborate and comfortable thatched hut. I met a surgical team just returned from the field looking bedraggled and tired. They'd spent a week operating in the village of Old Fangak up in the far north in Unity Province, not far from the border on a tributary of the White Nile. The team had lived in tents in a swamp area. It had been unbearably hot and they had been short of food and drinking water. They had endured black mambas – regarded by many as the most venomous snake in the world – plus scorpions and rats to contend with.

I had another briefing with Yves that afternoon. My programme had been decided. I was going to go with a team upcountry to see the snakes. I was going to Old Fangak. Thanks.

*Chapter 36*

# Old Fangak

The other members of the team were a surgeon, Amilcar from San Salvador; Ella, an Icelandic theatre nurse; John, a Kenyan nurse who recognized me from Lokichokio and Hoo, a woman from the Chinese Red Cross as field delegate who would handle security, team management and communications – she also wanted to do the cooking, It was the first time I'd come across a member of the Chinese Red Cross. It took a couple of days to prepare for the trip, arranging food, drinking water, sleeping bags, tents and a vast array of surgery supplies. The logistics officer asked us to rethink our list – it all had to fit into a small Islander plane.

Early in the morning we were driven to Juba airport where a large number of aid agency cargo planes were parked or preparing to leave for the field. We managed to squeeze everything into the ICRC Islander and ourselves with it. There was a long delay in the hot aircraft waiting for permission to take off. Some VIP was leaving at the same time. It was the vice-president, we heard, and he had priority. All aircraft movement was halted for security and after half an hour a large black car drove across the airfield followed by a jeep packed with soldiers and a machine gun mounted at the rear. After his plane had taken off there was another half hour until air traffic was allowed to resume. There was by now a long queue of aircraft. Our small plane taxied slowly behind two huge Ilyushin cargo planes like a chicken following two fat hens and we were eventually in the air and the temperature inside the cabin thankfully dropped.

We followed the meandering White Nile for over 300 miles across patchy grassland and isolated patches of brilliant green swamp. After almost two hours we started to descend. It was sparsely populated here, I could soon make out the occasional *tukul* hut, a few cattle and the odd shrub. The runway at Old Fangak was just a strip of cleared dirt. The pilot made two low passes above the runway, firstly to clear some people off the runway, and another to get them to clear their cattle. We landed on the red soil and unloaded. There were some thorn trees but no real shade except under the wing of the plane. A solitary white cow with long horns looked at us with little interest and a group of locals had come to see the aircraft. The pilot had one aborted take-off attempt and had to shout at the locals to get their children off the runway.

A river ran alongside the runway; the village of Old Fangak was upstream a short way along and across on the other side in a loop of the river. We had to get there by boat so had to wait for transport to take us there. A launch had been arranged, no more than a large canoe with an outboard motor and we crammed it with our supplies. The river was the Zaraf, a slowly-flowing tributary of the White Nile. It was about fifty metres wide at this point, bordered by thick tall grass and reeds that blocked the view and swayed with the wake of the boat as we passed, like a Mexican wave.

It was a short journey, about three quarters of a mile, to a small wooden jetty with the village hospital just beyond. We were met and welcomed by Jill Seaman, an American from Alaska. She was aged over 60 and had been at Old Fangak for twenty-eight years since she started work in Africa, originally with MSF. She was quite small with very long plaits and wore a permanent stethoscope round her neck and flashlight round her head. She was helped by a woman in her twenties, Kate, who was on a sabbatical, daughter of some old friends of Jill.

'It's cooler today,' said Jill, but it was still 40°C. She gave us tea and we chatted – she'd visited Lokichokio in Kenya in the past. She worked for most of the year in this village, running the hospital entirely by herself and taking a couple of months off a year to go back to Alaska.

The village itself was a distance away; there must have been a few thousand inhabitants in huts widely spread out but many more scattered in the surrounding area. The roads were dirt tracks, no vehicles visible, and a few simple shops.

The hospital was small and untidy. The small 'medical hut' had a cooking stove in a kitchen and a storeroom for food and medicines. It was locked both at night and when no one was around, otherwise things went missing, especially bottles of cola. There was litter everywhere and a large pile of non-degradable waste and plastic bottles. The wards were prefabricated concrete structures with corrugated-iron roofs. They were very crowded with patients and relatives on iron bedsteads with bare mattresses. There was no need for much in the way of blankets in this heat, even at night. The patients stared at us new arrivals. The operating theatre was primitive, very basic with an old operating table and a small table with anaesthetic equipment, mostly ketamine. I noticed what looked like rat droppings on the table. Some medicines were missing, there wasn't the best type of local anaesthetic for spinals and no ephedrine in case the blood pressure dropped too low. I would have to make do.

Amilcar was very keen to start and after tea we did a ward round so Jill could show us the patients she thought needed operation. The first patient was the most difficult: a man with a gunshot to his jaw a few days before, his face and neck were swollen, and he was unable to open his mouth; he was dripping saliva.

This was a nightmare for an anaesthetist and his airway would very likely be compromised if I tried to put him to sleep. I still feared these cases even after all these years. In fact, in the end, he was alright and we subsequently reset his jaw and he survived There was a 12-year-old girl who had appendicitis. We had officially only come to operate on war-wounded patients but as always we could hardly refuse to take out her appendix, otherwise she could very likely die. She would be operated on tomorrow. She did well.

It was a busy time. We operated each day as long as we could, making full use of the daylight, but taking an hour off in the middle of the day when the temperature just got too hot to work. We dealt with gunshot wounds, shell wounds and burns. We even performed a hysterectomy on a woman who wouldn't stop bleeding after giving birth. There were more difficult cases. A woman with a suspiciously large tonsil which was occupying a large part of her mouth. We had to decline operating on her. It could be a cancer, she would be a very high anaesthetic risk and if the cancer was stuck to a blood vessel, maybe eroding it, she could easily bleed to death if we tried cutting it out and we weren't Ear, Nose and Throat experts. It was a difficult decision but we could do very little for her. There was no long-term surgical help for the patients here and in the coming rainy season no help at all.

The temperature inside the theatre went up to 50°C and became very uncomfortable. We had a large fridge in the theatre run by a generator, the only one in the hospital, where we kept some of the medicines. It also stored the plastic bags of intravenous fluids. I used to surreptitiously stuff an ice-cold bag up my shirt to try to keep cool. Then swap it for another cold one. Amilcar was a fast, no-nonsense surgeon and we got a move on. It was a good feeling.

We had our main meal at dusk. We would sit outside where it was cooler, smothered with unpleasant-smelling anti-mosquito cream. Hoo cooked an excellent spaghetti bolognaise for our first meal. But as we brought our food out of the kitchen hut, we were dive-bombed by large birds, kites I think, that would try to grab the food from the plates with their talons and wheel away with spaghetti hanging from them. One of them drew blood from my hand. I scrubbed it vigorously with antiseptic. Heaven knows what germs it carried.

We slept in tents on the hard ground under a tamarind tree. The tents were too hot and mine had a broken zip so I soon put up a mosquito dome and slept inside that instead. The fine-mesh nylon material kept the insects out but allowed a slight breeze in. It got dark quickly and was completely black by 7 p.m. It wasn't possible to read for long by head torch as we had to conserve batteries. It was a long night. I slept a little but woke around 6 a.m. and was surprised. I'd put the dome up in the dark and had forgotten it was transparent –

I opened my eyes to see above me a brilliant, deep-red sky through the branches of the tamarind tree, a chorus of unfamiliar birdsong and a croaking stately ibis bird flying past. A true African sunrise.

We had primitive showers: a bucket of water in a concrete shack. Despite the hard ground we had to sleep on, it wasn't an unpleasant place and I loved the feeling of being in the real Africa, so far from any tourist areas and to a small extent experiencing life as the natives knew it

We were all worried about snakes especially the infamously aggressive and very poisonous black mamba. We woke one morning to find that the locals had killed one right outside the medical hut. I always wore stout boots because it's easy to step on a snake. The nights were worse when I felt a primordial fear that something might get into the tent. I was fanatical about making sure the zips were completely closed. A walk to the toilet hut fifty yards away in the middle of the night felt particularly hazardous. Snakes could hide easily in the grass and one never knew what was down the toilet hole. It was laborious putting on my boots in the dome for a visit but I wasn't going to risk flip-flops. Late one night, I heard Ella let out a cry from her tent. In the light of the moon she'd seen a long, thin shadow slithering up the outside of the wall of her tent. It was ominously waving from side to side, no doubt trying to get to the top and in through a vent. I hurriedly grabbed my flashlight and shone it on her tent. No snake, a stray dog was looking for food and its tail was lazily wagging against her tent.

Children always gather round us on any mission, out of curiosity. A small boy called Dwolle took a keen interest in us. It was difficult to tell his age – probably around 8 years old but undersized and underweight with stick-like legs. He had very severe strabismus – cross-eyed. He liked my magic tricks – I had to be careful not to scare him in case he thought I was a *maganga* – a witchdoctor. I heard that his mother was alcoholic and paid little attention to him, and there was no father around. He'd just been placed on the ground as a baby and largely ignored and hadn't learned to walk until he was five. No one had bothered to teach him. He was smart though. His favourite pastime was collecting tamarind seeds, crushing them and putting them in an old plastic water bottle and shaking it to make a more interesting drink. He was always on his own. Some older boys came along and tried to steal his drink, making fun of him. He gave as good as he got, had a fight with them and scowled at them, hugging his precious bottle as the boys got bored and walked away.

One night at around 2 a.m. there was rumbling in the distance, I could see flashes across the river, low on the horizon. I couldn't work out if it was thunder or artillery fire. An hour later there was a downpour. I was woken by rain on my face as it came in through the dome mesh. I found it quite pleasant. But I was getting very wet. I moved into a spare tent next door but the rain was becoming heavier and soon coming through a vent at the top. There was lightning, a simultaneous flash and an almighty bang very close. We were under a tree, not safe. We decided to move to a large equipment tent further away. I had to sleep next to some diesel barrels and woke with a bad headache from the fumes. The ground was wet now and there were more mosquitoes. The rainy season was coming, it would soon become flooded, and the toilet would be overflowing. Jill would soon go back to Alaska for a month or two for a rest and to fund-raise for the hospital.

The peaceful setting was really an illusion; we sometimes heard gunshots and one day distant shelling that definitely wasn't thunder. It reminded us that we were in a civil war and it wasn't far away. Jill took this in her stride, she'd heard it many times before and assured us that Fangak wasn't strategically important so there was no logical need for anyone to attack the village. But I'd heard that armed soldiers had entered the village some weeks before and things had become very tense. One thing I'd learned in all my past missions was that when it comes to war, logic doesn't play a significant part.

One day we were surprised to see a series of rafts going upriver past the jetty. They were made of reeds, branches and grass and loaded mostly with women, children and some elderly and packed with as much as they could carry, even bits of furniture. They were refugees from the fighting, perhaps from Malakal which was particularly unstable. The people on the boat were quiet, serious, afraid. They didn't stop, call or wave to us. They passed by silently searching for safety.

We were nearing the end of our time at Old Fangak but I didn't quite make it. I was suffering increasingly from diarrhoea with blood. I felt very dry and seemed to be constantly trying to rehydrate myself with water. Jill gave me a course of antibiotics to try to clear it up.

One evening, we'd had mince and onions for supper but I was feeling queasy, yet thirsty. I went to bed feeling weak and tired. I slept fitfully, and could still taste the mince and onions, I was longing for a fizzy drink to settle my stomach but the medical hut would be locked and I didn't want to wake Jill up. I'd have to wait till morning. By 3 a.m. I really needed water. I sat up and felt very faint. I was blacking out so I lay down again. I measured my pulse and it was 40 instead of the normal 60, and I could tell my blood pressure was very low. I was having a vasovagal fainting attack. I called to Ella in the next tent for help and soon all the team were awake. Jill came over and said I probably had amoebic dysentery – it commonly caused vasovagal episodes like this. We discussed the cause and agreed it wasn't the food here at Fangak but more likely the wretched hamburger I'd eaten when I first arrived in Juba. She put up an intravenous drip on me and after two litres of saline the faintness eased.

In the morning it was decided I needed to be evacuated. I protested. I was feeling a bit better and hated to cut the trip short and leave the rest of the team behind. But the rainy season was starting and if they couldn't land a plane on the sodden runway we could be stuck here for days or weeks. I needed tests to confirm the diagnosis and further treatment and they didn't want an invalid on their hands. I was dazed and not feeling well at all. The plane arrived by lunchtime and I was bundled into the launch and taken downriver to the airstrip. Lise, a Danish anaesthetist, had come to replace me for the last two days. I said I was really okay and would soon get over it with some intravenous fluids.

She said, 'Have you looked at yourself in a mirror? You look ghastly and white, like death. You're not staying.'

We took off and a Scandinavian medic looked after me on the flight. He put in another intravenous cannula in my other arm ready for more saline. But the bung on the end of the cannula wasn't on properly. It came off and I noticed in my dazed, detached, almost curious state that blood was pouring out of it onto my shirt, trousers and the aircraft seat. He apologized profusely. The nausea increased during the flight, the taste of the damned mince and onions was ever present and just as we were landing at Rumbeck airstrip for refuelling, I was copiously sick again and again. I felt sorry for the pilot what with making a mess of his clean aircraft but he never said a word except to reassure me it was all okay. I started to feel a lot better.

In Juba, I was taken to a small private hospital, St Luke's Medical Centre. There were only half a dozen beds and the place seemed empty. The doctor and two nurses were all from Uganda. It was good to lie on a mattress for a change and the staff seemed to know what they were doing. I was rehydrated and I slept a lot. It was hot and there was just a fan next to the bed. There were several dashes to the toilet carrying my drip on its stand with me. In the evening there was a violent rain storm, it was coming through the blinds on the glassless window. I let it spray onto me – it felt so good. They brought me some chicken soup, I said 'no thanks'. I left after thirty-six hours, feeling weak and feeble but comfortably well. I was surprised to be presented with a bill but realized there's no NHS in South Sudan – but the equivalent of £130 was very reasonable.

The rest of the team arrived back from Old Fangak. All except the indefatigable Amilcar who'd decided to stay and wait for the next team. Conditions were getting bad with the rains, and the runway might suddenly go out of action and they'd have been stranded. Things had gone quiet in the hospital for a day or so despite rumours of wounded people heading for the hospital. There was no sign of them. This is the inherent problem: a team goes out into the field – they find it's very quiet and have little to do, but slowly people in the surrounding areas hear about the surgical team and a week later the wounded begin arriving at the hospital only to find the team has already gone back to Juba. By the time reports of a big influx of patients has arrived and a team is sent out again, the patients have got tired of waiting and have gone elsewhere. And so the cycle tends to repeat itself.

# Chapter 37

# Juba

From St Luke's I was put in another hotel, The Rainbow, very clean and comfortable and had a further two days rest and recovery in an air-conditioned room. I started to eat a little, just a few biscuits then soup, and the next day a sandwich. But a hamburger? I think not. Then I was back to work. This time joining the teams at the Juba Military Hospital.

The ten of us left the delegation early in a convoy of two ICRC Land Cruisers. We stopped off to get drinks and biscuits at a favourite shop to keep us going during the day. We passed through town along the main dusty roads for two miles, then under a concrete arch standing in isolation – the fading paint announced the Sudan People's Liberation Army. Beyond was a large empty area of brown dirt, like a huge flattened reclamation area. In the centre was the military hospital. There were five or six old white stucco buildings with peeling paint which had seen better days: these were the wards, operating block and storerooms. We arrived to hear shooting. Our driver was cautious driving into the compound but said it was probably just a protest from the soldiers. They were getting restless as they hadn't been paid for a while. There were soldiers with guns walking around. I wasn't used to this. ICRC bans guns from its own hospitals. There were civilians as well, but it was difficult to tell them apart as some wore half-uniform, half-civvies. People got clothes from wherever they could. It was inevitably hot. There was a tree in the compound and there seemed to be a waiting list to sit underneath it for shade – inside the wards it could get even hotter. I got the impression there was a lot of vehicle maintenance going on, every military truck had three or four soldiers underneath but I was told they weren't engineers, they were just using the trucks as shade and were most likely all asleep. A goat ambled slowly through the compound – probably someone's supper, they said.

Like Fangak, the hospital was incredibly untidy with litter everywhere. We went into the main block which was a combined ward and operating theatre. A crowd gathered round to watch us. To get in we had to negotiate some make-shift shelters made from cardboard boxes and brushwood near the entrance and then up some steps. On either side were two large rubbish dumps of plastic IV bottles and discarded dressings. Someone had half-heartedly tried to incinerate them. The corridor inside was dimly lit by a single shadeless light bulb. It looked like the tiled floor had never been washed. A toilet/washroom/shower was on our right, the floor was swimming in water, the toilet seemed to be blocked and water was leaking into the main corridor. Off the corridor were some four-bedded wards but patients were also lying on the floor between the beds, doubling the capacity. There was a strong smell of wounds and decaying flesh mixed with disinfectant. There were more patients in the corridor on trolleys, and some unlucky ones on the wet floor. Everyone, staff and visitors, had to step across them. Another corridor was filled with cardboard boxes full of tangled equipment. It had been donated, probably by other well-meaning agencies or charities. It was all incompatible and non-interchangeable and couldn't be used. A box had split open revealing a suction machine with no connectors; an operating lamp of the wrong voltage; bits of clamps and brackets and corrugated rubber tubing, already perishing; an anaesthetic ether vapourizer, the latest in technology back in the 1950s; a metal tray with titanium screws and plates for internally fixing fractures. It would have cost a fortune in the UK but was useless here as we never internally fixed open wounds. No one had the energy or resources to sort any of it out or even throw it away so it lay there taking up room and getting in the way and gathering dust. The changing room was a store cupboard. There were two theatres and three operating tables with blessed air conditioning, a joy which made life bearable but there were no windows. A generator supplied electricity but less than half the electrical sockets worked. Strangely, some days it was the other half that worked – I suspected there were two generators doing alternate duty. Then there were some sockets which never worked at all. We had three ICRC surgeons, from Portugal, Italy and Ghana. The two local military surgeons had been overwhelmed by patients and were happy for us to take charge. We had three anaesthetists including myself, three theatre scrub nurses, and two ward nurses.

The conditions were primitive and the workload very heavy. The floor wasn't cleaned between cases. There were flies everywhere, it was a losing battle to swat them and the theatre smelled of fly spray. The operating rooms were packed with stored equipment and medicines as there was nowhere else to keep them. The surgery was basic, nothing fancy. But strangely it seemed to work. We tried to keep everything sterile, did a lot of hand washing in iodine, and we had surprisingly few infections considering the environment and the trauma. Two of the surgeons disagreed about operating on war wounds – one was meticulous and very slow, the other said that wasn't a luxury we could afford – there were too many patients waiting for operation … go in, come out, stitch up!

The head ward nurse, Kaye, from New Zealand was a treasure. But she was continuously harassed: patients didn't have name tags or they sometimes used their first name, sometimes their family name and it was difficult to tell which was which. Patients kept moving around not just to better beds but between the other three wards and it was often impossible to keep track of them when it came to bringing them to the operating room. She would try to make a list for operation but patients would be brought in as emergencies and would be moved up the queue as a priority. Some patients were kept nil by mouth pre-op but the relatives would feed them huge bowls of chicken and soup. She tried to organize the stores of dressings, but it was almost impossible to find anything when needed and there was no room. She'd asked a local nurse to get rid of all the boxes of useless donated equipment, but the nurse had spent all morning just moving them all to another corridor.

'No one says please or thank you,' said Kaye who told me with a long sigh that she had six months more of this left in her mission.

It was often a long day's operating, one patient after another: removal of a bullet, debridement of a shell wound, redressings, they kept coming. Then there was a very long case: a bullet wound through the patient's back and into the stomach. It had left a trail of destruction and dead tissue as the shock wave of the bullet passed through; the patient was not well at all, delirious. The surrounding skin was also dead and more skin and muscle had to be taken away every two days. It was all infected despite high doses of antibiotics. His immune system was failing. It's called necrosing fasciitis and it was eating away his tissues. All we could do was load him up with pethidine so he didn't feel the pain. Was he asleep or was he unconscious most of the time? He died within a week.

I got used to the daily hassles. Next to my anaesthetic machine, one of the wheels of the drip stand fell off. I had to prop it upright with a well-out-of-date medical textbook. Eventually I swapped it for one on the ward. They'd probably have to pinch one from another ward ... and so on ... and the thing goes round in a circle. It was back in the theatre within three days. The main theatre light failed completely and our headlights weren't very good. Yves brought another large lamp on a stand. It was new and had been donated by another aid agency. But it had the wrong plug, and there didn't seem to be another spare plug in the whole hospital, so he drove off to buy one in the town. When he came back the light was switched on, a bright light for a second then nothing – the fuse had blown. No spare fuses so off he went again to buy a pack of six. Full marks for tenacity. But each fuse blew as soon as it was inserted. The generator voltage was irregular and was probably 'spiky', so we were told. We gave up and used our headlights, the surgeon groping around in the poor dim light in a poor patient's abdomen looking for a bullet. The rains were becoming more frequent and days were getting more humid. The cardboard boxes used as houses outside the theatres had got soaked and collapsed and were now turning into a mass of papier-mâché.

We got into a routine. We would work right through the day, grab a drink and some biscuits at noon and afterwards either eat at the delegation where the food couldn't be faulted or in our hotels where my appetite returned with a vengeance. I was addicted to salty chips.

We would go back to the delegation at the end of the day as it wasn't safe to stay in the hospital overnight. We would gather at the two Land Cruisers outside the theatre waiting for Kaye to finish on the wards and join us. It was always intensely hot outside and inside the cars it was even hotter – the local driver wouldn't switch on the air-conditioning while he was stationary as he said it made the battery flat. Poor Kaye would be the last to finish – she'd make it to the Land Cruisers, we'd sigh with relief, then she'd get called back to the wards – a patient needed antibiotics perhaps and the local nurse didn't know what to do. She would rush to the ward while we stifled in the heat. Back to the cars, then she'd be called back because a nurse couldn't find any intravenous fluids. It became a regular occurrence, even a joke, every day. We were often tempted to lock her in the car and drive off. I was very fond of her and she appreciated it when after work I listened to her unloading all her hassles. Sometimes we left very late but always well before dark. It wasn't safe after sunset and there was a 9 o'clock curfew, strictly kept by the military. If we went to visit colleagues in a different hotel in the evening, we had to be sure that we could get a Red Cross car to get us home before the stroke of 9 p.m. otherwise we'd have to stay overnight.

It was a relief to relax on the journey across Juba back to the delegation after a hard day. The road was thankfully well surfaced without the usual potholes. We would pass simple shops, often just a wooden frame with a thatched roof: the ubiquitous drinks and biscuits shops, fruit stalls selling watermelons and mangos, cafés with just a few fold-up chairs round an old table serving tea. Ramshackle, dingy hotels made of mud bricks, perhaps only two or three bedrooms, with ambitious names … The Grand, Deluxe Empire, Comfort Hotel. We passed a furniture shop selling garish leather sofas, the colour fading in the intense sun, an ironmonger making and selling security gates and heavy railings and doing great business, beauty parlours, Chinese pharmacies that we were advised to avoid by a local worker who said they were unreliable. There was a Chinese hospital, an obscure Christian organization I'd never heard of, a motor-cycle shop – motorcycles and scooters filled the roads and they are dangerous with maybe two or more pillion passengers, helmets are rare. A mother was riding her scooter and not only carrying a baby but also a shopping bag, a watermelon and drinking a bottle of cola at the same time. We passed a small concrete building, signed 'Council Office' with room for just two chairs and a man asleep on the floor. There was a large police station and outside the gates was a letterbox curiously labelled 'Suggestions'. Along the road was a military barracks, rows of soldiers on parade were standing to attention in the heat – they always seemed to be there and I wondered if they were a permanent fixture. Past a major roundabout that was very dangerous as there was no concept of priority. The idea seemed to be to give way to the most brave or foolhardy. On two occasions the traffic snarled up as a main road was cleared for a cavalcade of black VIP cars to drive past at speed with military vehicles all around them, rich with armaments. Further on was a police checkpoint where the car ahead of us was once stopped and a furious driver got out together with his two female passengers and had a violent argument with the police, arms waving, and was promptly arrested. His car remained there, doors open, for three days.

In the evening it was a welcome break to sit in the hotel restaurant, an open, thatch-roofed, wooden structure, where the fresher evening breeze would waft through. We could chat with the rest of the teams and the other delegates – food relief, tracing, detention – or with the other aid agencies. We would sit and mildly complain that it took on average thirty minutes to send one email home because of the poor wi-fi. The rainy season was now upon Juba and occasionally there would be the most intense storms, lightning and downpours that were so heavy it was often difficult to talk over the noise, the rain would splash onto the restaurant tables and dilute the drinks, and canvas awnings would hurriedly be unfurled. But it would make the air much cooler, and so I could put up with the mud and puddles. I enjoyed these storms, I'd never seen heavier rains than in Africa, but I imagined how disrupting and unpleasant it would be for the inhabitants of Fangak. And before the season was over many of the streets in Juba would be completely flooded and impassable.

At breakfast one morning the large TV in the restaurant was on Al Jazeera showing an interview with the leader of the rebel army who announced they would soon be attacking Juba again. It was disquieting and we each thought, 'Not before we've finished our missions, thank you.'

My six weeks were up, a replacement anaesthetist arrived and it was time for me to leave and fly home. I had one last day at the military hospital. My team were leaving the same day to go out into the field again – to Bor to set up a temporary operating theatre. It wasn't very safe there. There can be an intense camaraderie in an ICRC surgical team especially in an unstable and insecure situation. I looked out at the stormy but vividly red African sunset with emotion and I suddenly desperately wished I was going with them, despite the uncomfortable conditions, the heat, the mosquitoes, the stomach upsets, the hard ground to sleep on, the warfare. But it was time to go. Perhaps I was getting too old for this. Older and I hoped wiser. I suspected this was the last time? Never again.

I took a last look round at the patients in the dirty crowded wards, the missing limbs the bloodied bandages, the heat and the flies and the smell. Overall we might not have made as much difference as we thought. Not just this mission but all the rest. But perhaps we'd lit another candle.

Never say never. Maybe there'll still be other candles to light.

# Index